1992

This book of fourteen essays – united here not by a common ideology but by the common subject matter, music and text – demonstrates how musical and literary scholarship can combine forces effectively on the common ground of contemporary literary theory and interpretive practice. Brought together for the first time in this volume, noted musicologists and literary critics explore diverse topics of shared concern such as literary theory as a model for music criticism, genre theories in literature and music, the criticism and analysis of texted music, and the role of aesthetic, historical, and cultural understanding in concepts of text–music convergence. The concluding essay by interdisciplinary historian Hayden White offers a magisterial, non-biased assessment of the individual contributions. By generalizing the critical issues raised, White locates this ambitious enterprise of contemplating "music and text" in the larger context of intellectual history.

Music and text: critical inquiries

Music and text:
critical inquiries

edited by

Steven Paul Scher

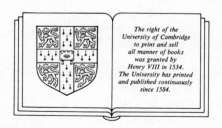

The right of the
University of Cambridge
to print and sell
all manner of books
was granted by
Henry VIII in 1534.
The University has printed
and published continuously
since 1584.

CAMBRIDGE UNIVERSITY PRESS

Cambridge

New York   Port Chester

Melbourne   Sydney

Published by the Press Syndicate of the University of Cambridge
The Pitt Building, Trumpington Street, Cambridge CB2 1RP
40 West 20th Street, New York, NY 10011–4211, USA
10 Stamford Road, Oakleigh, Victoria 3166, Australia

First published 1992

Printed in Great Britain at the University Press, Cambridge

British Library cataloguing in publication data
Music and text: critical inquiries.
1. Music related to literature
I. Scher, Steven Paul
780.08

Library of Congress cataloguing in publication data
Music and text: critical inquiries /
edited by Steven Paul Scher.
        p.   cm.
"Initial versions of the essays in this book were written for the
international conference held in May 1988 at Dartmouth College on
'Music and the Verbal Arts: Interactions'" – Acknowledgments.
Includes index.
ISBN 0 521 40158 5
1. Music and language. 2. Music and literature. 3. Music –
Philosophy and aesthetics. I. Scher, Steven P. (Steven Paul)
ML3849.M935 1991
780'.08 – dc20   90–23762   CIP   MN

ISBN 0 521 40158 5 hardback

CE

Contents

Figures

Contributors

PAUL ALPERS, Professor of English and Comparative Literature and Director of the Townsend Center for the Humanities at the University of California, Berkeley, is a specialist in Renaissance literature and the author of *The Poetry of "The Faerie Queene"* (1967), *The Singer of the Eclogues: A Study of Virgilian Pastoral* (1979), and the forthcoming *What Is Pastoral?*

MARSHALL BROWN, Professor of English and Comparative Literature at the University of Washington, is the author of *The Shape of German Romanticism* (Cornell, 1979), *Preromanticism* (Stanford, 1991), and essays on eighteenth- and nineteenth-century literature and literary theory, and co-editor of *La via al sublime* (Alinea, 1987).

EDWARD T. CONE, Professor of Music Emeritus at Princeton University, is a composer, pianist, and critic. His publications include *Musical Form and Musical Performance* (1968), *The Composer's Voice* (1974), and a volume of his selected essays entitled *Music: A View from Delft* (1989).

THOMAS GREY is an Assistant Professor of Music at Stanford University. He has published on various topics in nineteenth-century opera, and his principal area of research is the music and writings of Richard Wagner.

CHARLES HAMM, Arthur R. Virgin Professor of Music at Dartmouth College, is a past president of the American Musicological Society and has twice served as Chair of the Executive Committee of the International Association for the Study of Popular Music. His books include *Opera* (1966), *Yesterdays: Popular Song in America* (1979), and *Music in the New World* (1983).

LAWRENCE KRAMER is Professor of English and Comparative Literature at Fordham University, Lincoln Center. He is the author of *Music and Poetry: The Nineteenth Century and After* (1984), *Music as Cultural Practice: 1800–1900* (1990), and numerous essays and musical works.

DAVID LEWIN teaches music at Harvard University. He is the author of *Generalized Musical Intervals and Transformations* (1987), as well as numerous critical and theoretical studies treating works ranging from Rameau's *Traité de l'harmonie* to Wagner's *Parsifal* and Schoenberg's *Moses und Aron*.

JOHN NEUBAUER holds the chair in Comparative Literature at the University of Amsterdam. His publications include *Symbolismus und symbolische Logik: Die Idee der Ars Combinatoria in der Entwicklung der modernen Dichtung* (1978), *Novalis* (1980), and *The Emancipation of Music from Language: Departure from Mimesis in Eighteenth-Century Aesthetics* (1986).

ANTHONY NEWCOMB, Professor of Music and Dean of Humanities at the University of California at Berkeley and editor-in-chief of the *Journal of the American Musicological Association*, is the author of *The Madrigal at Ferrara* (1980). His principal fields of research are Italian texted music of the later sixteenth and early seventeenth centuries and the aesthetics and criticism of nineteenth-century German music.

PETER J. RABINOWITZ, Professor of Comparative Literature at Hamilton College, is a literary theorist and music critic. He is the author of *Before Reading: Narrative Conventions and the Politics of Interpretation* (1987) and has written on topics ranging from theories of reading to detective stories to Mahler symphonies. He is a contributing editor of *Fanfare*, and a regular columnist for *American Record Guide*.

ELLEN ROSAND, Professor of Music at Rutgers University, is the author of *Opera in Seventeenth-Century Venice: The Creation of a Genre* (1990). She has also published essays on topics of her major research interests, which include the music of Renaissance Venice, vocal chamber music, seventeenth-century singing, Handel, Verdi, and operatic dramaturgy.

STEVEN PAUL SCHER is Professor of German and Comparative Literature at Dartmouth College. His major areas of research are the interrelations of literature and music, European Romanticism, and literary theory. He is the author of *Verbal Music in German Literature* (1968) and editor of *Postwar German Culture* (1974), *Interpretationen zu E. T. A. Hoffmann* (1981), and *Literatur und Musik. Ein Handbuch zur Theorie und Praxis eines literarischen Grenzgebietes* (1984).

RUTH A. SOLIE is Professor of Music at Smith College, where she also teaches in the Women's Studies program. She is the co-editor of *Explorations in Music, the Arts, and Ideas* (1988), an associate editor of the journal *19th-Century Music*, and the author of essays and reviews concerning music in the history of ideas, criticism, and feminist studies.

CLAUDIA S. STANGER is Associate Professor of English at Berklee College of Music in Boston. Her research focuses primarily on nineteenth- and twentieth-century literature, with special emphasis on semiotics and theories of textuality in music and literature.

HAYDEN WHITE, Presidential Professor of Historical Studies at the University of California at Santa Cruz, is a scholar of modern European history, philosophy of history, and intellectual history with a special interest in the theory and criticism of literature and the other arts. His publications include *The Uses of History* (1968), *Metahistory: The Historical Imagination in Nineteenth-Century Europe* (1973), *Tropics of Discourse: Essays in Cultural Criticism* (1978), and *The Content of Form: Narrative Discourse and Historical Representation* (1987).

Preface

Steven Paul Scher

In recent decades, interdisciplinarity has had a profound impact upon humanistic studies and has occasioned exciting and innovative critical developments. As a result, more and more scholars and critics today are willing to probe the validity of traditional disciplinary premises, to reconceive the scope, aims, and interpretive trends of their own disciplines in relation to other fields, and to cross disciplinary boundaries while pursuing discrete research interests.

Methods that have emerged in literary criticism and theory since World War II have been particularly influential in charting the course of interdisciplinary inquiry. Since the early sixties, when New Criticism had lost its persuasiveness, there has been an unprecedented proliferation of theoretical approaches. Poststructuralism, hermeneutics, semiotics, reception aesthetics, and deconstruction, as well as Marxist, feminist, psychoanalytic, and reader-response criticism, and more recently New Historicism, are prominent examples. Diverse and disparate as these theories may be, their practitioners are generally willing to transcend disciplinary confines and apply insights and perspectives of other disciplines and media. Indeed, "the whole of what the French call the human sciences is being more or less rapidly transformed into something called theory, which encompasses not only literary criticism but also philosophy, history, art history, musicology, architecture, psychology, and social and political theory as well."[1] The notion of interdisciplinarity thus appears to be ubiquitous and compelling.

But while ample scholarly attention has been devoted to the interrelations of literature and the visual arts, not nearly as much effort has been expended on the reciprocal illumination of litera-

---

[1] Clayton Koelb and Susan Noakes, eds., *The Comparative Perspective on Literature: Approaches to Theory and Practice* (Ithaca and London, 1988), p. 6.

ture and music. In part this is because musicology itself commands
such a formidable technical apparatus for analysis; in part, its
nonrepresentationality makes music more difficult to view as an
analogue to literature than painting. Nevertheless, "melopoetics"
seems to fare well in the critical climate of postmodernism; during
the last decade or so, musico-literary study has become a respected
and increasingly popular field of interdisciplinary research. While
it is true that "extended comparative studies of musical and
literary works are still rare [and] good ones are downright
scarce,"[2] substantial progress has been made in the last few years
by musically sophisticated literary critics who have written on the
multifarious relations between music and text.[3]

On the musical side the rate of progress has been slower: until
recently, of all humanistic disciplines, the study of music has been
perhaps least receptive to novel critical approaches. Lately,
however, the potential interpretive, critical, and analytical benefits
of melopoetics as a rewarding area of cross-disciplinary research
have been recognized by a growing number of literary-minded
musical scholars of diverse persuasions and specialities.

That attitudes in musical scholarship concerning the function
and value of interdisciplinary critical strategies have indeed
changed significantly in recent years is a conviction shared by the
scholars writing in this volume. Taken together, the essays in *Music
and Text: Critical Inquiries* demonstrate how musical and literary
studies can combine forces effectively on the common ground of
contemporary critical theory and interpretive practice. For the
first time in a broadly conceived framework devoted entirely to
scrutiny of the interactions between music and text, noted musicologists and literary critics explore here specific affinities and shared

[2] Lawrence Kramer, "Dangerous Liaisons: The Literary Text in Musical Criticism,"
19th-Century Music 13 (1989), 159. The term "melopoetics," suggested here by Kramer to
designate the comparative discipline of "musico-literary study," is felicitous and should
gain wide currency among its practitioners.
[3] See especially Lawrence Kramer, *Music and Poetry: The Nineteenth Century and After*
(Berkeley, 1984); Steven Paul Scher, ed., *Literatur und Musik. Ein Handbuch zur Theorie und
Praxis eines komparatistischen Grenzgebietes* (Berlin, 1984); Herbert Lindenberger, *Opera: The
Extravagant Art* (Ithaca and London, 1984); Margaret M. Stoljar, *Poetry and Song in Late
Eighteenth-Century Germany* (London, 1985); Jean-Louis Cupers, *Aldous Huxley et la musique.
A la manière de Jean-Sebastian* (Brussels, 1985); John Neubauer, *The Emancipation of Music
from Language: Departure from Mimesis in Eighteenth-Century Aesthetics* (New Haven and
London, 1986); David M. Hertz, *The Tuning of the Word: The Musico-Literary Poetics of the
Symbolist Movement* (Carbondale, Ill., 1987); Robert Spaethling, *Music and Mozart in the
Life of Goethe* (Columbia, S. C., 1987); Jean-Louis Cupers, *Euterpe et Harpocrate ou le défi
littéraire de la musique. Aspects méthodologiques de l'approche musico-littéraire* (Brussels, 1988); and
Lawrence Kramer, *Music and Cultural Practice, 1800–1900* (Berkeley, 1990).

concerns. They do so by focusing on diverse topics such as literary theory as a model for musical criticism, genre theories in literature and music, the criticism and analysis of texted music, and the role of aesthetic, historical, and cultural understanding in concepts of text-music convergence. This list of salient topics, while indicative of areas and orientations of general concern in the individual essays, is by no means exhaustive. What is more, readers of these essays may well discern two ways to conceptualize specific issues: first, the conjunction of cultural and historical approaches which aim to interpret musical and literary works through the construction of the cultural contexts from which they arose and second, the refinement of interpretation by drawing from outside the work's immediate discipline on the many theoretical and critical methods that have emerged in recent years in both literary and musical studies. That these two modes of approach are not mutually exclusive but actually complement each other reinforces the relevance of such a critical enterprise.

Diversity and interdisciplinary breadth, as well as an overarching coherence of purpose, were the chief criteria for assembling these essays, presented originally as papers at a conference at Dartmouth College in 1988 and revised for the present volume. *Music and Text: Critical Inquiries* thus offers a wide range of innovative methodologies, critical directions, and new perspectives on familiar and more recent musical and literary works. Most importantly, the essays that follow are unified not by common ideology but by the common subject matter – music and text.[4] The rather generally formulated section headings are not meant to be prescriptive for the essays subsumed under them; they serve merely to highlight certain theoretical, critical, analytical, historical, thematic, rhetorical, or genre-oriented preoccupations and concerns shared by two or more of the authors.

An integral part of this book is the concluding essay by Hayden White in which he traces, with consummate skill, just how and to what extent the diverse preoccupations and concerns that determine the contributors' premises and interpretive strategies nevertheless cohere in presenting a musico-literary panorama consonant with contemporary theory and critical/historical praxis. As a prac-

---

[4] Throughout this book, the conjunction of "music and text" is used in its broadest sense which includes, but is not restricted to, matters of texted music such as musical settings of texts in opera and song. For example, the issue of *Contemporary Music Review* entitled *Music and Text* (vol. 5, 1989) focuses exclusively on problems of word-setting.

ticing interdisciplinary critic himself, the historian White offers a circumspect and non-biased opinion on the state of affairs in musical and literary scholarship. He reviews the individual essays in searching analytical detail and discusses them polemically in relation to each other, uncovers fundamental alliances that group them together, identifies specific trends and directions in both disciplines that are likely to lead to further scholarly exchange based on a more refined and viable musical–literary discourse; and finally, by generalizing the critical issues raised throughout, he locates the ambitious enterprise of contemplating "music and text" in the larger context of intellectual history.

It is our hope that this book will stimulate similar collaborative efforts that will strengthen the prospects of melopoetics as a comparative discipline: "What [this] still-incipient discipline might have to offer is not drastic innovation but greater explicitness, resources of enrichment, wider interpretive adventure."[5]

Steven Paul Scher
Dartmouth College

[5] Kramer, "Dangerous Liaisons," p. 167.

Acknowledgments

Initial versions of the essays in this book were written for the international conference held in May 1988 at Dartmouth College on "Music and the Verbal Arts: Interactions," generously sponsored by the Ted and Helen Geisel Third Century Professorship in the Humanities. I am grateful for the additional support provided by The William and Flora Hewlett Foundation and The Dickey Endowment for International Understanding.

Special thanks are due to the contributing authors as well as to the many individuals from whom I have received invaluable guidance and assistance during the completion of this volume, in particular to Joseph Kerman, William Summers, Gary Tomlinson, Margaret Robinson, Roberta Gran, and Magdale Labbe. Last but not least, I wish to thank Penny Souster of Cambridge University Press for her sustained interest in the project and her meticulous attention to every editorial detail along the way.

I gratefully acknowledge permission granted by the following to use material for this volume: Michael Fried for use of his poem "Depths," and John Harbison and G. Schirmer Inc. for extracts quoted from "Flower-Fed Buffaloes" by John Harbison.

Figures 2.2 to 2.8 in Charles Hamm's essay were taken by Marilyse Hamm.

Part I

Institutional dimensions and the contexts of listening

1

Music and literature: the
institutional dimensions

John Neubauer

Comparative studies may look at the contacts, overlappings, and interactions between fields, or they may consider general analogies and contrasts between them. The former undoubtedly provide a sounder base and surer methodology than general comparisons, which are often arbitrary in their choices and vague in their conclusions. But interactions and overlappings usually occur at the disciplinary margins, which tend to appear indeed marginal to those who work in the respective fields.

Like most comparatists, I question the epistemological value of disciplinary boundaries, but, as my very title indicates, I recognize that we live in institutions whose divisional boundaries, however arbitrary, are difficult to overcome. Genuinely successful inter-disciplinary studies of a "margin" will have to convince the scholars at the center that questions at the margin are actually central to their field. Such studies should foster then a perspectival shift of what is important in a field, a reinterpretation of what is center and what is margin.

Within mixed genres, like opera and the Lied, the music is more often part of the canonical musical repertoire than the text of the canonized literature. Though dual genres are both legitimate and important as subjects of comparative studies, they usually yield specialized results which do not lend themselves to the kind of generalized conclusions that are necessary to combat professional parochialism. If we are to convince our colleagues that the joint study of music and literature is important, we must demonstrate that our conclusions affect what they do.

These introductory remarks on "disciplinary politics" should give a taste of my institutional approach and indicate at the same time that I shall be concerned with broad comparisons and contrasts rather than with specific "interactions." The urgency of my topic is indicated by the great interest that both musicologists and literary critics have shown in institutional approaches to their own fields. The time may be ripe to explore these approaches on a comparative basis.

This recent interest is manifest in theoretical and historical studies of the institutions and conventions that govern the creation, dissemination, and reception of artworks, which is itself part of a general shift from subject-centred, idealist, intellectual, and diplomatic explanations to sociological studies from "below," be they of the Marxist, neo-Marxist, or the *Annales*-school variety. To this general, art-external factor we may add several art-internal, aesthetic factors, foremost among them the twentieth-century development of the arts itself, the renewed effort by each generation to wash out the structures and borders of artworks established by the previous generations.

This constant disassembling and parodying of previous art, emblematized by Duchamp's exhibiting of a real urinal, has made it all but impossible to define once and for all what artworks are. Although there have been many attempts in the twentieth century to define the essential features of the arts, such ontological definitions have proved to be an easy prey to critics. The failure of efforts to define what art *is* has led to newer approaches that ask rather how it *functions*.[1] And this leads to questions about institutions, for functioning always takes place within a social–institutional framework.

The shift from ontological towards functional approaches to art is evident in Arthur Danto's article on the "Artworld," which focuses on art that traditionally would not have been considered art at all. After considering the work of Warhol, Rauschenberg, and others, Danto concludes: "To see something as art requires something the eye cannot descry – an atmosphere of artistic theory, a knowledge of history of art: an artworld."[2] In other words, an object becomes art if it is placed within the historical, critical, and

---

[1] When asked what attracts him to Wittgenstein, John Cage answered that he had retained the sentence: "Something's meaning is how you use it." (Daniel Charles, ed., *For the Birds, John Cage in Conversation with Daniel Charles* [Boston and London, 1981], p. 153.) Cage presumable refers to Wittgenstein's statement on language: "Die Bedeutung eines Wortes ist sein Gebrauch in der Sprache" (Ludwig Wittgenstein, *Philosophical Investigations*, trans. G. E. M. Anscombe, 3rd edn. [New York, 1968], p. 20), but Wittgenstein adds that not all word-meanings are defined by use.

[2] Arthur Danto, "The Artworld," in *Culture and Art*, ed. Lars Aagard-Mogensen (Atlantic Highlands, 1976), p. 16. This article first appeared in the *Journal of Philosophy* 61 (1964), 571–84.

philosophical matrix of the artworld. Danto shifts from internal to external defining features, but the external matrix is for him intellectual rather than sociological. It is therefore appropriate that he should speak of an "artworld" rather than of an art institution.

George Dickie takes Danto's approach a step further by explicitly subtitling his book "An Institutional Analysis." Like Danto, Dickie turns to institutions because earlier attempts have failed to define artworks,[3] but, whereas Danto takes issue with those who want to define artworks in terms of special internal "aesthetic" features, Dickie polemicizes primarily against those who approach the issue from the reception side, seeking to define artworks by reference to the "aesthetic states of mind" they elicit. Furthermore, Dickie gives little attention to the intellectual conditions of art: he concentrates "on the practices and conventions used in presenting certain aspects of works of art to their audiences," because he believes that these "presentational conventions" locate or isolate the aesthetic objects.[4] Danto's intellectual "artworld" becomes in Dickie's adaptation an institution with "an established practice."[5] Works become aesthetic if they are objects of this institutional practice.

Thus Dickie's notion of institutional practice corresponds to the notion of literary competence and conventions that Jonathan Culler established coming from structuralist linguistics. For Culler wants to reformulate statements of "facts about literary texts" in terms of "conventions of literature and operations of reading" occurring within literature as an institution. Thus, for instance, instead of defining literary texts in terms of their internal features of fictionality, we may say "that to read a text as literature is to read it as fiction."[6] If a text is placed within the literary institution, we apply to it modes of understanding that treatments of fiction have conventionalized, and we may apply those modes even to historical, philosophical, or psychoanalytical texts that are not normally considered fictional. No text *is* fiction by virtue of its internal features; texts *become* fiction by being treated as such.

Another institutional approach to the arts can be traced through the works of the Frankfurt School, whose major landmarks are

---

[3] George Dickie, *Art and Aesthetic. An Institutional Analysis* (Ithaca, N. Y., 1974), p. 10.
[4] *Ibid.*, p. 12.   [5] *Ibid.*, p. 31.
[6] Jonathan Culler, *Structuralist Poetics* (Ithaca, N. Y., 1975), p. 128. Culler's reformulation may rid us of the problem of defining fiction in terms of internal features, but it continues to hold on to the equally problematic notion that literature is fiction.

Walter Benjamin's essay on the impact of the "reproducible" artforms of photography and film, Theodor Adorno's sociology of music, and Peter Bürger's notion of literature as institution.

Adorno's music sociology, which originated in the early 1930s and culminated in his 1961–62 introductory lectures, offers a wealth of brilliant ideas on the concrete musical institutions of opera, chamber music, music criticism, and the orchestra. Furthermore, it paves the way towards reception-oriented interpretations by repeatedly demonstrating that social practices may ill fit or abuse particular musical forms. Thus, for instance, Adorno's lecture on opera[7] sets out to disprove the traditional assumption that "der ästhetische Stand musikalischer Formen und Gebilde und ihre gesellschaftliche Funktion harmonierten ohne weiteres. Statt dessen kann die Rezeption von Gebilden von ihrem gesellschaftlichen Ursprung und Sinn bis zum Bruch sich entfernen."[8]

It should be obvious from this formulation that in Adorno's view intrinsic meaning remains the standard. The meaning acquired by institutional practices may deviate from this meaning, but it does not by itself create meaning, it does not endow previously as yet "meaningless" works with semantic content. Adorno repeatedly criticizes those who blithely ascribe concrete and definite semantic content to music, but he too believes that musical form can be transcribed into verbal meaning by way of a "materiale Formenlehre."[9] After all, the "ästhetische Stand musikalischer Formen und Gebilde" can clash with their social use only if these "Formen und Gebilde" have an intrinsic, use-independent (perhaps even intentional) meaning. Precisely this belief is questioned in recent, more radical institutional approaches to the arts.

The work of Adorno and Benjamin became Peter Bürger's point of departure in formulating an explicitly "institutional" analysis of the historical avant-garde. According to Bürger, "art as institution" (*Institution Kunst*) includes "the art-producing and art-distributing apparatus as well as the dominant ideas about art in a certain epoch, which essentially determine the reception of works."[10] This general definition serves as a basis for Bürger's two theses: first, that art's autonomy is the informing idea of the art-institution in the bourgeois epoch, and second, that this bourgeois institution was radically, but unsuccessfully, attacked by the

[7] Theodor W. Adorno, *Einleitung in die Musiksoziologie* (Frankfurt am Main, 1962), pp. 81–95.
[8] *Ibid.*, p. 81.   [9] *Ibid.*, p. 72.
[10] Peter Bürger, *Theorie der Avantgarde*, 3rd edn. (Frankfurt am Main, 1981), p. 29.

historical avant-garde in the early decades of this century. I shall return to these notions later.

We may look at the emergence of institutional theories from yet another angle, by following the twists and turns of twentieth-century critical conceptions. Musical analysis and New Criticism, the dominant modes of mid-century, focused on "the work in itself," its internal features; they questioned the notion that art was "expression" and they rejected the "genetic fallacy" that scholarship was to recover authorial intentions. Both musical and literary scholarship turned against the idealistic view that the author's transcendental subject was the defining origin and center of artworks, and maintained that one could identify a core of stable meaning in artworks without reference to the originating subject behind them. Reference to subjects as receptors or consumers of artworks was considered to be a similar, "affective" fallacy.

Postmodernists find the "work in itself" diffuse rather than organically coherent and meaningful. Their sensitivity to the "fuzziness" of literary texts may actually move literature closer to music, for it attributes a kind of elusive semantic content to literature that has traditionally been considered typical of music. From a postmodernist perspective, New Criticism's search for intrinsic meaning in texts is a form of fact-chasing that merely displaces the earlier positivist search for biographical and historical facts. Postmodernist critical theorists are apt to point out that both forms of positivism tend to camouflage the personal and ideological bias of interpretation.

That artworks have a "weak identity" is an idea that informs such widely differing conceptions as Gadamer's hermeneutics, Wolfgang Iser's "Leerstellen," Umberto Eco's "open works of art," Roland Barthes's "scriptible" texts, and various formulations of "expression," including Nelson Goodman's definition of it as "metaphoric exemplification."[11] All of these notions imply today's critical commonplace that artworks are inexhaustibly interpretable, but they draw different consequences from it. Deconstructionist critics like Derrida or de Man trace the indeterminacy of texts to the nature of language itself.[12] Their critique of logocentrism, their

---

[11] See Hans-Georg Gadamer, *Wahrheit und Methode* (Tübingen, 1960); Wolfgang Iser, *Der Akt des Lesens* (Munich, 1976); Umberto Eco, *The Role of the Reader* (Bloomington, 1979); Roland Barthes, *S/Z* (Paris, 1970); and Nelson Goodman, *Languages of Art*, 2nd edn. (Ind. 1976).

[12] The work of Michel Foucault represents a special case for two reasons. Following Nietzsche, Foucault occasionally takes a "deconstructionist" view of language, although

sophisticated exploration of the breaks, discrepancies, and contradictions in the "languages of art" (Goodman) have undermined
the age-old belief in the unity and determinacy of artworks and
offer no substitute for it. The lacking logical coherence in language
simultaneously signals the dissolution of the subject as a metaphysical entity, so that the indeterminate text cannot be given
stable meaning by referring "backward" to the creator's intention.
Artworks are richer than the meaning their authors imputed to
them.[13]

Of those who agree that authorial intention cannot be the
yardstick of meaning and artworks are intrinsically indeterminate,
many resist a radical deconstruction of meaning by making the
reader, the listener, and the critic or scholar the foundation of
meaning. But how stable can a meaning be if it is imputed by
historically and culturally bound recipients? To this question I
should want to turn by considering recent notions of performance.

II PERFORMANCE

Before the spread of printed books, all three literary genres – poetry
and prose as well as theater – were usually performed, often in
conjunction with some form of music. The silent reading of print
gradually replaced reciting and communal reading, and this led to
a gap between poetry and prose on the one hand, and drama,
which remained a performing art, on the other. Recent literary
criticism has recognized, however, that readers have a constructive
role in making a text, and it has become customary to speak of the
"reader's performance" as an act by which the text is actually
constituted, not unlike the performative constitution of music. Has
literature thereby moved back into the vicinity of music? The
performance-metaphor of literary reception is suggestive and
useful, although I suggest that we not abuse it.

Let us start with the role of notation in performance. If every
aspect of sound-production could be encoded in a score, performers

this is not the image that emerges from his *The Order of Things* (New York, 1971).
Furthermore, unlike most of the deconstructionists, Foucault is very much interested in
the functioning of institutions and institutional power, as witnessed, for instance, in his
work on the history of madness. Yet his work on institutions seems to run parallel to,
rather than inform, his work on the arts.

[13] E. D. Hirsch's well-known proposal, in his *Validity in Interpretation* (New Haven, 1967), to
distinguish between "meaning" (the author's original intention) and "significance" (a
work's interpretation by the author or anybody else) seems sensible to me but hardly a
practical way to get agreement, since the authorial intention is elusive.

would have no freedom; creative performance is made possible because of inadequacies in notation. Composers who no longer believe that they own and control their work can grant creative freedom to the performer by reducing or minimizing notation. This is indeed what John Cage, one of the most radical critics of "well-wrought" artworks, wants: "my task is to open up the personality; I also want to open up the work so that it may be interpreted in various ways"; "we should forget the relationship between writing and what is heard"; and "the extreme manifestation of this form of notation would be no more notation at all!"[14]

Performance is the medium of sign-communication, and hence an important dimension of semiotic pragmatics. Yet, in spite of its importance, performance has not received enough attention within musical semiotics so far. For example, recent volumes of *Semiotica* and the *Zeitschrift für Semiotik* (exclusively devoted to the semiotics of music) treat the semantics of musical structure and the inter-action between musical and verbal signs but they pay little attention to performance.[15] In order to discuss the semiotics of musical performance, I shall have recourse to Umberto Eco's somewhat dated article, "The Poetics of the Open Work," which now appears in his volume *The Role of the Reader* (1979), though its first version was published in 1959.

Eco discusses the aesthetics of certain pieces by Stockhausen, Berio, Pousseur, and Boulez, pieces that authorize the performer to determine the length of a note or to rearrange the sequence of sub-divisions. Such pieces, writes Eco, "reject the definitive, concluded message and multiply the formal possibilities of the distribution of their elements. They appeal to the initiative of the individual per-former, and hence they offer themselves, not as finite works which prescribe specific repetition along given structural coordinates, but as 'open' works, which are brought to their conclusion by the per-former."[16] Performers of these compositions may then reassemble the parts, as readers of Julio Cortázar's *Hopscotch* may rearrange the sequence of chapters. Eco believes that this new freedom granted to the performer opened "a new page in sociology and in pedagogy, as well as a new chapter in the history of art."[17] He compares it with the introduction of the complementarity principle in physics.[18]

---

[14] Charles, *For the Birds*, pp. 59, 60, and 171, respectively.
[15] See the special issues of *Semiotica* 66:1–3 (1987) entitled "Semiotics of Music," and *Zeitschrift für Semiotik* 9:3–4 (1987) entitled "Zeichen und Musik."
[16] Eco, *The Role of the Reader*, p. 49.   [17] *Ibid.*, p. 65.   [18] *Ibid.*, pp. 58 ff.

In retrospect, it seems remarkable that Eco should have formulated the notion of "open works," a central idea of postmodernist aesthetics, in terms of relatively traditional compositions that did not themselves create a tradition, let alone open "a new chapter in the history of art." It now seems ironic also that Eco was so eager to distinguish these so-called "works in progress" from "open works" in general, by claiming that the performer's freedom in "works in progress" is more radical than the freedom that readers always enjoyed, especially since the rise of Symbolism and Modernism. According to Eco, Baroque artists, Mallarmé, Joyce, Kafka, and Brecht wrote "open works," but Boulez, Stockhausen, Pousseur, and Berio composed "works in progress."[19]

The distinction seems to me highly questionable on several grounds. First, the "works in progress" mentioned firmly retain control over pitch and other musical dimensions and grant only limited freedom to the performer. John Cage, the true radical, remarks that Stockhausen's *Klavierstück IX* "only deals with the question of sequence. A kaleidoscopic juxtaposition of fixed fragments can't have anything more than merely ornamental value. . . . But everything would change, if, instead of playing the eleven groups organized by the composer one after the other you played them all at once . . . we wouldn't have to worry about relapsing into a predetermined organisation!"[20]

But we need not collapse diachrony into synchrony in the manner of Cage in order to empower the performer. A number of older literary works have granted readers the kind of freedom that Eco finds revolutionary in the mentioned "works in progress." As I have shown in my *Symbolismus und symbolische Logik*,[21] combinatorially reconstitutable poetry existed in the seventeenth century, for instance in the work of the German poet Quirinus Kuhlmann. Furthermore, a number of important literary works that may not have been *intended* as "works in progress" actually remained unfinished and unclear as to the sequence of their parts. The arrangement of the chapters in Kafka's *Castle*, for instance, has been a matter of scholarly debate. Hölderlin, Georg Trakl, and others eternally revised certain of their poems so that we now have several, radically different versions which constitute in their entirety a genuine "work in progress." While earlier scholarship

---

[19] *Ibid.*, p. 65.   [20] Charles, *For the Birds*, pp. 198–99.
[21] See John Neubauer, *Symbolismus und symbolische Logik. Die Idee der Ars Combinatoria in der Entwicklung der modernen Dichtung* (Munich, 1978).

monumentalized the last version, postmodernist readers, like the performers of Stockhausen and Berio, find in newer editions a series of alternative texts that cannot be ranked simply by chronology. Sensitivity to such choices has multiplied the number of versions even in cases where the text has hitherto been considered relatively simple and unique. In the case of *King Lear*, for instance, traditional editions conflated the 1608 Quarto and the 1623 Folio versions, whereas the recent Oxford edition prints both of them. Finally, and perhaps trivially, completed and definitive artworks may confront their public with far more radical interpretive alternatives than those available to the performers of the mentioned "works in progress."

It may no longer be possible to make ontological distinctions between "closed," "open," and "in progress" works. These labels seem to indicate intrinsic qualities in the works but the boundaries of the categories shift according to changes in our perception. Which label we choose for a particular work will largely depend on our interpretive stance, which in turn is deeply affected by conventions governing our age and our institutions. The current critical conventions sharpen our eyes and ears to the cracks and faults in monuments of the past, and as a consequence we see "works in progress" where our fathers found "open works" and our grandfathers "closed" ones. Future conventions may cement the cracks and faults, they may direct our vision once more to that which unites rather than separates. But for the time being even the staunchest defenders of stable meaning are sensitized to interpretability and the flux of critical perspectives. The diverse forms of postmodernist thought (including reception aesthetics, deconstruction, and neo-Marxism) all acknowledge that identity and meaning are no permanent properties of the work itself but eternally constituted and reconstituted in reading, seeing, and listening.

A brief excursus concerning authentic performance practices may illustrate my last point. As a resident of Amsterdam I have the frequent pleasure of listening to superb performances of seventeenth- and eighteenth-century music by Ton Koopman, Frans Brüggen, Nikolaus Harnoncourt and others. Preoccupied during the day with problems of postmodern theories of literature in my teaching and research, I enjoy such musical events also as occasions for reflection.

The intention to reconstitute music "the way it really was"

seems to involve the wish to reestablish the historical author's
intentions as the basis of interpretation. If so, this would counter
the trend to increase the performer's freedom, which could only be
achieved by deemphasizing the text and the authorial intentions. I
am aware, of course, that many currents within contemporary
musicology run counter to the philosophy underlying authentic
performance practices. However, this philosophy too has strong
institutional dimensions.

Performances are authenticated by means of historical scores,
instruments, and handbooks. But instruments belong to performers, not to composers, and the few handbooks that survive
cannot intimate the intentions of the many composers contempo-
raneous with them. The scores may be the most direct and extensive indication of what composers intended, but their evidence is
far from clear. Musical notation encodes only a fraction of what
composers have in their minds, and according to Harnoncourt, the
most articulate spokesman of authentic performance practices,
musical notation was sparser in the seventeenth and eighteenth
century. Only the romantic cult of originality and genius led to the
nineteenth-century ideal to record all instructions of the composer.[22]

Why this should be so is not quite clear from Harnoncourt's
argument. At times he says that performance instructions were less
needed earlier because the performance conventions were shared
by composer and performer alike; at other times he suggests that
earlier scores dispensed with performance indications in order to
grant greater freedom to the performer. Similarly, the advent of
Romanticism signifies to him both a cult of genius and a pedantic
standardization of training, and of playing and recording music –
standardizations he associates with the egalitarian spirit that dominated the Parisian *Conservatoire* during the revolution.

Be that as it may, Harnoncourt believes that this "creative
freedom of the interpreter, which made every performance into a
unique, inimitable event," is totally alien to the musicians of our
time.[23] He favors, then, the eighteenth-century musical conventions because they granted freedom to the performers, and he
advocates their revival in order to rid the performer of the straight-
jacket of *contemporary* conventions. Thus Harnoncourt is no anti-
quarian: he wants "authentic" performance in order to "emanci-

[22] Nikolaus Harnoncourt, *Musik als Klangrede* (Salzburg, 1982), p. 43.   [23] *Ibid.*, p. 47.

pate" the performer, something which parallels literary attempts that aim at the emancipation of the reader: "Der Musiker sollte doch das Recht haben, jedes Werk mit dem Instrument zu spielen, das ihm dafür am besten geeignet erscheint, oder die ihm ideal dünkende Klangkombination zu wählen."[24]

A more orthodox and purist revival of the older musical conventions would demand reestablishing all aspects of the old institution. Besides the use of authentic instruments it would have to involve a return to the historical locations of performance and even a resuscitation of the historical listener – a listener whose mind has been bleached of nineteenth- and twentieth-century music. Yet, no matter how much we listen to authentic performances or, for that matter, how enthusiastically we respond to Harnoncourt's book, our listening to Rameau and Bach is conditioned by the experience of Beethoven, Wagner, and Stravinsky, the sound of the modern orchestra, and the modern instruments. As T. S. Eliot wrote in "Tradition and the Individual Talent," "The difference between the present and the past is that the conscious present is an awareness of the past in a way and to an extent which the past's awareness of itself cannot show."[25]

Like Schiller's sentimental poet, advocates of authentic performance practices seek to recreate a lost pristine tradition, a *Klangrede* of the individual voice that has been drowned out by the ready-made noise of mass society. But actually they offer exhilarating new interpretations that manifest a contemporary preoccupation with performance. Authentic performance practices destabilize the text by privileging the performer and blurring the line that separates him from the author.[26]

The enfranchisement of literary readers, which parallels the "emancipation" of performers in music, may be indicated by a shift in the musical metaphor applied to reading. If readers were formerly enjoined to "listen" to the author's "voice," they are now encouraged to "perform" acts of reading.

How similar is a reading "performance" to a musical one? Creative reading and listening may be called performance inasmuch as they bring to life what exists only on paper. Are then

[24] *Ibid.*, p. 95.
[25] T. S. Eliot, "Tradition and the Individual Talent," in *The Sacred Wood* (London, 1920), p. 52.
[26] On contemporary discussions of authentic performance practices see Peter Redemeister, *Historische Aufführungspraxis. Eine Einführung* (Darmstadt, 1988) which includes a bibliography of 644 items.

creative musical listeners, music critics, or musicologists also performers? And if so, how do their performances differ from a violinist's? Furthermore, performances in their traditional sense are more than just creative interpretations. Playing or practicing alone is no performance in the usual sense, for this implies display and necessitates an audience. Of course, reading, listening, and viewing may be directed towards an audience – for instance if one discusses a painting with a companion in the museum or publishes an interpretation of a novel – but they typically occur in private.

Reader-response criticism seldom considers such distinctions between musical and reading performances. Eco, for instance, foregrounds the performance metaphor by giving the reader a *role*, yet he devotes only a short footnote to the comparison between recipients and performers. He distinguishes there "the practical intervention of a 'performer' (the instrumentalist who plays a piece of music or the actor who recites a passage)," from the act of the interpreter–consumer, who "looks at a picture, silently reads a poem, or listens to a musical composition performed by somebody else." But, having thus associated reception with privacy, and performance with a public, Eco adds that "for the purposes of *aesthetic analysis*" (my italics) both cases "can be seen as different manifestations of the same interpretative attitude. Every 'reading,' 'contemplation,' or 'enjoyment' of a work of art represents a tacit or private form of 'performance.'"[27]

To engage in "aesthetic analysis" without considering the institutional conditions of performance is to ignore much more than just its public or private character. Let me name just a few of the institutional conditions. There are levels of performance, determined by the performer's competence, which, in turn, depends on experience and training, as well as individual talent. The reading performance of a literary critic will differ from the performance of a naive reader of popular novels, just as the listening performances of a casual concert-goer will differ from those of a music critic or scholar. The nature and level of the performance will heavily depend on institutional affiliations, conventions, and training practices.

Musicians, who perform "literally," and literary readers, who perform only by way of a metaphor, are trained in vastly different ways. Musicians need a lengthy technical training to acquire

[27] Eco, *The Role of the Reader*, p. 65.

certain *bodily* skills, for which the *mental* training in literary criticism has no equivalent. Furthermore, musicians prepare their performances in arduous practices and rehearsals, thereby giving their *public* performance considerable stability. Reading has no rehearsals and we improvise, so to speak, as we go along, even though we may re-read and re-consider once we are finished or in a second reading. On the other hand, an interpretation that emerges from a series of readings and reflections may be more rigorously cumulative than a musical performance – unless we include recorded performances which may be improved.

Institutions are subject to change, and institutional approaches to the arts must be historically and culturally relativistic. I have just claimed, for instance, that reading is a silent and essentially private act, yet in earlier ages reading and reciting for others was common. Music listening also became more private in our century, with the advent of recording. Earlier, music listening could only take place in the presence of a live performer. The new possibility of listening to recordings in privacy fundamentally changed our listening habits, but the nature of that impact has hardly been studied and is difficult to assess. Following Benjamin's essay on technical reproducibility, we may associate this impact with the disappearance of "aura." Although we may still listen to music in the traditional religious or festive secular places, we habitually listen to it in our home and in our car. Earlier generations also listened to music at meals, but only we can listen to it while cleaning our teeth or jogging. Most of our music listening has become a secondary activity, an accompaniment or background to something else, and this surely profanes the experience. Yet listening was always a "social" event, and the institutional circumstances of its earlier performance at a meal or in the opera did not leave its aura untarnished. Could the privacy of listening, now made possible by recordings, not endow music with a new kind of aura?

Is there something in the realm of reading that parallels the impact of recording? The training of writers and musicians, the various forms of patronage throughout the ages, the institutions of performance and publishing, the role of criticism and scholarship in molding public taste – how do all these differ in the two arts? Such are the issues that comparative studies of institutions could explore by using the accumulated historical and sociological material now available in each field separately.

III   INSTITUTIONS

My discussion has gradually shifted from performance to the institutions within which performances and their preparation occur.
Performances and institutions are interlinked, yet they also point
towards alternative sociological approaches to the arts. The choice
is evident, for instance, in Harnoncourt's hesitation between reviving the performer's freedom and reviving older conventions. The
two may partially coincide if, as Harnoncourt claims, the older
convention gave greater freedom to the performer than the existing
one, but conventions always limit individual freedom. Similarly,
according to Harnoncourt, post-eighteenth-century music is dominated both by the romantic notion of genius and by institutional
conventionalization and standardization promulgated by the Parisian *Conservatoire*.

Does the individual performer endow the work with an identity
or are the performance and its reception pre-programmed by the
conventions of the existing institutions? The first view is attractive
because it empowers the individual, but it easily tips over into
idealistic glorifications of the subject. Reader-response theories
have tended to move from the first to the second view, to replace
the performer's individual creativity with social and institutional
conventions.[28]

The shift to institutional conventions is evident in the work of
Stanley Fish, which is often labelled deconstructionist though it
shares with deconstruction only the premise that texts have no
unequivocal intrinsic meaning. Fish actually claims to counter
those charges of rampant relativism that have been raised against
the deconstructionist weakening of the text. His notions of institution and convention are meant to recover the stability of meaning
previously based on authorial intention and historical circumstances.

Fish asks whether there is a text and answers, "there is and there
isn't": there is none if we mean by it "an entity which always

---

[28] The movement away from idealistic notions of the subject is evident also in the thought of
those, like John Cage, who do not turn to institutional models. Cage playfully defines his
philosophy as "Get out of whatever cage you find yourself in," and this implies an
emancipation of the performer and the listener. But this must be understood in the
framework of Taoism, which principally opposes the imposition of any human will on
sounds: "Impose nothing. Live and let live. Permit each person, as well as each sound, to
be the center of creation"; and "the opening up of everything that is possible and to
everything that is possible is, I believe, what I am seeking." Charles, *For the Birds*,
pp. 239, 100, and 147, respectively.

remains the same from one moment to the next," but there is one "if one means by the text the structure of meanings that is obvious and inescapable from the perspective of whatever interpretive assumptions happen to be in force."[29]

Thus Fish argues that inherently indeterminate texts are concretized within institutions, by "the authority of interpretive communities" that permits only certain kinds of approaches and interpretations. These institutionally enforced meanings are, in Fish's words, "obvious and inescapable" within that particular interpretive community; once we leave it we shall adopt other, equally "obvious and inescapable" conventions in another community, for we never escape the coercing power of institutional practices.

Fish, together with many others, seems to have deconstructed the autonomous subject, only to posit in place of it an equally reified and rigid institution. But, surely, only totalitarian institutions (and often not even they) are consistent, intentionally unequivocal, and meaningful. "Normal" institutions and their practices are as pluriform, inconsistent, and permanently fluctuating as the norms and values of subjects. The Catholic Church is Inquisition as well as a message of love. And if its "obvious and inescapable" norms leave such a latitude of choices, what are we to say of New Criticism, which had no Ten Commandments, no rituals, and no organized membership?

While we are swayed by institutional norms, we are subject to several different ones. Earlier, monolithic cultures and modern totalitarian states may have exclusive power to control us, but pluralistic cultures divide us. Apart from those few who fully submit to a single dogma and its institution, the vast majority holds pluralistic allegiances, as candidates for elections well know. Fish's claim that the institutional norms of humanistic scholarship are "obvious and inescapable" is an erroneous adaptation of Thomas Kuhn's theory of scientific paradigms.[30]

If paradigms and interpretive communities had absolute sway over us, it would be difficult to explain why and how institutions and individuals change. Such changes can only occur if we assume that individual norms seldom conform totally to the norms of a single institution, that people usually adhere to different sets of institutional norms, that institutions are not the sole factor in

[29] Stanley Fish, *Is There a Text in This Class?* (Cambridge, Mass., 1980), p. vii.
[30] See Thomas Kuhn, *The Structure of Scientific Revolutions* (Chicago, 1962).

determining human judgment, and, finally, that institutions themselves are not monolithic. In fact, as I have shown in an article on
critical pluralism,[31] Fish claims for himself a critical freedom that is
incompatible with his institutional theory.

Interpretive communities and traditions – whether those of
music analysis, historicism, New Criticism, or deconstruction –
focus our attention on certain features of an artwork. They place a
differential value on different parts, and suggest certain networks
of association between them. To most twentieth-century listeners
the interpretive conventions of the eighteenth-century *Affektenlehre*
are a closed book, but we bring to Bach's music norms, values, and
expectations that were unavailable to his contemporary listeners.
If we recover some of the conventions of *Affektenlehre* by means of
studying historical documents and listening to authentic performances, we shall have one ear, so to speak, for the eighteenth- and
one for the twentieth-century conventions. Most of our listening,
performing, and reading occurs in a pluralistic institutional setting
and our responses are correspondingly multi-perspectival. Fish has
no adequate explanation for this.

Similar objections can be raised to the other institutional theories. To conceive, as Bürger does, of a bourgeois "institution of
literature" that stretches from the end of the eighteenth century to
our days is to subsume under one concept a continuously changing
system that always encompassed several centers and several conflicting trends. Furthermore, Bürger derives the autonomy idea of
the bourgeois institution of literature from the aesthetic views of
Karl Philipp Moritz, Schiller, and a few other late-eighteenth-
century writers, and not from the history of real institutions.
Though Bürger is regarded as a neo-Marxist, in this he seems to be
a latter-day Hegelian, whom Marx has not as yet "turned upside
down." For, surely, the bourgeois publishers and teachers of literature (to name two institutional representatives) were deeply
enmeshed in the fabric of bourgeois society, even if they believed
that the arts were autonomous.

In sum, today's institutional theories tend to remain abstract
and schematic, and share many of the weaknesses for which theories of the Zeitgeist have rightly been criticized. If they are to
become effective, they will have to develop further the mechanisms
of institutional change, and they will have to admit that the

31 See John Neubauer, "Critical Pluralism and the Confrontation of Interpretations,"
   Poetics 14 (1985), 433–44.

institutions and conventions of the artworld do not shape exclusively the production and reception of artworks.

A genuine institutional perspective on the arts ought to acknowledge that we participate in many social, political, and intellectual institutions, whose extra-art conventions and ideologies deeply affect the judgments we make within the artworld. The artworld is enmeshed in a system of other institutions, a system that is in constant flux and hardly ever free of inner contradictions. Furthermore, institutional theories of the arts will have to offer a more supple account of the behavior of individuals within such institutional constellations. The meaning of artworks will neither be "obvious" nor "inescapable" if we have several conflicting institutional loyalties; and it seems only reasonable to assume that our judgments will, as a rule, not be determined by such loyalties alone. Faced with a choice, we respond not only to social pressure, we are swayed also by the coherence of an argument, the quantity and quality of the evidence, our personal fears, wishes, and momentary moods. The latter are affected, but not exclusively determined, by institutions and their conventions. Lest institutions become fetishes, comparable to the text-fetishes and subject-fetishes of the past, we must find their mechanism of change, which will have to include some account of how institutions are shaped by individuals.

A responsible institutional theory of interpretation will have to allow that the meaning we attribute to an artwork is co-determined by properties of the work, the intellectual and emotional disposition of the observer, and the guiding conventions in the relevant institution(s). Neither of these is fixed and powerful enough by itself to define meaning. The numerous and complex properties of an artwork are always selected and selectively foregrounded from a particular perspective that is co-determined by our personal preferences and by the governing institutional conventions of the moment and location. In terms of Nelson Goodman's theory,[32] artworks have a very large, though limited, set of qualities, and they will *exemplify* a certain subset of these according to the particular circumstances. Thus the sound of the clarinet may exemplify a particular timbre or pitch, and it may also exemplify the sweetness or melancholy of a certain musical motif. Timbre and pitch are measurable qualities of the sound, sweetness and melan-

---

[32] See Goodman, *Languages of Art*, pp. 45–67.

choly are metaphorical emotional labels we apply to the configuration of sounds, so that the sounds will *express* sweetness or melancholy for us. Only certain qualities of the sound will be exemplified to us (metaphorically or literally) in any particular situation, others will remain dormant, so to speak. Which particular qualities these will be is indeed dependent on the listening conventions of our institution(s). But it will also depend on the personal and momentary disposition of the listener. Institutional and personal forces interact in focusing selectively on qualities in the artwork. Working out a model for this is one of the most challenging tasks for an institutional theory and an aesthetics of both music and literature.

2

Privileging the moment of reception: music and radio in South Africa

Charles Hamm

Joseph Kerman observed in 1985 that "semiotics, hermeneutics, and phenomenology are being drawn upon only by some of the boldest of musical studies today, [and] post-structuralism, deconstruction, and serious feminism have yet to make their debuts in musicology."[1] As accurate as this statement may have been then for mainstream historical musicology in the United States, it was not applicable to the study of popular music, which was marked throughout the 1980s by attempts to apply these and other recent theories and methodologies to musical scholarship, largely through the agencies of the International Association for the Study of Popular Music (IASPM), established in 1981 during a first International Conference on Popular Music Research held in Amsterdam, and the journal *Popular Music*, published by Cambridge University Press since 1981.

Music exists as a three-fold series of processes: a first stage of creation, or composition; a middle stage of mediation, involving publication, production, performance, and dissemination; and a final one of reception and perception. Historical musicologists, particularly in the United States, with their propensity for accumulating "more and more facts, [with] less and less confidence in interpreting them," as Kerman put it,[2] have tended to privilege the first of these processes to the virtual exclusion of the others, while scholars of the mass media and certain social scientists focus their attention on the second. My intent here is modest: to isolate a single moment of reception – one piece of music heard at a given time in a specific place – and to test what socio-historical analysis can tell us about what is being perceived at this moment and what

---

[1] Joseph Kerman, *Contemplating Music: Challenges to Musicology* (Cambridge, Mass., 1985), p. 17. (Also published by Fontana as *Musicology* [London, 1985].)
[2] *Ibid.*, p. 54.

relationship this perception bears to what was intended by the creator of the piece, and to the persons or agencies involved in its mediation. I've chosen the song "All Night Long (All Night)," written by the American singer–songwriter Lionel Richie in 1983 and recorded that year for the Motown Record Corporation.

THE COMPOSITION

Dave Harker's admonition that "unless we locate cultural products in history, we cannot hope to understand culture or history"[3] is a useful starting point for our analysis, though his seminal study of the early nineteenth-century English song "Bob Cranky" is of little further use to us because, like most studies of popular songs,[4] it focuses chiefly on the text. More fruitful as a model is Bill Austin's book-length analysis of three songs by Stephen Foster which explores in exhaustive detail the various socio-historical contexts in which the songs are embedded and the several resultant levels of meaning which can be teased out by close analysis.[5]

At a first contextual level, the words of our song, and in fact its very title, invoke the most venerable symbolism in rock music: music and dance as sexual imagery. Such lines as "Everybody sing, everybody dance, lose yourself in wild romance, all night long," are in a tradition extending back to Bill Haley's "Rock Around the Clock" of 1953 – "We're going to rock around the clock tonight, we're going to rock, rock, rock till broad daylight."

But while Haley's song, like so much early rock 'n' roll, draws on the black dance hall culture of rhythm and blues of the 1940s and '50s, "All Night Long," thirty years later, is more complex and ambiguous in cultural reference. The text, on paper, often suggests contemporary, colloquial American usage: "Well my friends the time has come, to raise the roof and have some fun ..." But soon words and phrases from other cultures begin to appear: "parti" is a Caribbean term for a celebration involving music, dancing, eating, and drinking; "karamu" is a Swahili term for feasting and

[3] David Harker, "The Original Bob Cranky?," *Folk Music Journal* 5:1 (1985), 76.
[4] See, for instance, Sean Cubitt, "*Maybellene*: Meaning and the Listening Subject," *Popular Music* 4 (1984), 207–24; Umberto Fiori, "Listening to Peter Gabriel's *I Have the Touch*," *Popular Music* 6 (1987), 37–44; and Michael Roos and Don O'Meara, "Is Your Love in Vain? – Dialectical Dilemmas in Bob Dylan's Recent Love Songs," *Popular Music* 7 (1988), 35–50.
[5] See William Austin, *"Susanna," "Jeanie," and "The Old Folk at Home": The Songs of Stephen C. Foster from His Time to Ours* (New York and London, 1975).

enjoyment within a community; "fiesta" is of course a Spanish word for a celebration, widely used throughout Latin America; "liming" is an English Caribbean slang expression for "hanging out," as for example at a party. The text of the second verse, beginning with "People dancing all in the street, see the rhythm all in their feet," invokes a street fest, more typical of Latin America than the United States. An apparently multi-lingual "chant" appears halfway through the song:

> Tom bo li de say de moi ya
> Yeah, Jambo Jumbo
> Way to parti' o we goin'
> Oh, jambali
> Tom bo li de say de moi ya
> Yeah, JUMBO JUMBO!

Neither I nor my colleagues can make sense of this text beyond the fact that it is densely packed with words and phrases from various black cultures: English Caribbean, Spanish-speaking Latin American, creole, African. More specific meaning seems to depend on one's linguistic and cultural heritage. For instance, one colleague suggested that the opening phrase "Tom bo li de say" may be heard by a Trinidadian as a corruption of "Liumbo lilissay" – Liumbo being a notorious thief and folk hero in Trinidad in the second quarter of the twentieth century, "lilissay" meaning to "slide into one's premises without being caught."

Musically, Afro-Caribbean drumming patterns by percussionists Paulinho Da Costa and John Robinson, not clearly identifiable with any specific ethnic tradition, serve as an introduction and continue throughout the song. This drumming, combined with Richie's accented English and the gradual introduction of foreign words, suggests a vaguely Caribbean location, though the string and horn accompaniment (arranged by James Anthony Carmichael) is vintage 1980s Motown. The refrain, "All night long," introduces a rudimentary call-and-response pattern between Richie and his seven background vocalists, reinforced by more prominent and complex drumming, again vaguely Afro-Caribbean. The "chant," introduced by crowd sounds and blaring horns suggesting a Carnival parade, is accompanied only by percussion and shouting. Crowd noises continue intermittently as the song moves towards its close; an instrumental interlude near the end is dominated by a xylophone, invoking a steel band from Trinidad or perhaps the marimbas of Mexico and Guatemala;

more blaring horns and shouts from Richie's "Hoopa Hollers" continue to suggest a street fest, up to the final fadeout.

Thus the music of "All Night Long," like the text, is shot through with references to various Afro-Caribbean and Afro-Latin cultures; there are hints of Latin street fests, of reggae, of calypso; but the song as a whole is none of these things.

Motown Records, established in the early 1960s, first produced music by black musicians in a regional black musical style, aimed at an urban black working-class audience in the industrial upper Mideast. In the mid-1960s the company targeted a national, more affluent, and mostly white audience, with outstanding commercial success. By 1983, when this record was produced, Motown had moved from Detroit to Hollywood and had entered into a long-term licensing agreement in the UK, with RCA. Thus the marketing strategies of Motown had been aimed successively at regional, national, and then international markets, and in the process the "Motown sound" had become increasingly generalized.[6] This LP was produced to be equally marketable in the USA, in Europe, in Commonwealth countries, in Latin America, and in Africa; even the iconography of the cover photo makes no visual references to a specific culture or geographic location.

Reggae music had become widely popular at this time in Latin America, Africa, and the UK,[7] particularly after Bob Marley's death in 1981. The texts of reggae songs were heard in many Third World countries as authentic expressions of the struggle of the populations of underdeveloped countries against the "new imperialism" of the late twentieth century. In the United States, reggae had remained a "cult genre ... with limited commercial appeal. [Recording companies] had little use for these perennially stoned wild-hairs with their lackadaisical recording methods and invariably late-starting, Grateful Dead-length concerts."[8] But Americans were nevertheless exposed to the characteristic rhythms and sonorities of this music, if not its ideology, through such reggae-influenced groups as the Police ("Zenyatta Mondatta" [1980], "Ghost in the Machine" [1980], "Synchronicity" [1983])

---

6 See Charles Hamm, "The Transformation of Folk into Popular Music through Mass Dissemination." Paper delivered at the Fourteenth Congress of the International Musicological Society, Bologna, September 1987.

7 Roger Wallis and Krister Malm, *Big Sounds from Small Peoples: The Music Industry in Small Countries* (New York, 1984), pp. 98–99 and 303.

8 Ed Ward, Geoffrey Stokes, and Ken Tucker, *Rock of Ages: The Rolling Stone History of Rock & Roll* (New York, 1986), p. 543.

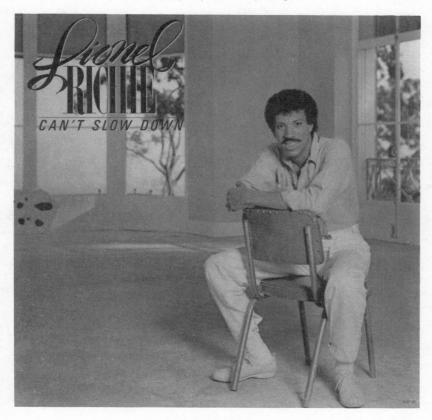

Figure 2.1 Cover for Lionel Richie's album Can't Slow Down *(1983)*

and the Talking Heads ("Fear of Music" [1979], "Remain in Light" [1980], "Speaking in Tongues" [1983]). Even such perennial stars as Stevie Wonder, Paul Simon, and Bob Dylan introduced elements of reggae into their music in the early 1980s. Thus Lionel Richie, writing a song in 1983 intended for international distribution, could have done no better than to sprinkle it with references to Caribbean music in general and reggae in particular.

We can understand "All Night Long (All Night)," then, as a deliberately generalized product, a generic pop song of the early 1980s. The text is non-narrative, repetitious, and episodic; its essence is stated in the first few lines, actually in the title itself, and there is no dramatic progression as the song unfolds. The music is likewise episodic, additive, open-ended. Since neither text nor

Figure 2.2 Two young women and radio, Fingo Village, Grahamstown, 1984

music is constructed in linear fashion, and neither moves to dramatic or structural climaxes, analytical systems developed to make
sense of linear, goal-oriented European classical music cannot be
expected to reveal structural or expressive relationships between
music and text, both packed with references to specific cultures.
More precise meaning comes only at the moment of reception,
shaped by the cultural capital of the listener.

RECEPTION

My analysis will be concerned with this song at the moment it was
heard over the radio by two young black women in November of
1984 in a black township in the Republic of South Africa.

We must first note that our moment of reception takes place
through the agency of one of the contemporary mass media, in this
case radio.

One strand of contemporary critical thought holds that the
electronic mass media have had an anti-social, dehumanizing
impact on listeners, and that these media have been used to
reinforce political and economic power. Attali suggests that in the
present era of "repetition," "each spectator has a solitary relation
with a material object: the consumption of music is individualized

... The network is no longer a form of sociality, an opportunity for spectators to meet and communicate."[9] As a result, he says, we live in a "world now devoid of meaning," in a "present made of abstraction, nonsense, and silence," as a result of the "strategic use of music by power to *silence*, [through] mass-producing a deafening, syncretic kind of music, and censoring all other human noises."[10] Allan Bloom is even less hopeful. Taking as the symbol of our era "a 13-year-old boy sitting in the living room of his family home doing his math assignment while wearing his Walkman headphones or watching MTV," he laments that Western civilization now culminates in

a pubescent child whose body throbs with orgasmic rhythms; whose feelings are made inarticulate in hymns to the joy of onanism or the killing of parents; whose ambition is to win fame and wealth in imitating the drag-queen who makes the music. In short, his life is made into a nonstop, commercially pre-packaged masturbational fantasy ... As long as [he] has the Walkman on, he cannot hear what the Great Tradition has to say. And, after its prolonged use, when he takes it off, he finds he is deaf.[11]

But Shuhei Hosokawa, among others, rejects the view that "with industrialisation and urbanisation, especially in recent decades, [people] lose that healthy relationship with the environment, become alienated and turn into [a] 'lonely crowd,' suffering from incommunicability."[12] Rather, he agrees with Lyotard that "the *self* [in the post-modern era] is small, but it is not isolated: it is held in a texture of relations which are more complex and more mobile than ever before."[13] For Hosokawa, the radio in general and the Walkman in particular are merely the latest, and possibly the ultimate, devices allowing one to have music at home, at work, while traveling. The listener has become the *minimum, mobile, and intelligent unit* in the contemporary landscape, at the center of an "intersection of *singularities*."[14] In other words, the person using a radio, television set, or a Walkman is not isolated and alienated from the contemporary world, but is connected to it through access to a multiplicity of simultaneously-available channels of information. And far from being a solitary occupation, the consumption

[9] Jacques Attali, *Noise: The Political Economy of Music* (Minneapolis, 1985), p. 32. First published as *Bruits: essai sur l'économie politique de la musique* (Paris, 1977).
[10] *Ibid.*, pp. 3, 5, and 19.
[11] Allan Bloom, *The Closing of the American Mind* (New York, 1987), pp. 74–5 and 81.
[12] Shuhei Hosokawa, "The Walkman Effect," *Popular Music* 4 (1984), 165.
[13] Jean-François Lyotard, *La Condition postmoderne* (Paris, 1979), p. 31.
[14] Hosokawa, p. 165.

Figure 2.3 Landscape with radio, Port Alfred township, 1984

of music through the mass media has become a social and visible part of the contemporary landscape and soundscape, most certainly in South Africa, where the radio is omnipresent.

Gary Burns has argued that the reception of any single piece of media-disseminated music must be examined in the context of several levels of programming. That is, a song heard on radio or television is a component of a specific program, which in turn is one part of a day's scheduling, and the radio or television service carrying this program is part of a complex of available channels.[15] An analysis of our moment of reception based on this model reveals that:

[15] See Gary Burns, "Music Video: An Analysis on Three Levels". Paper delivered at the Third International Conference on Popular Music Studies, Montreal, 10 July 1985.

Figure 2.4 Landscape with radio, Northern Transvaal, 1984

i. "All Night Long (All Night)" at this moment of reception was heard on a request program, with listeners phoning the radio station to ask that a certain piece of music be played for specified friends or family members, and engaging the presenter in conversation and banter.

ii. The radio service in question, Radio Zulu, is devoted to omnibus, round-the-clock programming in the Zulu language; music, news, sporting events, religious messages, political commentary, announcements of deaths, children's programs, radio dramas, game shows. It is a commercial service, with frequent advertisements of consumer products.

iii. Radio Zulu is one of a network of nine "vernacular" services produced by the government-controlled South African Broadcasting Corporation (SABC), collectively called Radio Bantu.

iv. Radio Bantu is an important agent of Separate Development, a policy formulated by theorists of the ruling National Party

Figure 2.5 Jiving on the job, Northern Transvaal, 1984

in 1960 as a more sophisticated refinement of racial segregation, or apartheid. The ultimate goal of Separate Development is for citizenship in the Republic of South Africa to be restricted to whites, some 4–5 million of them benefiting from the rich mineral and agricultural wealth of the region. Blacks would be forced to live in, and become citizens of, ten impoverished "homelands" (or "National States") occupying a small fraction of the land area of South Africa, as seen in Figure 2.6. They would be allowed into "white" South Africa only as temporary, cheap labor, and while there would be forced to live in racially segregated townships.

Radio Bantu was designed to intensify ethnic and "national" identity among the various black "tribes" of the region, in order to make each of them receptive to the idea of having their own "National State," and to inhibit black unity. Its nine separate services, each in the language of the ethnic group assigned to a given "homeland," are beamed in highly selective geographical patterns, by FM transmission, to the ten ethnically segregated "homelands" and to the segregated townships in nearby "white" urban areas. The network of Radio Bantu is laid out in Table 2.1.

Thus the moment of reception with which we are concerned takes place in a context designed to elicit audience response and participation through a phone-in format; to maximize the sales

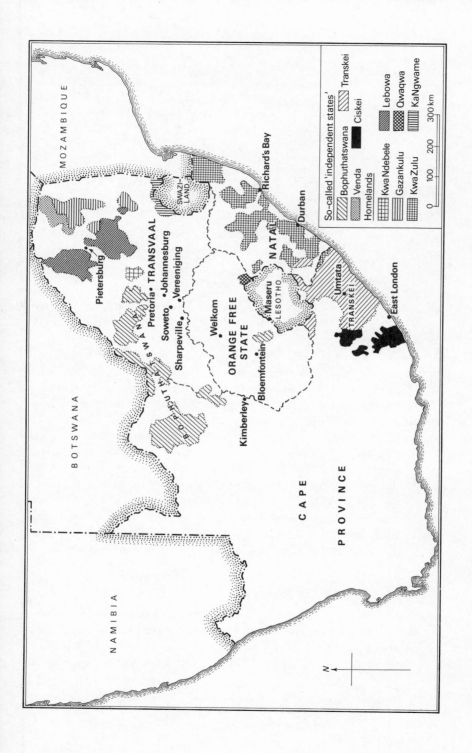

MOZAMBIQUE

BOTSWANA

NAMIBIA

SWAZI-
LAND

TRANSVAAL
Pietersburg
Pretoria • Johannesburg
Soweto •
Sharpeville • • Vereeniging

B O P H U T H A T S W A N A

NATAL
Richard's Bay
Durban

Welkom
•
ORANGE FREE
STATE
Bloemfontein •
Kimberley •

Maseru
LESOTHO

Umtata
TRANSKEI
East London

C A P E

P R O V I N C E

N

So-called 'independent states'
Bophuthatswana   Transkei
Venda   Ciskei
Homelands
KwaNdebele   Lebowa
Gazankulu   Qwaqwa
KwaZulu   KaNgwame

0   100   200   300 km

Table 2.1. *Radio Bantu*

Service	Language	Dissemination
Radio Zulu	Zulu	*Kwazulu*,[1] Natal, the Rand[2]
Radio Xhosa	Xhosa	*Transkei, Ciskei*, Eastern Cape
Radio Tswana	SeTswana	*Bophutathswana*, the Rand
Radio SeSotho	Southern Sotho	*Qwaqwa*, the Rand, Free State
Radio Lebowa	Northern Sotho	*Lebowa*, Northern Transvaal
Radio Tsonga	Tsonga	*Gazankulu*, Northern Transvaal
Radio Venda	LuVenda	*Venda*, Northern Transvaal
Radio Swazi	SiSwati	*KaNgwane*, Eastern Transvaal
Radio Ndebele	Ndebele	*KwaNdebele*, Central Transvaal

Notes
[1] The "homeland" for each ethnic group is italicized
[2] "The Rand" designates the area around Johannesburg, which has a high concentration of mines and other industry and thus a heavy demand for black workers, drawn from many different ethnic groups

among the black population of commodities produced by white-controlled capital; and to intensify the ethnic identity of its Zulu-speaking audience, as part of a larger political strategy.[16]

In this case, then, as Attali suggests, the mass medium of radio is being used by power to promote its own objectives. The SABC saturates its black listeners with "deafening, syncretic" music, dulling their sensibilities, making them more receptive to its own propaganda. "All Night Long (All Night)" was chosen for play on Radio Bantu because its text seemed innocent of political content, and Lionel Richie had no visible history of political activity. Its musical style likewise seemed devoid of political implications, and since music by black Americans is widely popular among South African blacks, it would help attract listeners to Radio Bantu.

PERCEPTION, RECEPTION

We are concerned with an individual moment of reception. If one accepts "the provocative claim made by extreme relativists that there are as many "Eroica" Symphonies as there are listeners in our concert halls,"[17] it is impossible to move beyond this movement

[16] See Hamm, *Afro-American Music, South Africa, and Apartheid* (Brooklyn, 1988).
[17] Carl Dahlhaus, *Foundations of Music History* (Cambridge, 1983), p. 152. First published as *Grundlagen der Musikgeschichte* (Cologne, 1967).

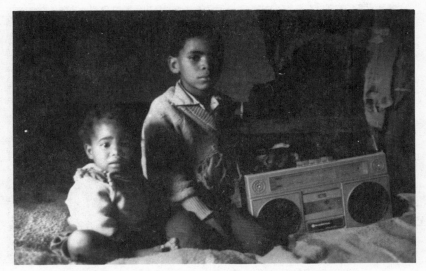

Figure 2.7 Two children and radio, Eastern Cape, 1984

in our analysis. But while it is all very well for John Cage to suggest that "now structure is not put into a work, but comes up in the person who perceives it. There is therefore no problem of understanding but the possibility of awareness. ... Here we are. Let us say Yes to our presence together in Chaos,"[18] musicologists are not at home with chaos and some of them have struggled to find a middle ground between rampant relativism and restrictive positivism. Felix Vodicka, for example, argues "that the object of reception history does not lie in individual reactions but in norms and normative systems that determine how surviving texts are perceived *within groups or strata conditioned by history, society and ethnic origin.*"[19]

We must, then, locate our moment of reception in the context of such a "group or stratum conditioned by history, society and ethnic origin." To do so, I propose moving outwards in concentric circles from the individual who is the subject of our moment of reception to larger social and political structures, until we reach clear breaking points.

One can locate any number of other individual moments of

[18] John Cage, *Silence* (Middletown, 1961), pp. 259 and 195.
[19] Quoted in Dahlhaus, *Foundations of Music History*, p. 152. Vodicka's essay "Die Konkretisation des literarischen Werks. Zur Problematik der Rezeption von Nerudas Werk" was first published in Rainer Warning, ed., *Rezeptionsästhetik* (Munich, 1975), pp. 84–112.

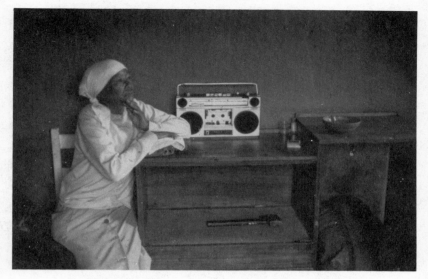

Figure 2.8 Woman and radio, Grahamstown, 1984

reception of Lionel Richie's song which would correspond to our original.

In each case the common factors are that the subjects are black; they live in South Africa, in a black township or one of the ten so-called "National States"; each speaks an African language, and usually has some knowledge of English as a second language; each has access to a Radio Bantu service in his or her own language; each is subject to racial restrictions imposed by the Population Registration Act, the Group Areas Act, Influx Control, and the other legal bastions of Separate Development; each is denied political input into the governing of community, region, and nation. These similarities cut across so-called "tribal" distinctions in South Africa, and in any event the notion of "tribe" is now understood as being an insupportable ethnographic concept, and as having been used by the government for its own political purposes.[20]

If our subjects were to be chosen from white South Africans, however, all these conditions would change: they would be free to live wherever they choose; their first language would be European (English or Afrikaans), and they would have little or no knowledge

[20] Monica Wilson and Leonard Thompson, eds., *A History of South Africa to 1870* (Cape Town and Johannesburg, 1985), pp. 75–186.

of any African language; they do not listen to Radio Bantu; they are the beneficiaries, not the victims, of the government's racial policies and laws; they help determine the political direction of South Africa by voting for local and national representatives. Likewise if one chose subjects from beyond the political boundaries of the Republic of South Africa, from Zimbabwe or Botswana for instance, conditions would once again be different.

The question now is to define precise ways in which the "history, society and ethnic origin" of our subjects affect the moment of reception with which we are concerned.

To begin with, references to rock music's mythology and history, to Bill Haley's "Rock Around the Clock" and similar songs which equate dancing with sex, do not come into play. An historical study of the dissemination of early rock 'n' roll in South Africa reveals that few blacks had access to this music in the 1950s and '60s, that it was rejected by those who did, and that it did not exist in the consciousness of black South Africans in the 1980s.[21]

Our listener(s) can be expected to understand enough English to grasp the general thrust of Richie's song – "Everybody sing, everybody dance, come on and sing along ... People dancing all in the street, see the rhythm all in their feet." But rather than understanding this as a metaphor for sex, our African listeners will take the text literally, as a description of communal dancing and singing – not only because the references to rock's mythology are not understood, but also because communal, celebratory singing and dancing is an important part of their traditional culture.[22]

Specific African words sprinkled through the text – karamu, jambo, jambali – are from Swahili, a language unknown this far south, and thus would not be understood literally, though they might be perceived as generically African. The "chant," however, would have a powerful resonance in South Africa. Whatever "Tom bo" means literally, it would have been perceived immediately by blacks, at this moment in South African history, as "Tambo": a reference to Oliver Tambo, the head of the outlawed African National Congress, in exile in Zambia.

The entire chorus and the extended coda of Richie's song are built on alternation between two notes (the tonic and the supertonic) and the two chords built on these pitches. As it happens, the musical bow, used to accompany much solo and choral singing in

[21] See Hamm, "Rock 'n' Roll in a Very Strange Society," *Popular Music* 5 (1985), 159–74.
[22] See Peter Larlham, *Black Theater, Dance, and Ritual in South Africa* (Ann Arbor, 1985).

Figure 2.9 "Beware Botha. Tambo is coming." Craddock township, 1984

traditional South African musical cultures, is capable of playing
only two notes, a major second apart. Musical patterns based on
alternation of two notes and/or two chords with roots a second
apart permeate other genres of traditional South African music as
well, and persist in such acculturated forms of the present century
as marabi, jive, and mbaqanga. Though it was surely not Richie's
intention, extended sections of "All Night Long (All Night)" had a
quite specific musical resonance among the black population of
South Africa.

　　Thus, at our moment of reception, the ambiguities deliberately
built into Richie's song are particularized by specific conditions of
history, society, and ethnicity. The song could have been heard as
a communal celebration of an exiled political leader, with several
musical details appropriate to this culture. This perception could
well have contributed to the enormous popularity of the song in
South Africa.

　　More generally, individual listeners at our moment of reception,
and the larger group of which they were part, knew that Richie
was black, and largely through music they had a sense of belonging
to a global black community encompassing Africa, the Caribbean,

and black America, North and South. Even though they had not been allowed to hear reggae songs with overtly political texts, they understood the issues involved in this music, and any piece of reggae – or even a piece with clear references to Caribbean music, like Richie's – carried a clear and quite specific reference to "the wrath, aspirations and hopelessness of [black] people who feel downtrodden," whatever the literal content of the text.[23]

Thus, just as the individual moment of reception of a song can result in a perception quite different from that intended by the composer, it can also empower a piece with meaning quite different from that apparently implied by its text and musical style, and thus alter the impact of media-disseminated music intended by "power."

Most historical musicologists have assumed that the composers of the great canonical works of Western musical history created "ideal objects with an immutable and unshifting 'real' meaning," and that the function of the scholar "consists in the gradual unfolding of [this] meaning."[24]

With "All Night Long (All Night)" we are dealing with a composer who deliberately created a generic piece, constructing it in such a way as to make it accessible to audiences of various cultural backgrounds, while at the same time packing it with details allowing it to be culture-specific at different moments of reception. The composer accepts and even utilizes the notion that more specific meaning will come only at reception, conditioned by factors of history, society, and ethnic origin.

A final question, then, is whether the situation described here results from some fundamental difference between the conditions of classical and popular music, or whether the suggestions made here might also be applicable to discussions of the reception and perception of classical music.

23 Wallis and Malm, *Big Sounds*, p. 66.
24 Dahlhaus, *Foundations of Music History*, pp. 150 and 155.

3

Chord and discourse: listening through the written word

Peter J. Rabinowitz

In an admirably pugnacious essay dealing with such matters as dust-jackets and *Cliff's Notes*, Gerald Graff argues that "'texts in themselves' ... have become harder to distinguish from the interpretations made of them" because they "come to us 'always already' pre-screened, so that we often know what texts mean before reading them."[1] I would like to make a related argument about listening – about the ways that music is implicated in a network of discursive practices so powerful that the very notion of "the music itself" becomes problematic. But lest it float away in theoretical abstractions, let me anchor my argument in a concrete cultural juxtaposition that I call the "purity and parasite" phenomenon. This was crystallized in a strange conjunction that marked the recording scene in the late 1980s: just as Christopher Hogwood began to extend his purifications ("authentic" performances with period instruments and performance practice) to the symphonies of Beethoven, Harmonia Mundi released the first complete cycle of those same symphonies in the notoriously impure piano transcriptions by Franz Liszt.[2] This was not an isolated coincidence. For some time, we have been deluged with recordings that try to get back to the composer's original intentions (and I would include here not only period performances of Bach, Mozart, and Beethoven, but also recordings of the "first versions" of the Bruckner symphonies). But we are simultaneously witnessing a resurgence of interest in parasitic rewritings of all kinds – Godowsky's twists of the Chopin Etudes, the completions of the

---

[1] Gerald Graff, "Narrative and the Unofficial Interpretive Culture," in James Phelan, ed., *Reading Narrative: Form, Ethics, Ideology* (Columbus, Ohio, 1989), p. 5.

[2] One might argue that the Liszt transcriptions are "authentic" since, in the nineteenth century, more people heard the music played on the piano than by an orchestra. But that is not how they are being packaged – and that argument would not explain the other parasitic trends I note below.

Schubert Tenth and Bruckner Ninth, Mahler's transcription of Schubert's "Death and the Maiden" Quartet, piano versions of *Le Sacre*.

In the present volume, among such colleagues as John Neubauer, it may not be shocking to suggest that we can account for this apparent contradiction only if we look at context – specifically, as Charles Hamm argues elsewhere in this volume, the context of listening. After all, whatever else happens when we listen to "authentic" Beethoven, we aren't listening with nineteenth-century ears. But I would like to look more closely at that truism: in what precise ways are our ears really different from those of Beethoven's listeners? Specifically, I am going to start to sketch out a model for the act of listening that I have been developing in collaboration with Jay Reise.[3] Like Lawrence Kramer, I started with the observation that "the way I read" was "intimately bound up with the way I heard".[4] But from there I have moved in a different direction. Rather than seeking "convergences" between the arts themselves, I have asked whether there are useful connections in the ways that they are talked about. That is, I have not been concerned with the relation between literature and music as much as with the question of what recent theorizing about how we read might teach us about how we listen.

My claim is that neither the score as written nor the sounds as performed offers sufficient grounds for interpretation or analysis; and my position derives, in part, from the work of such literary theorists as Jonathan Culler and Mary Louise Pratt, as well as from my own work on narrative convention. It is not that I am trying to make the score disappear, as Stanley Fish often seems to be doing to the literary text. But I do believe that what you hear and experience is largely dependent upon the presuppositions with which you approach it, and that those presuppositions are to a generally unrecognized degree verbal in origin. For if, as Ruth Solie points out, "language is not merely reflective but actually constitutive of our awareness," the "constellations of language" not only, as she puts it, "tend to shape and control the observations

---

[3] The collaborative nature of my work makes it hard to know when to use the first person singular, when the plural. Since the specific arguments in the paper that follows are, for the most part, my own, I have written it in the singular – but the essay should be recognized as part of an ongoing, joint venture.

[4] Lawrence Kramer, *Music and Poetry: The Nineteenth Century and After* (Berkeley and Los Angeles, 1984), p. vii.

of the analyst using them," but also tend to shape and control the experiences of the listener as well.[5]

This model of listening, like my own model of reading, involves several interlocking levels, and I would like to focus on two of them. First, there is what Reise and I call the *technical*: what is specifically represented by the musical notation. Examples of technical "facts" include: "The first note of the Beethoven Violin Concerto is a quarter note D timpani stroke on the first beat of a measure" or "The marking *lento* in the Funeral March of Chopin's Second Sonata means that we should play slowly." The technical is the usual fuel for musical analysis – or, at least, *appears* to be the usual fuel for musical analysis. For most analysis still concerns, as Joseph Kerman puts it, "the detailed 'internalist' explication of the structure of particular compositions."[6] That is, analysts often assume that the listener's experience is a more or less direct consequence of the technical. As W. J. Henderson puts it in his late nineteenth-century guide to listening, "The highest form of music is that in which music stands alone, and exercises her sway upon us wholly by means of her own unaided powers."[7]

---

5 Ruth A. Solie, "The Living Work: Organicism and Musical Analysis," *19th-Century Music* 4 (1980), 147–56; the cited passage is on p. 147. If Solie's word "tend" fudges the issue, I sympathize, for it is not clear how far the influence goes. Thus, while I accept the thrust of Hayden White's argument that "discourse *constitutes* the objects which it pretends only to describe realistically and to analyze objectively" (*Tropics of Discourse: Essays in Cultural Criticism* [Baltimore, 1978], p. 2), I am not ready to accept the most radical implications of that claim. *To a certain extent* discourse "tends" to constitute objects – the issue remains that of finding out how much and in what precise ways. Still, I would argue that musicians are insufficiently aware of the impact of discourse on the way music is experienced. Thus, for instance, the distinction between what a listener is "hearing" and what he or she has "learned" may be messier than Edward T. Cone imagines. See, for instance, Cone's "Three Ways of Reading a Detective Story – or a Brahms Intermezzo," *Georgia Review* 31 (1977), 554–74, in particular p. 565.

6 Joseph Kerman, *Contemplating Music: Challenges to Musicology* (Cambridge, Mass., 1985), p. 17. See also his "How We Got Into Analysis, and How to Get Out," *Critical Inquiry* 7 (1980), 311–31. See also Susan McClary's deconstruction of "the Master Narrative of 'Absolute Music,' ... [the] denial of meaning in the instrumental repertory" ("Sexual Politics in Classical Music," in *Feminine Endings: Music, Gender, and Sexuality* [Minn., 1991], pp. 53–79), and Gary Tomlinson's attack on "internalism" ("ethnocentrisism with a vengeance") in "The Web of Culture: A Context for Musicology," *19th-Century Music* 7 (1984), 350–62; the passage cited is on p. 360. For other critiques of analysis's formalist underpinnings, see Robert P. Morgan, "Theory, Analysis, and Criticism," *The Journal of Musicology* 1 (1982), 15–18 and Leo Treitler, "'To Worship that Celestial Sound': Motives for Analysis," *Journal of Musicology* 1 (1982), 153–70. Although Rose Rosengard Subotnik's "The Role of Ideology in the Study of Western Music" specifically addresses musicology, her arguments apply to analysis as well (*The Journal of Musicology* 2 [1983], 1–12).

7 W. J. Henderson, *What is Good Music? Suggestions to Persons Desiring to Cultivate a Taste in Musical Art*, 3rd edn. (New York, 1899), p. 87. Or, to be more up-to-date, see Milton

Granted, certain musical gestures *do* seem to have a direct causal effect on our experience. Nielsen's Third, for instance, begins with fourteen measures of repeated As in ever more rapid succession – and our sense of urgency seems a fairly unmediated result of that rhythmic gesture. But even if this is an instinctual, rather than a learned, response, such moments are rare. As Kramer suggestively puts it, "To hear [Chopin's] Op. 28 Preludes as an integral work ... requires" a particular "interpretive attitude"[8] – and the same holds true for our ability to hear *any* piece of music as anything. That is, listeners *process* the technical: they mediate "the notes themselves" through a series of interpretive strategies that allow them to make sense out of them. These strategies come from a second level that Reise and I call the *attributive* level, a level that is extra-compositional (although not always extra-musical), and that *precedes* the act of listening itself.

The ideal source for evidence about interpretive strategies would be actual listeners.[9] But I haven't the expertise necessary to run proper experiments. Nor, even with that expertise, could I uncover *historical* differences in listening, since there is no way to survey past experience. I have turned, therefore, to the next best thing (with a recognition of its limitations): writings *about* listening. And since my primary concern is not specialized listeners, but what used to be called the "average concert-goer," I have for the most part been exploring popular sources, especially books aimed at guiding the uninitiated.

In these texts, the attributive often appears in the outward guise of "factual" statements – what speech-act theorists often call constatives. Included here are such historical statements as "Mozart lived in the Classical period," such supposedly analytical statements as "rondo form consists of a series of A sections with contrasting material between," and such fanciful descriptions as those discussed by Thomas Grey in his essay elsewhere in this volume. In reality, though, their illocutionary force is *advisory*: that is, they serve not as facts but as instructions for listening. They thus provide a verbal structure through which the experience of sound

---

Babbitt: musical compositions can "completely and accurately" be viewed as "events occurring at time-points." ("The Structure and Function of Musical Theory," in Benjamin Boretz and Edward T. Cone, eds., *Perspectives on Contemporary Music Theory* [New York, 1972], p. 14).

[8] Kramer, *Music and Poetry*, p. 103.

[9] For a discussion in literary terms, see Janice Radway, *Reading the Romance: Women, Patriarchy, and Popular Literature* (Chapel Hill, 1984).

is processed, a structure that not only provides a grid through which listeners organize the sounds that they hear, but that also in part determines what those sounds are thought to be in the first place. But let us not separate ourselves too neatly from these "untrained" listeners. While the nature of the attributive level is clearest when we think of the listeners implied by these popular guides, the same principles govern the listening process we all go through. When we hear music, we always hear a complex combination of chord and discourse.[10]

As we consider the distinction between the technical and the attributive, it's important to remember that what is at issue is not where the *object* of musical meaning lies. The technical/attributive distinction is thus not a recasting of what Leonard Meyer calls the absolutist/referentialist split, "between those who insist that musical meaning lies exclusively within the context of the work itself ... and those who contend that, in addition ... music also communicates meanings which in some way refer to the extramusical world of concepts, actions, emotional states, and character."[11] Meyer is concerned with what kinds of meaning sounds can have; I, rather, am talking about the processes by which musical meaning is perceived. Even the most *absolute* musical experiences in Meyer's terms depend on an attributive level, even if there is no "outside" reference involved at all.

The two levels can be clarified by an analogy with cards. You can watch people playing a game you don't know and make technical statements: Gustav puts down a three of clubs, Alma plays a four of clubs on top of it. But that "event" is *in itself* meaningless. What meaning it has is *attributed to it*, not found in it; and it is attributed according to a conventional structure codified in the rules of the particular game. Of course, once you know a

---

[10] For a good discussion of the power of discourse in the reception of Mahler, see Marc A. Weiner, "Mahler and America: A Paradigm of Cultural Reception," *Modern Austrian Literature* 20 (1987), 155–69. Although I have difficulty with Weiner's neat distinctions between "musical" and "unmusical" concerns, his description of the way stories about Mahler influenced ways of listening is compelling. Since my concern here is with the written word, I will be emphasizing primarily (but not exclusively) the verbal manifestations of attributive discourse. It should be remembered, though, that the attributive level also includes non-verbal "statements": for instance, performance decisions as to just how long the second beat in a Viennese waltz should last. For a fascinating study, see Alf Gabrielsson, "Interplay Between Analysis and Synthesis in Studies of Music Performance and Music Experience," *Music Perception* 3 (1985), 59–86.

[11] Leonard B. Meyer, *Emotion and Meaning in Music* (Chicago, 1956), p. 1. See also the four levels of reference set out by Janice E. Kleeman in "The Parameters of Musical Transmission," *Journal of Musicology* 4 (1985), 1–22, esp. pp. 17–20.

large number of games, you have a background that allows you to make reasonable guesses about the particular meanings involved here – just as knowledge of Donne and Milton prepares you, to some extent, to read Herrick, or knowledge of Beethoven and Mendelssohn prepares you, to some extent, to listen to Mozart. But no matter how quick you are, there is always an attributive level, even if it is only postulated from analogous experiences. You may be right or wrong in your assumption about what that four on top of that three "means" – but it only "means" *in the first place* because of assumptions that attribute meaning to it.

The attributive does not overlay "the music itself" (like the colorization of black-and-white films); it is, rather, an essential *part of* the music. Indeed, it even helps determine "what" the technical level consists of. Again, to analogize from cards: a Jack of Spades is a "one-eyed Jack" in certain kinds of poker, but not in bridge; that is, its "one-eyed-ness" is *turned into* a relevant quality by the rules in force upon it.

If the attributive level is not an overlay, even less should it be seen as a contamination that the good listener tries to wash off. The day is past when literary people argue that a text itself tells the objective reader what to make of it. But we have not yet gotten as far in music, and we hence do not quite so readily see through Aaron Copland when he defines the "gifted listener" as one who, "without theories and without preconceived notions of what music ought to be ... lends himself as a sentient human being to the power of music."[12] Listening is less passive than that; in fact, it is *only* the "theories" and "preconceived notions of what music ought to be" that allow a listener to turn the raw material of sound into a musical experience at all.

If the attributive level resembles the rules of a card game, what sorts of rules are in fact involved? Of course, we should not take the metaphor too literally. The rules of listening – in contrast to those for cards – are not prescriptive; that is, they are conventional strategies for making sense of things, not laws of behavior, and they thus have an *ad hoc*, often personal, quality. Granted, composers compose with the expectation (conscious or unconscious) that their listeners will make sense of their notes through a particular set of interpretive strategies – so, in terms of authorial intention, we can perhaps speak about "proper" listening. But the rules are always

---

[12] Aaron Copland, *Music and Imagination: The Charles Eliot Norton Lectures 1951–1952* (New York, 1959), p. 23.

implicit, and listeners do not always listen as intended. The rules are also so numerous that it is not easy to get a grip on them. Thus, in my work on narrative, I have found it convenient to classify the equivalent rules or strategies for reading according to a four-part scheme.[13]

First, there are rules of notice. Despite the critical litany that "everything counts" in good literature, we cannot possibly keep track of all the details. We have learned to live with this profusion because we have rules that give priority to certain details, and that thus tell us where to direct our attention. Some rules of notice cover a wide spectrum of texts: for instance, the rule that openings are privileged. Others are specific to smaller groups of texts: we are, for instance, expected to pay more attention to the anagrammatic possibilities of characters' names in Nabokov than we are in James Cain.

Second, there are rules of signification. These rules allow us to transform the elements that the first set of rules has brought to our attention. Included here, for example, are rules for determining symbolic meaning (like the rules that tell us when to invoke the sexual connotations of words) or psychological meaning (for instance, the rules that permit us to draw conclusions about characters' thoughts from their deeds).

Third, there are rules of configuration. Certain complexes of literary features tend to occur together; and, because of our familiarity with such groupings, we can predict patterns while they are in the process of emerging. We can thus both develop expectations and experience closure.

Finally, there are rules of coherence, which allow us to convert a text into a meaningful whole. Included here are rules that deal, for instance, with textual disjunctures, permitting us to repair apparent inconsistencies by transforming them into metaphors, subtleties, ironies, and themes. Even deconstructive readings, which widen rather than bridge textual gaps, often find some overarching theme or philosophical point in terms of which the discontinuities "make sense."

In ordering the rules in this way, I am not suggesting that we apply them one after another: they interact with each other in ways that may well be beyond neat analysis. Thus, logically, rules of notice would seem to come before rules of configuration, since we

[13] For a fuller discussion, see my *Before Reading: Narrative Conventions and the Politics of Interpretation* (Ithaca, N.Y., 1987).

cannot perceive a pattern until we notice the elements out of which it is formed. But, in practice, one of the ways elements become visible is that they form parts of a recognizable pattern. By postulating these four types, therefore, I intend neither a descriptive model of the way the human mind actually operates nor an absolute and exhaustive classification. The scheme is, rather, a practical analytic device, of value to the extent that it helps answer particular questions.

Let me stress again that I am not using the word "rule" prescriptively. Although a given author is bound, consciously or unconsciously, to expect or desire readers to apply a given set of rules, I am not concerned today with whether readers do or should apply them (or any other particular set). Rather, my point is that application of *some* rules is an inevitable part of reading, and that the activity of *applying* the rules to a certain extent *creates what it is that we understand the text to be*. Interpretive strategies, in other words, are *part of* the "work itself" in the sense that they will always figure (explicitly or implicitly) in any description that purports to be a description of the work itself. But while they are part of the work itself, they are not *in* the work itself – and therein lies the source of much interpretive disagreement.

I don't want to be the sort of theorist who grinds up all aesthetic artifacts in the art-processor of a single system; but it does seem that my four literary categories have musical analogues as well.

Let me start with notice. Kerman argues that "Schenkerian analysis repeatedly slights salient features in the music"[14]: but the very notion of salience is slippery. Although we like to believe that the score makes us hear what is important, in fact what we know *about* a piece also influences what we highlight. It's no accident that the phrase "what to listen for" is so common in primers on listening (indeed, Copland used it as the title for one of his books). I remember, as a child, hearing a Leonard Bernstein lecture in which he showed how Strauss, in *Till Eulenspiegel*, had buried the opening theme, rhythmically dismembered, in the horns, beneath a complex music fabric. Without that verbal guidance, I could have gone on listening to that piece without ever focusing on that horn part. As it is, though, I'm on the lookout for it, so it's always

---

[14] Kerman, *Contemplating Music*, p. 82; see also p. 152. Of course, Kerman is not unaware of this difficulty: "The first thing to ask about theory in any historical period is what musical elements theorists felt it necessary to speculate about" (p. 60).

what I hear when that passage is played. The horn part itself, of course, is inherently in the score; but its *importance* is not. Rather, in listening, I *attribute* importance to it because of what I already know about it. If Strauss intended me to do so, that may make that attribution "correct" in a certain sense of the word; but it doesn't make its importance a technical matter.[15]

Not only does knowledge of specific facts allow us to perceive or to stress particular musical details; notice works in more general ways, too. Henry Edward Krehbiel, in his once-popular *How to Listen to Music*, suggested that counterpoint was out-of-date, an "elaborate and ingenious," but "soulless" technique that effectively "fettered" melodies. Robert Erickson, in contrast, *begins* his listener's guide with counterpoint, which he treats as the essential musical technique.[16] Obviously, listeners who follow the advice of these different teachers will hear the interplay of melodic material in different ways. It is not only that different texts and different listeners as individuals engage in different operations of notice. Furthermore, in different periods, different rules of notice tend to predominate. I will come back to this point later on.

Let me turn now to signification. Specific themes or gestures take on musical meanings which stem not only from their particular character (yet another area of musical signification) but also from their relationship to other gestures, either within the same piece or in other pieces. Thus, Kramer argues that the finale of the Mahler Second works as it does at least in part because it closes "with a variant of the lyrical melody of the first movement."[17] And the middle of "Golliwog's Cakewalk" works as it does in part because of Debussy's slap at *Tristan*.

There are, in fact, three distinct operations going on in these attributions of significance. First, you have to be able to recognize the different musical events as somehow "the same theme." Were the two Mahler themes identical, were the Debussy an exact quotation, such recognition would be a matter of memory. But in

---

15 As stated in note 10, my concern here is with verbal manifestations of the attributive; but I should point out that the same information can be conveyed through performance – which is why performance history too becomes part of the attributive level. Still, Bernstein's verbal guidance influences my hearing even of performances by conductors who do not share his views about the importance of that horn part. Thanks to Harold Fromm for helping me clarify this point.

16 Henry Edward Krehbiel, *How to Listen to Music: Hints and Suggestions to Untaught Lovers of the Art* (New York, 1896; New York, 1931), p. 277 and Robert Erickson, *The Structure of Music: A Listener's Guide* (New York, 1955).

17 Kramer, *Music and Poetry*, p. 88.

these examples, we're dealing not with identity, but with *similarity*, which is not inherent in objects, but is rather a matter of perception: a decision to see two musical gestures as similar requires being able to "transform" one into the other. Like grammatical transformation, such transformations are rule-bound, although it is not easy to specify precisely what the rules at work are.[18] Second, even two listeners who share the same transformational rules will assign different thematic meanings depending on what other themes they have available for association. That is not, presumably, a problem when the thematic links are internal to a given piece, as they are in the Mahler. But it *is* an issue in the Debussy: someone who doesn't know Wagner – or isn't prepared to summon up Wagner when listening to this piece – simply will not get the point. The sense we have of a particular musical gesture thus depends in part on the "intercompositional grid" on which we place it – that is, on the other music we have in our minds as we listen, and against which we measure it. And, to a large extent, that grid is determined by the verbal texts we read – by journalistic criticism, by musicological treatises, by guides that chart out the masterworks that "cultivated" people should know, by lists for Ph.D. exams. Third, even among listeners with the same intercompositional grid, reactions will depend on the quality of associations with those other works. In order to hear the Debussy as intended, you not only need to know *Tristan*, but also need to have the "right" associations with it, associations (as is often true in such cases) that are quite different from those intended by the original composer of the quoted material.[19]

The intercompositional grid is even more important when it comes to configuration – a term I use not to refer to what Anthony Newcomb calls "static schema" or what Edward T. Cone calls "a synoptic overview," but rather to what Newcomb calls "formal process" – that is, our constantly changing projection of a future as a piece "unfolds in time."[20] To the extent that we in fact listen to

[18] See, for instance, the complex maneuverings as Marshall Portnoy tries to prove connections between Elgar and Bach ("The Answer to Elgar's *Enigma*," *Musical Quarterly* 71 [1985], 205–10) or the even more arbitrary manipulations of Alan Walker in *An Anatomy of Musical Criticism* (London, 1966).

[19] As I have argued elsewhere (see, in particular, "Fictional Music: Toward a Theory of Listening," in Harry R. Garvin, ed., *Theories of Reading, Looking and Listening* [Lewisburg, Penn., 1981], pp. 193–208), traditional analysis has special trouble explaining how the same notes can take on different meanings.

[20] Anthony Newcomb, "Those Images That Yet Fresh Images Beget," *Journal of Musicology* 2 (1983), 227–45, esp. pp. 235 and 232 and Cone, "Three Ways," p. 557.

music not as a string of events but rather as a series of expectations as to what will follow, the "meaning" of a particular piece is largely a function of the pattern of the satisfactions – and, as Newcomb emphasizes, the frustrations – of those expectations.

Those expectations, of course, work on several levels – from the most immediate expectation that a particular chord will resolve in a particular way through larger-scale expectations about antecedent and consequent phrases, to the grandest architectural designs. But, as Kramer puts it "Avant-garde experiments aside, virtually all works of music or poetry move toward closure by referring to a normative pattern."[21] On whatever level, expectation is only possible in terms of norms that precede, and exist outside, the work in question. And since music is a constantly changing social practice rather than a natural occurrence, those norms always vary according to context, as is demonstrated elsewhere in this volume by Ellen Rosand's discussion of disruption of norms in mad-scenes.

Thus the probabilities of the various possible resolutions of a given chord – and hence the experiential meaning of a composer's particular choice of one of them – depends on whether we hear that chord against the harmonic practice of Haydn and Mozart, or against the harmonic practice of Debussy and Bax. That is, the experiential meaning is not entirely in the progressions themselves, but is to a largely unappreciated extent attributed to them by the listener, through the terms in which he or she chooses to listen. The same is true with expectations regarding larger formal units. Suppose we are listening to a sectional piece which, after an introduction in B♭, starts with an A section in B♭, followed by a B section in B♭, a repeat of the A section in B♭, and a C section in E♭. What expectations are set up? Listening according to Mozartian norms, we expect a return to the original material and the original key – and would therefore experience both surprise and lack of closure if the piece concluded with a D section, also in E♭. But that surprise is not inherent in that structure – it is the result of a prior decision we make (perhaps unconsciously) about how to listen to it. We might well make a different initial choice. Listening, for instance, according to the norms that Scott Joplin expected his listeners to apply, the conclusion would be unsurprising and closed, as it was intended to be, say, in "Pineapple Rag," which follows that pattern. In other words, the ending

21 Kramer, *Music and Poetry*, p. 16.

of "Pineapple Rag" is, *in itself*, neither satisfyingly closed nor ambiguously open (although Joplin intended it to be closed). To a large extent, the listener *gives* the piece its configurational character by the presuppositions with which he or she listens to it.

Rules of configuration tell us what to expect as we go through a piece of music; rules of coherence allow us, once we're finished, to reconsider what we've heard (including the pattern of frustrations and satisfactions that the rules of configuration have allowed us to experience), and give it some kind of broader, more generalized "meaning." Rules of coherence are the most difficult to articulate. But it is easy to see them in action: when we listen to the *Liebestod* and sense it as the orgasmic relief of the sexual tensions that have characterized *Tristan* from the beginning of the Prelude; when we discover that the "meaning" of the Adagio of the Bruckner Ninth shifts when a reconstruction of his unfinished Finale is added to the traditional three-movement score; when we hear a piece and recognize it as "a product of the seventeenth century": in all of these cases we are applying rules of coherence. Kramer's brilliant discussions of "structural rhythms" are, in my terms, descriptions not of inherent structures at all, but of rules of coherence, strategies of listening through which he makes, rather than finds, the sense of the music he hears.

Since sonata form has such a well developed attributive history in our culture, we can get an especially clear sense of the ways that the attributive level influences listening by looking at the different ways in which it is presented in elementary guides to listening. In particular, I would like to examine what might be called the "narrative" side of sonata form's attributive layer. One thing the attributive level does is help us make sense out of music by providing a roadmap or story. And the events in a sonata-form movement stand out, take meaning, satisfy or frustrate our experiences, and ultimately cohere at least in part according to their correspondence to the privileged points mapped out by a "master/mistress story" of reconciliation.

Actually, such a claim about this master story is not quite accurate. Rather, sonata form is presented as one or another of several *different* stories about reconciliation – and it is precisely the coexistence of these different stories that makes clear that they are attributions and not descriptions. To be sure, since the nineteenth century, the most popular versions divide a sonata-form movement in more or less the same spots: most musicians agree that sonata form consists of an optional introduction, an exposition of the primary material, a development section that expands on that material, and a recapitulation, perhaps followed by a coda.[22] But within those general divisions, guides to listening tell substantially different stories – which means that the experiences they urge the listener to create are substantially different, too.

Since space is limited, I am going to simplify and treat these narratives under two general rubrics. One of these is what I call the thematic story. According to this plot, the exposition sets out two themes, which are of contrasting nature in order to minimize the listener's boredom. In many versions, the first theme is described as "masculine," the second as "feminine."[23] The dramatic conflict in this tale occurs in the development, where one or both themes are torn apart and reworked in a way that increases tension – a tension resolved in the recapitulation, where the themes are re-presented in more or less their original guise. What results is an ABA structure of stability/tension/restabilization. Thus, for W. J. Henderson, the essentials of a sonata are "its tripartite form, its contrast of thematic material, its development of that material, and its *return to the original proposition*."[24]

Krehbiel, one of the theme-story advocates, points out the recapitulation "is devoted to a repetition, *with modifications*" of the exposition.[25] For him, those modifications are decorative; but for critics who tell the other story – the one that I call the key-story – it is precisely in the "modifications" so lightly brushed aside by Krehbiel that we find the essence of the form. As Erickson, one of

22 Of course, earlier visions of sonata form were different, and often difficult to translate into nineteenth-century terminology. See Jane R. Stevens, "Georg Joseph Vogler and the 'Second Theme' in Sonata Form," *Journal of Musicology* 2 (1983), 278–304.

23 As Ethel Peyser puts it, "The first theme could be called the male theme because it is usually virile, while the second theme, in lovely contrast, is usually gentle and winning" (*How to Enjoy Music: A First Aid to Music Listeners* [New York, 1933], p. 55). Although many theme-story tellers will note in passing that the themes are initially in different keys, that difference is played down as secondary. See, for instance, Peyser, *How to Enjoy Music*, p. 55; Henderson, *What is Good Music*, p. 48; Percy A. Scholes, *The Listener's Guide to Music, With a Concert-Goer's Glossary* (London, 1919; 8th edn, London, 1933), p. 37; and Krehbiel *How to Listen to Music*, ... p. 130.

24 Henderson, *What is Good Music*, pp. 54–55 (italics added). Or, as Peyser puts it, "The composer likes to repeat and to recapitulate at the end so that you and I may remember his piece (perhaps). This recapitulation in music is like the summary of a prose work" (*How to Enjoy Music*, p. 44). See also John Hallstrom, *Relax and Listen: How to Enjoy Music Through Records* (New York, 1947), p. 42: in "the recapitulation, ... the first part, involving the statement of the two themes, is virtually repeated."

25 Krehbiel, *How to Listen to Music*, p. 131 (italics added).

the more vigorous champions of this story, puts it, "The sonata-allegro form, the grand formal idea of the classicists, was not essentially a matter of themes at all, but of key areas."[26] According to this alternative narrative, sonata form starts out with an exposition not so much of basic material to be developed, but of an *initial instability* in the form of a juxtaposition of two conflicting key areas. This initial tension is further increased during the development, which not only twists the themes but, more important, ventures into more distant harmonic areas. The recapitulation ultimately resolves these tensions (and this is the crucial "modification" for the key-story people) by erasing the key conflict – for, in the recapitulation, both the first and the second themes reappear in the tonic. As Helen Kaufmann puts it, "After the giddy, often puzzling whirl of the development section, B, the return to the theme A, called the recapitulation, falleth as the gentle rain from heaven. Especially does it so appear inasmuch as, when restated, both themes have the same tonal center or key ... The return of those harmonies restores the sense of rounding out and completion of the story." We thus have an ABA′ structure of instability/greater instability/resolution.[27]

These stories are not variants of one another, nor even of some Proppian Ur-tale. They are, rather, mutually incompatible. With regard to notice, the two encourage listeners into experiences that are almost photographic negatives of one another – for each takes as the figure what the other takes as ground. Similarly, they attribute different significations to the key layout of the exposition, one setting it up as an ornamental contrast, the other as a dramatic conflict. In terms of configuration, they provide different norms against which to judge particular compositional choices as deviations or not. And they posit two different "coherences" for a given movement – two different "meanings" for our total experience: the theme story is a story of a *return* to an initial idyll; the key story is the story of the resolution of an initial conflict. Yet, for a hundred years or so, they have seemed (to different listeners, at least)

---

[26] Erickson, *The Structure of Music*, p. 82. Or as Edwin John Stringham puts it, in sonata form "key and modulation" are "the very determinants of form" (*Listening to Music Creatively*, 2nd edn. [Englewood Cliffs, New Jersey, 1959], p. 373).

[27] Helen L. Kaufmann, *You Can Enjoy Music* (New York, 1940), p. 69. For a more sophisticated account, see Kramer, *Music and Poetry*, p. 35: "The overall pattern of tension and release in a Classical sonata-allegro movement ordinarily depends on two things: an exposition that establishes the tonic with reasonable stability, then produces harmonic tension with a move to the dominant or its substitute, and a recapitulation that discharges the accumulated tension with a stable return to the tonic."

equally satisfactory ways of mapping out the terrain of sonata form. This suggests that actual people experience a given sonata-form movement differently, depending on which master-plot they are following as they listen.

It would be easy to draw a purely subjectivist conclusion from this argument, claiming that each listener creates a given piece in his or her own way. And to a certain extent this is true. But we all live in (and are partly formed by) a culture (or cultures). And different cultures, different historical periods, tend to support particular ways of listening. To put it in other terms, certain kinds of attributional activity are found more commonly in some periods than in others. It is for this reason that Berlioz could fool some of his contemporaries into thinking that the "Farewell of the Shepherds" from *L'Enfance du Christ* was a seventeenth-century piece, even though, to most experienced listeners today, its nineteenth-century origins are clear. For Berlioz's listeners had attributive screens that allowed them to "put it together" in a way that made it congruent with the seventeenth-century pieces they had put together before. Nowadays, most listeners work with different strategies, and no longer create that piece so that it "sounds" like our creations of the seventeenth-century pieces we know.

Nowadays, we have a different intercompositional grid to work with, too, and this also greatly affects the kind of musical experiences we create. Indeed, adding pieces to our standard repertoire – or subtracting them – has the potential to change the meaning of all the other pieces that we hear. Thus, even *new* pieces can influence the experienced meaning of pieces written before them. Certain passages in Schubert and Alkan, for instance, can now sound distinctly Mahlerian – although they obviously could not have sounded that way when they were written.[28]

This brings me back to the purity and parasite phenomenon I mentioned at the outset. Once we think of listening as an attributive act that in part creates the work of art according to prior rules that we apply to the musical sounds at hand, it is clear why reproducing the actual sounds of an early nineteenth-century "Eroica" will not result in our hearing it "as Beethoven intended."

---

[28] See Leonard Meyer: "It is not so much the past that shapes the present, but the present that, by selecting from the abundant possibilities of the past ... chooses what will influence it and, in so doing, 'decides' what its past will be" ("Innovation, Choice, and the History of Music," *Critical Inquiry* 9 [1983], 517–44; the passage cited is on p. 540).

I don't have the space to do a complete analysis of the act of listening to that piece. But let me point out a few of the ways in which we are likely to make a "new" piece out of the "Eroica". Take rules of notice: most contemporary listeners, of course, who are apt to be interested in a period-instrument performance of the "Eroica" have already heard it more times than Beethoven thought possible – and so, especially if the exposition repeat is taken, they are likely to focus on the details with more concentration than the composer expected.[29] More important, as I suggested earlier, listeners who are placed in different historical periods are likely to assign a different hierarchy to the fundamental musical elements. Copland points out, for instance, "Nowadays we tend to look upon transcriptions with suspicion because we consider the composer's expressive idea to be reflected in a precise way by its tonal investiture." He contrasts this with the eighteenth century, when "What instruments it was played by seems often to have been dictated by the requirements of a particular occasion."[30] Granted, this difference is truer for Bach and Mozart than for Beethoven; but even the "Eroica" does not depend on its orchestration in anything like the way that *La Mer* does. Yet, for most lay listeners, the primary interest in authentic performances lies precisely in the "tonal investiture," which would have been less important (and would certainly sound far less novel) to Beethoven's intended listeners.

The rules of signification and configuration that we apply to this authentic Beethoven performance, too, are apt to differ from those the composer intended. The intercompositional grid here is especially important. Beethoven's music takes much of its meaning from its differentiation from a background against which he expected his listeners to hear it: not only Mozart and Haydn, but also Clementi, Hummel, Dussek, Vorisek, Stamitz, and a host of others who are no longer generally familiar. As we listen now, we hear the music against a different background – including later symphonists like Schumann, Bruckner, and Shostakovich. As a consequence, Beethoven's compositional choices are measured by different norms, and we engage different expectations.

[29] The difficulty of deciding what to do about exposition repeats in modern performances stems, in part, from the new attributional rules most commonly in force. Current rules of notice would encourage us not to take the repeats, at least in pieces that are familiar; current rules of configuration, in contrast, may create the expectation of the kind of balance that the repeat provides.

[30] Copland, *Music and Imagination*, p. 35.

Because we are using different rules of notice, signification, and configuration, of course, we would be apt to produce a different coherence for the "Eroica" Symphony than Beethoven's audience did, even if we had the same rules of coherence to work with. But, in fact, much of what we know about the listening habits of the period suggests that we order things in a different way. Certainly, listeners comfortable with Berg, Berio, and Babbitt have developed a whole arsenal for dealing with musical disjuncture that Beethoven's audience never had. Beethoven may well not have wanted his work to be heard as "a very long drawn-out, daring, and wild fantasy" that "often ... seems to lose itself in anarchy," as one of the original critics heard it.[31] But I suspect he wanted it to sound more daring, wild, and even anarchic than it sounds today.

In sum, what is most significant about these performances in the context of the late 1980s and early 1990s is their newness, not their authenticity: they work for us *not* because they recapture the past, but because, as Richard Taruskin puts it, "They are quintessentially modern performances ... the product of an aesthetic wholly of our own era."[32] That is, they are right for our time – just as the Stokowski versions of Bach were right for the 1920s and 1930s. Furthermore (and this is where the purity and parasite paradox resolves), they are right for the same reason that the Liszt versions of the Beethoven symphonies are: they give us a fresh view of something we value that was growing stale. They serve a momentary, historical purpose – and they will not do so forever.

My conclusion is not that we ought to stop trying to explore and understand the past. Although I do not believe that "historically correct" interpretations are inherently better than anachronistic ones,[33] I do believe that there is real (if limited) value to be gained from recuperating the author's intentions – and that historical reconstruction is therefore a valid (although not the only valid)

---

31 The anonymous critics of the *Allgemeine Musikalische Zeitung*, quoted, via Schindler, in H. C. Robbins Landon, ed., *Beethoven: A Documentary Study* (New York, 1970), p. 155.

32 Richard Taruskin, "On Letting the Music Speak for Itself: Some Reflections on Musicology and Performance," *The Journal of Musicology* 1 (1982), 338–49; the cited passage is on p. 346.

33 Obviously, I do not agree with Malcolm Bilson that authentic practice takes us "ever closer to what the composer intended" ("The Vienna Fortepiano of the Late 18th Century," *Early Music* 8 [1980], 162), or with Kerman that "No one who has heard Beethoven's 'Moonlight' Sonata or the Sonata in D minor, opus 31 no. 2, well played on the fortepiano will ever be entirely happy with them again on the modern piano" (*Contemplating Music*, p. 213). Were that the case, the modern piano would never have taken its position of prominence.

musical aim. But to the extent that we *are* interested in recovering the past, the issues are now being framed in misleading ways. For historical reconstruction has less to do with determining the number, pitch, and type of instruments that produced the sounds at the premiere, or even with determining the practices that governed their performance, than with discovering the attributive screens through which they were processed by their intended listeners.

What would such recovery involve? Let me close with the example of Beethoven's Violin Concerto. When it was premiered in 1806 by the Viennese virtuoso Franz Clement, he not only played it, according to some reports, without rehearsal; more striking, the program also featured a few works by Clement himself, including a sonata played on one string with the violin upside down. Today, of course, everyone disparages Clement's shenanigans as a supreme instance of aesthetic blundering that made a mockery of Beethoven's sublime masterpiece. But is our easy dismissal appropriate? Not if we are really interested in authenticity. Clement, after all, was no buffoon. Even as a child, he was admired by Haydn; and his memory, which allowed him to produce a piano reduction of *The Creation* on the basis of a few hearings, was legendary.[34] So instead of worrying about the pitch of that performance, we should be asking a different and more important question: what strategies of listening shaped the experiences of those early listeners (and performers), and led them to accept the juxtaposition of concerto and virtuoso vaudeville?

Of course, we can never recover these strategies completely. In part that is because we live in the twentieth century and cannot "forget" all that has happened in the last 185 years. It is also, in part, because many of the operative rules of listening were implicit for the original listeners and hence left only indirect traces. Still, we *can* learn to look at those indirect traces more carefully. Specifically, if the theory of listening I have presented is correct, then part of "the music," as the composer originally intended it, lies in the commonplaces and metaphors listeners were likely to use to organize their aesthetic experiences. And we can come closer to sharing those experiences by taking more seriously the discourse that surrounded the music when it was new. In other words, if we are interested in truly *informed* interpretation (interpretation by

[34] See Robert Haas, "The Viennese Violinist, Franz Clement," trans. Willis Wager, *Musical Quarterly* 34 (1948), 15–27.

informed listeners as well as by informed performers), it is time to think less about reconstructing the precise sounds represented by the score (that is, reproducing the technical) and to concern ourselves more with reconstructing the attributive screens through which they were heard.

Part II

Literary models for musical understanding: music, lyric, narrative, and metaphor

4

Lyrical modes

Paul Alpers

This essay concerns the way the term "mode" is used in literary criticism, and is conceived as lying somewhere between two areas pertinent to this volume: literary theory as a model for music criticism and genre theories in literature and music. It is unlikely that what I say will be a *model* for the analysis and interpretation of music, but I hope that it will interest interpreters of music. As for genre theory, the concept of mode enters literary discourse partly as a way of dealing with certain impasses that arise from thinking in strictly generic terms, and it may be that some real analogies with musical analysis will be evident. Whatever these may be, I will not try to say anything about the musical term "mode." Having worked my way through Harold Powers' article in the *New Grove Dictionary of Music and Musicians* (Vol. 12, pp. 376–450), I know enough to leave to others the discovery of possible relations and analogies.

In literary studies, the theory of genres often seems a whirligig of reifying and hair-splitting, but in work of the past few decades there is something of a shared sense of what is meant by a genre. Most theorists and critics do not now use the term for the ultimate categories – the most familiar of which are narrative, drama, and lyric – which Goethe called *Naturformen* and which include all that we mean by literature. Genres are now generally agreed to be historical phenomena, and there is a tendency to think of them as well demarcated, both historically and aesthetically. Genre is sometimes defined as a principle of matching matter and form or a way of connecting topic and treatment; these definitions understand the term in a way which is most usefully formulated by Wellek and Warren, in their *Theory of Literature*. "Genre should be conceived," they say, "as a grouping of literary works based, theoretically, upon both outer form (specific metre or structure) and also upon inner form (attitude, tone, purpose)."[1]

Identifying genre by both "outer" and "inner" features corresponds to our intuitive sense of the term and reduces the confusion caused by the fact that generic characteristics tend to be of many different sorts. It does, however, make for an emphasis on literary kinds that are particularly well defined. Wellek and Warren single out the Gothic novel as "a genre by all the criteria one can invoke": "there is not only a limited and continuous subject-matter or thematics, but there is a stock of devices ... [and] there is, still further, a *Kunstwollen*, an aesthetic intent."[2] The genres which one now encounters in criticism and theory tend to be as well defined as the Gothic novel – for example, the eighteenth-century descriptive poem, the detective novel, and the medieval pastourelle. If anything, there is a bias toward genres that are narrow and circumscribed, and it is not surprising that the multiplying of entities has led to the concept of "subgenre."

For our purposes, the distinction between genre and subgenre is unimportant. What matters is the principle that a genre (and a fortiori, one of its subdivisions) is a specific, definable, readily identified literary form: one that has clear superficial features or marks of identification and that is sufficiently conventional or rule-governed to enable us to say, for example, that a given work is a pastoral elegy or a Petrarchan love poem or a verse satire or a Plautine comedy or an encomium, and not another thing. But if we conceive genres this way, then it seems there are a number of literary types which have generic-sounding names but which are more inclusive and general than genres proper. Among these are tragedy, comedy, novel, romance, satire, ode, and pastoral. Literary pastoral, for example, includes not only the whole range of formal eclogues – pastoral elegies, love complaints, singing-contests, and the like – but also pastoral romances, pastoral lyrics, pastoral comedies, and pastoral novels. Hence it has become commonplace to say that pastoral is not a genre, but a mode.[3]

---

[1] René Wellek and Austin Warren, *Theory of Literature*, 2nd edn. (New York, 1956), p. 221. On matching matter and form, Claudio Guillen, *Literature as System* (Princeton, 1970), p. 111; on connecting topic and treatment, Rosalie L. Colie, *The Resources of Kind: Genre-Theory in the Renaissance*, ed. Barbara K. Lewalski (Berkeley and Los Angeles, 1973), p. 29

[2] Wellek and Warren, *Theory of Literature*, p. 223.

[3] See the survey of modern definitions of pastoral in David M. Halperin, *Before Pastoral: Theocritus and the Ancient Tradition of Bucolic Poetry* (New Haven, 1983), esp. pp. 33–35.

But what do we mean by calling a literary type a mode? The answers to this question are very vague, and at times seem to be so on principle. Paul H. Fry has the following to say about "ode" as the name of the poetic type that concerns him:

The reason why the words "elegy" and "satire" seem more usefully to rope off poetic kinds than "ode" does is that "elegy" and "satire" are *modal* terms that allow enormous flexibility of reference. They describe orientations but tend not to prescribe a set style, form, or occasion – or even, necessarily, a set theme. It is in the loose spirit of such terms that I propose the "ode of presentation" as a mode.[4]

It is, if anything, an understatement to speak of the "loose spirit" of modal terms. There is positively a tradition of not defining the concept. You will not find a definition of "mode" in Angus Fletcher's *Allegory: The Theory of a Symbolic Mode* or in Earl Miner's books on seventeenth-century poetry, *The Metaphysical Mode* and *The Cavalier Mode*, or in the introduction and selections of a recent anthology of criticism called *The Pastoral Mode*.[5] The definitional plight of this term is unwittingly summed up by one critic, who says, "A work's mode, then, let us say, is whatever it seems to be in its most general aspect."[6]

When critics do define "mode," they tend to equate it with "attitude." The critic last quoted goes on to say: "In general, ... the mode of a work will be largely a matter of attitude or tone rather than style or form of writing." A prominent theorist of narrative proposes that the "primary modes of fiction" derive from the way fictional worlds "imply attitudes." He emphasizes that "in this modal consideration," terms like "tragedy" and "comedy" "refer to the quality of the fictional world and not to any form of story customarily associated with the term."[7] Mode is taken to refer to feelings and attitudes as such, as distinguished from their realization or manifestation in specific devices, conventions, and structures.

If mode really is an "inner" matter of attitude or philosophical conception, then it is hard to see how it can be continuous with the concept of genre, in which "outer form" is of the essence. But in fact the term is preeminently one that connects "inner form" and "outer form," indeed treats them as inseparable. We can see this

[4] Paul H. Fry, *The Poet's Calling in the English Ode* (New Haven, 1980), p. 5.
[5] Bryan Loughrey, ed., *The Pastoral Mode: A Casebook* (London, 1984).
[6] Allan Rodway, "Generic Criticism," in Malcolm Bradbury and David Palmer, eds., *Contemporary Criticism* (London, 1970), p. 94. The sentence quoted below is on p. 95.
[7] Robert Scholes, *Structuralism in Literature* (New Haven, 1974), pp. 132–33.

not by gleaning statements from theoretical discussions, but by
examining the way the word is used in practice. To take just one
example, Helen Vendler invokes it to qualify her paraphrase of a
section of Stevens' "The Man with the Blue Guitar."

> Such a paraphrase of the poem does not reveal its mode ... The poem is not tragic,
> but drawn and wry ... Rhythm is practically abrogated; rhyme is prohibited;
> syntax seems reduced to the simple declarative sentence ... rhetoric is cramped
> to simple indication ... "And" is dropped from the language. The sentences
> stand like epitaphs, in strict autonomy.[8]

Vendler's main attention is on qualities of diction, syntax, and
rhythm. These are not represented as *expressing* an attitude, but
rather as somehow encoding it, as having an attitude implicit in
them. It is precisely this sense of literary language – that there is a
reciprocal relation between usages and attitude – that makes critics
invoke the term "mode" to give a summary sense of a work or
passage. It is the term to use when one wants to suggest that the
ethos of a work informs its technique and that techniques imply an
ethos. In practical criticism, the idea of "mode" *connects* outer and
inner form; it assumes that form and content entail each other and
cannot, finally, be separated. This is the sense of the term that is
registered when Josephine Miles says, "We should look for a new
mode where a new complex of idea, material, and structure clearly
began,"[9] or when Richard Cody observes of Tasso's *Aminta* that it
went "far enough to establish the pastoral as a whole literary
mode, with an ethos and style of its own."[10]

Miles's and Cody's remarks show an awareness of what a mode
is, but they do not constitute definitions of the term. For that we
must turn to the most important treatment of the concept, the
chapter of Northrop Frye's *Anatomy of Criticism* entitled "Historical
Criticism: Theory of Modes." Frye says:

> In literary fictions the plot consists of somebody doing something. The somebody,
> if an individual, is the hero, and the something he does or fails to do is what he can
> do, or could have done, on the level of the postulates made about him by the
> author and the consequent expectations of the audience. Fictions, therefore, may
> be classified, not morally, but by the hero's power of action, which may be greater
> than ours, less, or roughly the same.[11]

---

[8] Helen Hennessy Vendler, *On Extended Wings: Wallace Stevens' Longer Poems* (Cambridge,
Mass., 1969), p. 130.

[9] Josephine Miles, *Eras and Modes in English Poetry* (Berkeley and Los Angeles, 1957), p. 115.

[10] Richard Cody, *The Landscape of the Mind: Pastoralism and Platonic Theory in Tasso's
"Aminta" and Shakespeare's Early Comedies* (Oxford, 1969), p. 78.

[11] Northrop Frye, *Anatomy of Criticism* (Princeton, 1957), p. 33.

Frye goes on to specify five modes – myth, romance, high mimetic (epic and tragedy), low mimetic (comedy and the novel), and ironic – according to the hero's stature in relation to other men and to the environment of other men. After surveying these fictional modes, as he calls them, Frye turns from "the internal fiction of the hero and his society" to the relation between writer and audience or writer and reader. "There can hardly be a work of literature," he rightly observes, "without some kind of relation, implied or expressed, between its creator and its auditors."[12] He then outlines a scheme of five "thematic modes," which have the same rationale as the "fictional modes."

Frye himself never tells us why he calls these categories "modes." But we find an explanation in Angus Fletcher's wonderfully illuminating comment on the idea that fictions may be classified according to the hero's power of action. "The term 'mode' is appropriate," Fletcher says, "because in each of the five the hero is a protagonist with a given strength relative to his world, and as such each hero – whether mythic, romantic, high mimetic, low mimetic, or ironic – is a *modulor* for verbal architectonics; man is the measure, the *modus* of myth."[13] On the basis of this formulation, we can define mode in the following way: it is *the literary manifestation, in a given work*, not of its attitudes in a loose sense, but *of its assumptions about human nature and our situation in the world*. This definition provides the question we implicitly put to any work we interpret: what notions of human strength, possibilities, pleasures, dilemmas, and so forth are manifested in the represented realities and in the emphases, devices, organization, pleasures and so forth of this work? The key to these questions, as Fletcher says, is the implicit view of the protagonist's or speaker's or reader's strength relative to his or her world. I specify all three of these figures, because we need not maintain Frye's separation of fictional and thematic. He distinguishes the two for theoretical reasons, but as he himself says, "every work of literature has both a fictional and a thematic aspect."[14]

[12] *Ibid.*, pp. 52–53.
[13] Angus Fletcher, "Utopian History and the Anatomy of Criticism," in Murray Krieger, ed., *Northrop Frye in Modern Criticism* (New York, 1966), pp. 34–35.
[14] Frye, *Anatomy of Criticism*, p. 53.

II

The term "mode" properly refers to the interconnection of usages and attitudes, but, as my account has suggested, it can be used in two different ways. It can be an inclusive term, a way of grouping satires or pastorals or romances in ways that go beyond generic specifications but that still make for coherent associations and distinctions. It can also be used as a summary term in practical criticism, drawing together the various elements that go into the interpretation of a particular work. My emphasis will be on the force and scope of three poems, and I will thus be using "mode" as a term of practical criticism. But these analyses are compatible with – and could be used in – locating each of these poems in one of the numerous modes of lyric. With the purposes of the present volume in mind, I have chosen poems that one can imagine being set as songs, and I want to begin with a comparison of two seventeenth-century poems, George Herbert's "Vertue" and Robert Herrick's "To Daffadills":

Vertue

Sweet day, so cool, so calm, so bright,
The bridall of the earth and skie:
The dew shall weep thy fall to night;
        For thou must die.
Sweet rose, whose hue angrie and brave
Bids the rash gazer wipe his eye:
Thy root is ever in its grave,
        And thou must die.
Sweet spring, full of sweet dayes and roses,
A box where sweets compacted lie;
My musick shows ye have your closes,
        And all must die.
Onely a sweet and vertuous soul,
Like season'd timber, never gives;
But though the whole world turn to coal,
        Then chiefly lives.[15]

To Daffadills

1. Faire Daffadills, we weep to see
    You haste away so soone:
As yet the early-rising Sun
    Has not attain'd his Noone.
    Stay, stay,

15 *The Works of George Herbert*, ed. F. E. Hutchinson (Oxford, 1941), pp. 87–88.

Untill the hasting day
Has run
But to the Even-song;
And, having pray'd together, we
Will goe with you along.

2. We have short time to stay, as you,
We have as short a Spring;
As quick a growth to meet Decay,
As you, or any thing.
We die,
As your hours doe, and drie
Away,
Like to the Summers raine;
Or as the pearles of Mornings dew
Ne'r to be found againe.[16]

These poems have a good many likenesses, which is what makes them comparable, but they also seem very different, and it is that felt difference – which in the case of these poems has no evident generic basis – that prompts a literary critic to discriminations of mode. Both concern innocent phenomena that show the evanescence and mortality of the natural world. They share a set of images – the day, flowers, springtime – which taken together represent mortal loveliness and which inform the thematics and structure of both poems. The poems also have in common the rhetorical device of addressing the attractive but fragile realities that engage them. And yet the two poems are strikingly different. The most important difference is the one registered by the title of Herbert's poem and by its last stanza. A reader might at first say that Herbert, unlike Herrick, points a moral. But if we are extracting morals, Herrick's poem has one of its own to draw about human life, and it is not that different from Herbert's. Rather, it is the tender pathos of "To Daffadills," as the title suggests, that makes it different from "Vertue."

We can begin by considering the stanzas of the two poems. (We might remind ourselves that given the whole range of lyric – which includes Pindar's odes, Petrarch's *canzoni*, Donne's major love poems, and Keats's odes – the stanzas of both these poems are small-scale and could even be called delicate.) Herbert's stanzas give an impression of regularity, which is due not simply to verse form but to every aspect of lyric rhetoric. The effect comes partly from the repetitions at the beginning and end of each stanza, but

16 *The Poems of Robert Herrick*, ed. L. C. Martin (London, 1965), p. 125.

also from the relation between sentence structure and the lineation of the verse. The lines are almost all end-stopped; there is
very little tension between the grammatical elements of each sentence and the way they are disposed in lines of verse; and there is a
strong pause, due to both syntax and verse rhythm, after the
second line of each stanza. This stanzaic rhetoric, as we may call
it, encodes or expresses the spiritual firmness that is praised in the
last stanza. A similar firmness is conveyed by the poem's rhetoric
in the ordinary sense of that term – the way it establishes a
relation to the objects of its address. The attraction and solicitude
registered in the first two lines of each stanza are converted, in the
third line (where the main verb occurs) and in the refrain, into the
uniform and severe sentence of mortality. The last of these
moments brings together the two rhetorics, of verse form and of
utterance:

> My musick shows ye have your closes,
> And all must die.

By contrast, the verse form and rhetoric of "To Daffadills" suggest
a very different strength relative to the speaker's world. The
middle lines particularly are determined by the brief *cursus vitae* of
the flowers. Two of the lines are only one foot long, and the
grammar sustains the effects of fluidity and evanescence, which are
thematized in the short lines, "Has run," "We die," and "Away."
The speaker seems thoroughly assimilated to the flowers he
addresses; even the way the poem refines its pathos – turning the
weeping that begins the first stanza into the moral that begins the
second – can be thought to be determined by the delicacy of the
daffodils.

So far as I know, no seventeenth-century settings survive for
either of these poems. Both, however, seem eligible for musical
setting, and presumably these settings would reflect the character
of the poems as we have described and differentiated them. Our
literary analysis so far has been fairly elementary, and therefore
implies only elementary musical consequences – of the sort, let us
say, that characterize the relation between words and music in
popular song. As we continue to analyze the two poems, the modal
question of strength relative to world will enable us to see their
literary complexity. I hope this analysis will suggest – though I will
not attempt to substantiate it – their interest as texts for art song.
What I have in mind is not only the expressive powers of art song,
but also the various ways, as Lawrence Kramer has discussed them,

in which the music of art song can contest the texts it sets, or seek out their tensions and dilemmas.[17]

In "Vertue," I have suggested a fairly direct equation of rhetorical and spiritual firmness. But the last line quoted, "My musick shows ye have your closes," shows that the poem is more interestingly entangled in its sense of strength relative to world. We have so far taken the line to mean simply, "my verse makes your endings clear." But in seventeenth-century English, "close" also means "musical cadence." This second meaning – which is unavoidably brought to mind by the phrase, "my musick" – suggests that not only the poet's physical being but also his poetry is subject to mortality. The implication that the speaker's firm conclusions share the mutability of natural things affects the poem deeply and intimately, not just as a moral point to be registered. To represent the death of natural beauty as a sequence of musical cadences means that a sense of vulnerability is central to the poem's rhetoric. The pathos of "The dew shall weep thy fall tonight" and the lavishing of the word "sweet" in the third stanza are only its most evident manifestations.

How does the poem negotiate the tension between spiritual vulnerability and firmness? It claims that they are compatible by joining them in the climactic phrase, "a sweet and vertuous soul." ("Virtue" in the seventeenth century meant strength as well as moral goodness, a meaning brought out by the comparison to "seasoned timber.") It has sometimes been felt that the poem does not succeed in joining these qualities – by Coleridge, for example, who quoted this as an exemplary poem but omitted the last stanza.[18] If the poem does not split in two this way, it is because it everywhere displays and engages its double sense of human capacity. On the one hand, there are the weeping dew of the first stanza, with more than a hint of self-representation, and the confrontation between the rose and the "rash gazer" in the second, where energetic rhythm and enjambment momentarily disturb the poem's regular lineations and betray, as Helen Vendler says, the passion underlying it.[19] Over against these are the manifestations

---

[17] Lawrence Kramer, *Music and Poetry: The Nineteenth Century and After* (Berkeley and Los Angeles, 1984), pp. 125–70.

[18] *Biographia Literaria*, ch. 19; ed. James Engell and W. Jackson Bate (Princeton, 1983), vol. 2, p. 95.

[19] Helen Vendler, *The Poetry of George Herbert* (Cambridge, Mass., 1975), p. 14. I am much indebted to Vendler's reading of the poem, though my interpretation differs from hers in some respects.

of firmness we have already noted. As Vendler says, "This is a voice
which 'never gives'."[20] But there is something odd about this as a
lyric voice: its speaker does not represent himself in the first person.
The only use of the first person is the possessive in the phrase, "my
musick." In displacing the first person pronoun by this phrase, the
poem suggests that the speaker's self is not prior to its utterance,
but resides wholly in the various gestures and orderings of verse
and rhetoric. It is for this reason, one would think, that the voice
never gives. But music has order because it has its closes: in this
poem, at least, it cannot escape the condition of the mortal who
makes it. It is still "*my* musick." Hence the apparent turn away
from mortality in the final stanza still contains the tensions that
occasion the poem. The last stanza makes a new music by its
variant placing of what was the initial word "sweet" and by
reversing the refrain, which now speaks of living. Furthermore, the
turn to general statement in the last stanza can be said to thematize
the absorption of the first person into an impersonal music. At the
same time, however, there is a strong sense of spiritual drama, most
noticeable in "But though the whole world turn to coal" – that
crucial third line, where the moral of mortality is sounded in each
of the preceding stanzas. The general, apparently impersonal
statement is made to have the feeling of personal recognition and
resolution. The full voicing felt in "Then chiefly lives" makes the
poem decisive in *its* close, but it also bears witness to the urgencies
that make this a mortal music.

The complicating element in "To Daffadills" is registered in
"Stay, stay," the first of the one-foot lines and the only one that
does not directly represent the evanescence that the speaker shares
with the flowers. In its voicing and its metrical virtuosity (a long
one-foot line – spondaic monometer?) it bears witness to a distinct
human need, both resisting the flowers' evanescence and seeking to
join it. This human presence is more elusively represented at the
end of the first stanza:

> And, having pray'd together, we
> Will goe with you along.

This looks like the pathetic fallacy, but wit counteracts the sentimental fancy of actually praying with the flowers. Since the first
person subject of this poem is from the first a plural "we," all these
lines need mean is that when we humans have prayed together, we

[20] *Ibid.*, p. 19.

will accompany you flowers to our common destination. This may still seem pretty willing to indulge the pathetic fallacy, but the lines are underpinned first by the fact that it is a main function of church services to prepare the soul for death and second by the fact that we need imagine accompanying the flowers only into night and sleep, the images of death. It is the felt *likeness* between humans and flowers, not a naively assumed identity, that gives authority to the moral statement: "We have short time to stay, as you." Hence, the fullness and formal satisfaction of the stanza can counteract, without contradicting, the haste the middle lines thematize: the stanzas make a stay. They make plausible the notion introduced in the second stanza, that our brief lives can be imagined not as mere transience, but as a genuine space:

> We have short time to stay, as you,
>> We have as short a Spring;
> As quick a growth to meet Decay,
>> As you, or any thing.

The somewhat paradoxical locution "short time to stay" is magnified into "as short a Spring," where despite the adjective the season is longer than any unit of time previously envisaged. The next line again allows a *spatium*, as well as a *cursus vitae*: it represents decay not as a process but as something met (like Even-song and the flowers) by the erotic eagerness first expressed in "Stay, stay" and here by "quick."

The sense that the poem conceives and represents a human space is confirmed by the images that close it:

> We die,
> As your hours doe, and drie
>> Away,
> Like to the Summers raine;
> Or as the pearles of Mornings dew
> Ne'r to be found againe.

The summer's rain suggests the flowing away of our life, but also adds another season to its conceived duration. It is associated with the moisture of tears but it also leads to their transformation in the final image. Herrick's and Herbert's poems overlap in this detail. The dew weeping the end of the day is the first of the speaker's self-representations in "Vertue," and the one most expressive of his vulnerability. The oblique self-representation leaves room for the sense that he has strengths in reserve. The greater sense of fragility in "To Daffadills" is evident from the beginning, where the explicitly human weeping over natural loveliness suggests that lyric capacity goes no farther than the tender encounter of men and flowers. Yet the powers implicit in human separateness are made evident in the image of "the pearles of Mornings dew." This line recalls our weeping at daybreak, but, by returning us to the beginning of the poem, it also provides formal satisfactions. Just as the fluent middle lines of each stanza lead to greater rhetorical stability and a sense of closure, so the human tears that flow at the outset are transferred to the natural scene and become precious objects, these pearls of dew. Their beauty both reflects and resists the sense of transience that prompts our tears but that we can memorialize in a poem.

The next poem I want to discuss engages musical issues differently from "Vertue" and "To Daffadills," which I have imagined, though I have not analyzed, as potential song texts. Wordsworth's "The Solitary Reaper" has an important role in the excellent and illuminating chapter on song, which I have already mentioned, in Lawrence Kramer's *Music and Poetry*. Kramer presents the poem as, in a sense, the reverse of a song text. For him it shows how music's tendency to efface text by voice, which he calls overvocalizing, can invade poetry itself as an imagined effect of music. In some Romantic poems, he says,

the poet hears a song that assumes epiphanic power precisely because it is unintelligible, and often at the very point where it passes the threshold of intelligibility ... The poet's imagination is initially aroused by the impulse to insert his own words in the linguistic gap opened by the song. Once in place, these words gradually dissolve like the song's own, leaving the poet mute and transfixed, usually in a posture of intenser listening.[21]

The question is whether this generic plot is enacted by the poem itself:

> Behold her, single in the field,
> Yon solitary Highland Lass!
> Reaping and singing by herself;
> Stop here, or gently pass!
> Alone she cuts and binds the grain,
> And sings a melancholy strain;
> O listen! for the Vale profound
> Is overflowing with the sound.
>
> No Nightingale did ever chaunt
> More welcome notes to weary bands

[21] Kramer, *Music and Poetry*, p. 139.

Of travellers in some shady haunt,
Among Arabian sands:
A voice so thrilling ne'er was heard
In spring-time from the Cuckoo-bird,
Breaking the silence of the seas
Among the farthest Hebrides.

Will no one tell me what she sings? –
Perhaps the plaintive numbers flow
For old, unhappy, far-off things,
And battles long ago:
Or is it some more humble lay,
Familiar matter of to-day?
Some natural sorrow, loss, or pain,
That has been, and may be again?

Whate'er the theme, the Maiden sang
As if her song could have no ending;
I saw her singing at her work,
And o'er the sickle bending: –
I listened, motionless and still;
And, as I mounted up the hill,
The music in my heart I bore,
Long after it was heard no more.[22]

We can focus our attention, as Kramer does, on the third stanza. The possibilities stated there are what Geoffrey Hartman calls "surmises": not mere speculations or reflections but imaginings that are caused by something striking or mysterious and that retain something of the troubling power that prompted them.[23] The question is how the poem represents and conveys these surmises. Kramer wants it to exemplify a "large-scale rhythm of verbal effort and exalted release from it," and he therefore speaks of it as attaining "a speculative rapture, an epiphanic act of hearing." He thus emphasizes what he calls "the imaginative overflow" of the third stanza: "the near and the far, past and present, heroic and humble all blend together as the possible subjects of the song."[24] But blending and overflow are not allowed to occur. The speaker's surmises are presented as alternative possibilities, and registering

[22] E. de Selincourt and Helen Darbishire, eds., *The Poetical Works of William Wordsworth*, 5 vols. (Oxford, 1940–49), vol. 3, p. 77. This is the final version of the poem first published in 1807. Unlike other poems by Wordsworth, "The Solitary Reaper" does not benefit from the recent movement to reinstate the poet's first versions. Anyone who reads this poem in the excellent volume in the "Oxford Authors" series – *William Wordsworth*, ed. Stephen Gill (Oxford, 1984), p. 319 – will have some rude surprises in the second and fourth stanzas.

[23] Geoffrey H. Hartman, *Wordsworth's Poetry 1787–1814* (New Haven, 1964), pp. 8–12.

[24] Kramer, *Music and Poetry*, p. 140.

alternatives is at the heart of the formal and representational
workings of both this and the second stanza. It is not simply the
statement of alternatives, but the way these stanzas balance their
surmises as equal possibilities. Both the rhyme scheme and the
short fourth line make for a clear division of the stanzas into halves,
and this effect is supported by the high degree of end-stopping in
the lines. Kramer's terms, blending and overflow, respond to
elements of the poem but are only partially appropriate to them.
The poem *begins* with this sense of musical experience – "O listen!
for the Vale profound/ Is overflowing with the sound" – but it
proceeds to bring music within the scope of language: precisely the
reverse of what happens in the poems with which Kramer associates it. The second stanza's social image of welcome notes and
bands of travellers suggests this accommodation to language,
which is sustained by the lineation of the verse. The lines do not
seem notably end-stopped, but as one moves through the stanza, it
would be possible to stop – not the stanza, of course, but the
particular sentence – after every line but the first. The effect of the
versification is to turn the initial overflowing of the reaper's song
into a well modulated "flow," the word used in the third stanza of
her "plaintive numbers" (a word which itself suggests ordered
utterance).

These counter-arguments to Kramer amount to saying that his
account of this poem does not fully answer to its character or our
experience of it. I think that the issues involved – not only here, but
in many such matters of practical criticism – are most coherently
and usefully stated in terms of mode. For what Kramer misconce-
ives, as it seems to me, is the way the usages and workings of "The
Solitary Reaper" manifest the way the poem conceives the human
singer's strength relative to world. He himself supplies the relevant
correction when he says, "One thing that is missing from Wordsworth's poem, however, is a recognition of the emotional and erotic
violence implicit in moments of overvocalizing."[25] That is certainly so, and he then shows what he means in a passage from
Whitman, in which the first-person speaker takes into himself, both
submitting and containing, the voices and sounds of an entire
opera. Whitmanian verse, one imagines, would be the supreme
instrument of verbal overvocalizing. But the verse and structure of
"The Solitary Reaper" answer to a quite different conception of

[25] *Ibid.*, p. 141.

poetic powers, for the figure of the poet, far from being all-inclusive, is divided between the reaper and the speaker. The reaper has, and represents for the speaker, the capacity to be at home in the world, even though alone. The first stanza emphasizes her solitariness, and in the imagined scenes of the second stanza, voices of nature relieve humans in desolate situations. Whatever its theme, the reaper's song must be a ballad, the form of poetry that most caught the Romantic imagination by its local and historical rootedness and its nature as a communal expression. When the speaker goes on to surmise its content, his imaginings bring out the importance, to him, of this lone figure's being in touch with the world of the past and the human world around her. Understood in this way, the reaper can be seen to set the agenda of the poem, which is to dispel solitude by utterance.

At the same time, there is no replicating the force and significance of the reaper's song except through the speaker. In Schiller's terms, this is a sentimental poem about a naive song. The power of the reaper's song is unavailable to her as conciousness: she is simply "reaping and singing by herself," as the poet says at the beginning. Even the immediate power of her song, which is what stops the poet dead – to adapt Hartman's connection of this poem with epitaphs – is conveyed, in the second half of the first stanza, as it impinges on the observer's mind and feelings. But the poem does not simply accommodate unintelligible song to language and consciousness; it maintains its double sense of the powers of human utterance, by suggesting the difference the reaper's voice makes to the poet's. The speaker seems most himself, and most in the character of a poet, in the second stanza. Song is there felt to be a power of nature to relieve an existential plight, and the stanza is unique, in this poem, in capturing some of the magical intensity of Romantic poetry.[26] The third stanza can be thought to reduce this imaginative scope and intensity, and at the same time to rescue the speaker from depending on the remote and exotic, on the mere symbolism of nature. It not only restores to the reaper her human form, but has the effect of modifying the observer's utterance by hers. For consider: would the reaper recognize the distinction the speaker draws between the two kinds of song? Would she consider the second kind of song "more humble" than an old ballad?

[26] A. C. Bradley, the great Victorian critic, cited this stanza to show that Wordsworth was not "deficient in romance": "the 'Arabian sands' had the same glamour for him as for others." *Oxford Lectures on Poetry* (Bloomington, 1961), p. 114.

Presumably not – these are the speaker's distinctions and hierarch-
ies. But the important thing is that the poem itself, though apparently unavoidably committed to making such distinctions, allows
the speaker, by the strength and felicity of his surmises, to mitigate
their force and approach the condition of the naive singer. The old
songs – far from being merely primitive or exotic, as "battles long
ago" may suggest – are assimilated to present utterance in the
second half of the stanza. For if we are still singing the old ballads,
it is because their "old, unhappy, far-off things" express "some
natural sorrow, loss, or pain/ That has been, and may be again."
And if these songs are being sung as one works, they are, in an
important sense, "familiar matter of to-day." This is not to say that
the reaper's song becomes the poet's, much less that it takes it over.
The mode of surmise remains too evident, indicating how deci-
sively the poet's power of representing another is determined by his
social, cultural, and physical situation. Hence, in the final stanza,
the moment of utter absorption – "I listened, motionless and still"
– gives way to the realities of time and physical motion, and the
poem, in which there has been not a word of mimetic sounding,
endows us with the only music of which it is capable, that which
sounds in the silence of the heart.

5

Origins of modernism: musical structures and narrative forms

Marshall Brown

Comparison of literature and the visual arts is much more common than comparison of literature and music. For, as Roland Barthes wrote in a late essay that in part exemplifies the problem, "It is . . . very difficult to speak about music. Many writers have spoken well about painting; none, I believe, has spoken well about music, not even Proust. The reason is that it is very difficult to link language, which is of the order of the general, and music, which is of the order of difference." Music, as Barthes says in another essay, is "inactual," or, as I should put it, abstract.[1] Non-specialists often feel that they can look at a painting and discern what it represents; and even those who know nothing about painting techniques are liable to have imbibed a few useful elementary notions of pictorial form. Far fewer stare at a musical score with anything but discomfort. Music suffers doubly: first from being nonrepresentational, and second from being written in a script that is arduous to learn. Even the most avid listeners would no sooner write about a piece of music than about a poem in a language they cannot read.

Yet despite Barthes's engagement on behalf of a purely affective approach, the analysis of music holds great potential. For what music lacks in external referentiality, it gains in the distinctness of internal relationships. If it is the most abstract art, it is also the most highly formalized. Or, to put this in yet a third way, while the *meaning* or denotation of a piece of music is far less explicit than that of a work of verbal or pictorial art, the *structure* is far more explicit.

This contrast among the arts can be described in semiotic terms. Language has what is known as a double articulation: a limited system of discrete sounds out of which is composed an essentially

---

[1] Roland Barthes, "La Musique, la voix, la langue" and "Le Chant romantique," in *L'Obvie et l'obtus* (Paris, 1982), pp. 247 and 253. See further the useful survey by Françoise Escal, "Roland Barthes: Fragments d'un discours sur la musique," *Semiotica* 66 (1987), 57–68. All translations in this essay are my own.

unlimited and unsystematic lexicon of discrete words. While literature intermittently exploits the phonetic system, it primarily communicates through the much more fluid lexical register. Painting,
of course, has at its disposal only the lexical or conceptual articulation. A painting may represent discrete objects or actions, but its
material basis is an unarticulated continuum of colors, brush-
strokes, and the like. No general system of "huemes" and "value-
emes" corresponds to the phonemes of language. Music, finally,
has in general only the lower or systematic articulation. The
elements of a musical composition are pitches, rhythms, instruments, dynamic levels, and types of articulation: more elements, in
other words, than there are phonemes in any natural language, but
a finite number nevertheless. That is why music can be notated.
The extensive writing on musical semiotics rarely seems to
acknowledge the basic fact that music does not, in general, have
words.[2] More specifically, since music sporadically has symbolic
motifs, one should say that music does not distinguish words from
sentences. Music has its own identity because it is not like language, and in consequence the manipulations of its building blocks
can be described far more concretely than the manipulations of
words, whose meanings and formal properties are by nature
complex and overlapping.[3]

Therefore, if we are interested in the formal sense of a period or a
movement, we may well look to its music for the clearest, most

[2] An exception to the word-envy of musical semiotics is Theodor Adorno's essay, "Frag-
ment über Musik und Sprache," from *Quasi una Fantasia*, in *Gesammelte Schriften*, ed. Rolf
Tiedemann, vol. 16 (Frankfurt am Main, 1978), pp. 251–56. Most prominent among the
examples of the yearning to assimilate music to language is perhaps Jean-Jacques Nattiez,
Fondements d'une sémiologie de la musique (Paris, 1975), esp. pp. 76–82. More extreme is B. M.
Gasparov, "Nekotorye deskriptivnye problemy muzykalnoi semantiki," *Trudy po znakovym
sistemam* 8 (1977), 120–37. More attuned to the specificity of music is Vladimir Karbu-
sicky; see, most recently, his "Zeichen und Musik," *Zeitschrift für Musik* 9 (1987), 227–49,
though even here we read: "Since musical symbols are more nearly [iconic] characteri-
zations than arbitrary encodings ["eher Charakteristika als willkürliche Chiffren"], they
point toward early stages in the development of language" (p. 240). In "Das Verstehen
der verbalen Sprache und das 'Verstehen der Musik,'" in *Musik und Verstehen*, ed. Peter
Faltin and Hans-Peter Reinecke (Cologne, 1973), pp. 276–88, Adam Schaff says that
music has phonemes but not words. He then argues that whereas language communicates
meanings, music therefore communicates only feelings. The reduction is like that of
Barthes or, before him, of Suzanne Langer. This volume contains numerous valuable
essays of a general nature that are relevant to the present discussion.

[3] These comments apply to musical texts, not to musical performance. Consequently, it has
been argued that no formal semiotic analysis is possible of music as actually realized: see
François Delalande, "L'Analyse des conduites musicales: une étape de programme
sémiologique," *Semiotica* 66 (1987), 99–107. The objection is true, but not relevant, since
the same objection would apply to plays as performed or to poems – or even novels – as
read aloud.

easily describable examples. By formal sense I mean such characteristics as the types of closure that are permitted, the nature of segmentation and transition (relationship between adjacent parts), the relative importance of local and long-distance relationships, the types of hierarchy or equivalence that are recognized. Geoffrey Tillotson's *Augustan Studies* contains a well-known essay on the "manner of proceeding" in eighteenth-century poetry, and his phrase conveniently sums up what I mean by style.[4] In all the arts there are characteristic manners of proceeding or formal principles by which we recognize the style of a creator, a group, or a period. In literary works these principles take the form of norms, often only loosely defined and frequently unrecognized in analysis. In music, on the other hand, the formal outlines of a piece can generally be described with a high degree of precision (or a low degree of ambiguity), and the generalizations based on a group of such formal descriptions appear much more like laws than like the flexible norms of literary form.

A preliminary example of structuring principles can usefully precede the main exposition in this essay. One norm of plot structure in the nineteenth century is surely that there must be a satisfactory resolution. Vladimir Propp has shown that this norm has the force of an invariable law in the case of fairy tales – or at least of those collected during that epoch. But the resolutions in novels and short stories do not always take the canonical forms of marriage or death; it is not easy to define the limited number of plot functions and thereby to specify acceptable outcomes. With music, on the other hand, we are on firm ground. There is a precise, inflexible law for most music of this period that everyone acknowledges, even though few bother to state something so obvious: every piece must end with a cadence in the same key in which it began. Schumann and Chopin, to be sure, experimented with what Charles Rosen has called "tonal unity" without a focused "central tonality,"[5] but only under carefully controlled conditions: in "romantic" forms, but not in sonatas, and with the prevailing keys a third apart, usually a major and its relative minor. More radical departures from the law – in a couple of iconoclastic forays by Beethoven and in programmatic gestures by Schubert, in songs exclusively – remain even more isolated. Such

---

[4] Geoffrey Tillotson, "The Manner of Proceeding in Certain Eighteenth- and Early Nineteenth-Century Poems," in *Augustan Studies* (London, 1961), 111–46.
[5] Charles Rosen, *Sonata Forms* (New York, 1980), p. 295.

departures, furthermore, acknowledge the law of resolution through their attempt either to amend it or to motivate a repeal. Even these few works, that is, have determinate, not suspended or cyclical endings.[6] In the absence of obviously Shandean character-istics (as in "Variety without Method," a late eighteenth-century setting in various keys and meters of the psalm, "O God thou hast been displeased," by the American hymnist William Billings), should one meet a nineteenth-century piece where the first move-ment ends in F major while the last movement ends in D major, one would have no recourse but to conclude that the composer was terminally syphilitic. Indeed, in this particular instance – the Second String Quartet of Smetana – the contributors to the earlier editions of *Grove's Dictionary of Music and Musicians* were unable to face the music; J. A. Fuller Maitland, the general editor of the second edition, put the piece in C major (vol. 4, p. 486), while Rosa Newmarch in the third edition put it in C minor (vol. 4, p. 789). Now it is not difficult to see how a closely related norm of closure likewise applies to the nineteenth-century novel. Flamboy-ant exceptions like Charlotte Brontë's *Villette* and Melville's *The Confidence-Man*, of course, confirm the norm by the self-conscious way the reject it. But we might risk losing our critical nerve with what seem like half-cadences or half-hearted conventionality in the works of Flaubert, Eliot, Hardy – indeed in an increasingly long list of major writers. Here the musical parallel should encourage us to view the endings as adequate resolutions of problems to be criti-cally identified. It teaches us the principle of reading the novels in the light of their conclusions, just as we analyze a symphony from the perspective of its tonal resolution, rather than, say, in the light of prevailing textures or of organizational symmetries.[7]

---

[6] Harold Krebs discusses examples of wandering tonality in Schubert songs and in Chopin in "Alternatives to Monotonality in Early Nineteenth-Century Music," *Journal of Music Theory* 25 (1981), 1–15. In some cases, he argues, Schenkerian analysis reveals the initial sonority to be a false tonic; in the others the harmonic movement is genuine and is textually motivated. The key relation between beginning and end in the latter cases is always a third. Even rarer are the works (always songs or programmatic character pieces) that end on a suspension; see the list in Vladimir Jankélévitch, *Fauré et l'inexprimable* (Paris, 1974), p. 26. One domain where the law of tonal consistency does not regularly apply is opera, particularly in the *bel canto* tradition and in Wagner.

[7] Drawing on Peter Brooks's book, *Reading for the Plot*, Anthony Newcomb's essay in this volume illustrates the origin of a modernist sense of closure in Mahler's Ninth Symphony. For another interesting modernist account that regards closure as a repression see D. A. Miller, *Narrative and Its Discontents: Problems of Closure in the Traditional Novel* (Princeton, 1981). I have criticized this approach on other grounds in "Plan Vs. Plot: Chapter Symmetries and the Mission of Form," *Stanford Literature Review* 4 (1987), 103–36.

In the spirit of this example, then, let us consider a central paradigm in nineteenth-century music, its parallel in literary form, and its fate in the twentieth century. What follows is an experiment at compactly surveying the prehistory of modernism. The intention is to show how the patterns of music history can help to organize our understanding of the more fluid patterns of literary history.

The language of nineteenth-century music was based on a series of polar oppositions that had gradually crystallized from the musical practice of the preceding centuries: the contrast of consonance with dissonance, tonic with dominant (or other non-tonic) harmonies, symmetrical with asymmetrical phrasing, melodic outline with rhythmic configuration, treble with bass, strong with weak beats, solo with accompaniment, string with wind sonorities. Each such polarity functions somewhat differently from the others, and their complex interplay defines the inner form of any given piece. But all have in common that one term is the normal, neutral, stable, or principal one, while the other is abnormal, expressive, unstable, or subordinate.

String sound, to expand on one of the oppositions, is neutral. Winds characteristically gain prominence in the more excited or colorful inner sections of a movement or a piece, and they are lavishly used in ballet and opera to accompany visual spectacles.[8] Yet wind-band music virtually disappears from main-stream composition, since it would have the effect of being all message and no code – it is a sign of unreality when Mendelssohn's Overture to *A Midsummer Night's Dream* opens with wind chords, and an obvious archaism when the theme of Brahms's *Variations on a Theme of Haydn* is stated by winds alone over no more string stability than is offered by cello and bass pizzicato. The string quartet, on the other hand, is the most neutral or purest medium, used only for fully structured abstract pieces, and never for short character pieces or for program music. (A list of exceptions shows how rare they are: apart from two or three quartet movements by Beethoven, Wolf's *Italian Serenade*, and Tchaikovsky's sextet, "Souvenirs de Florence," you have to descend to the level of Afanasiev's quartet, "The Volga," or return to the hapless Smetana to find programmatic or evocative

---

[8] Cf. Jerome J. de Momigny, *Cours complet d'harmonie et de composition* (Paris, 1806), p. 585, cited in Leonard Ratner, *Classic Music: Expression, Form, and Style* (London, 1980), p. 146: "the general plan is established by these instruments [the strings] and the wind instruments, when they are not assigned a leading part, only serve to reinforce the plan with a clearer or more decisive color." The string–wind polarity is invoked in David Lewin's essay in this volume.

string music. And it could be argued that Schoenberg's first decisive attack on nineteenth-century musical language came with his
writing a full-scale symphonic poem for string sextet, *Verklärte
Nacht.*)

Taken as a whole, all the various oppositions define a manner of
proceeding that every listener recognizes as the nineteenth-century
norm: most simply, pieces oscillate between stability or resolution
and excitement or expressivity, and, in particular, pieces begin in
normality (in the tonic key) and move through areas of greater or
lesser tension in the middle until they arrive at a concluding
resolution. These patterns of what linguists call markedness are
obvious; just as obviously they do not structure much of the most
characteristic music of our century, and they apply only in a
partial and weaker way to music of the Baroque era, which
depends more heavily on symmetrical balance than on pointed
contrast.

The formal structures of nineteenth-century fiction are likewise
defined by oppositions between tension and relaxation, complication and resolution, colorful dissonance and restored harmony.
The categories for analyzing these structures are, to be sure, more
flexible and imprecise than the musical categories, but they were
acknowledged at the time, they remain discernible now, and,
however approximate they may be, I believe that they are nevertheless essential to an understanding of nineteenth-century fiction.

The structural oppositions in nineteenth-century fiction can
only be illustrated here; a full description must be left for another
occasion. The terms that we most often find in nineteenth-century
discussions are the true or the real and the interesting or the
romantic. The struggle of the nineteenth-century writer is to
accommodate both the true and the interesting or – to borrow the
musical terms – both consonance and dissonance, tonic and dominant. Trollope, for instance, objects to the designation of himself as
realistic and Wilkie Collins as sensationalistic: "a good novel
should be both, and both in the highest degree."[9] Hardy says,
"The writer's problem is, how to strike the balance between the
uncommon and the ordinary so as on the one hand to give interest,
on the other to give reality"; *Bleak House* was intended to portray
"the romantic side of familiar things," and Henry James is employ-
ing only a superficially different vocabulary when he writes,

[9] Anthony Trollope, *An Autobiography* (1883; ed. Michael Sadleir, London, 1953), p. 194.

"Every good story is of course both a picture and an idea, and the more they are interfused the better the problem is solved."[10]

Just as certain composers lay bare the skeleton of the period's formal sense by simplifying and rigidifying the polarizations in harmony and rhythm,[11] so certain authors and works likewise render the polarizations of literary form in a purified and thus unmistakable way. *Bleak House* experiments with juxtaposing a pitiless, objective, foggy narrator with a romantic and sunny one and moves toward reconciling the two at the end. Stevenson's best-known work pits the real scientist Dr. Jekyll against the nightmarish romantic villain Mr. Hyde. And detective stories in the mold of Arthur Conan Doyle regularly fall into two main parts: the recital of the actual situation in the present tense with all the scattered clues of the crime, and the recital in the past tense of the romantic and exciting history of the criminal and the crime.

At the end of the nineteenth century these polarized forms become formulaic. Their interest slips, and eventually they lose their coherence. The artist who preserves the traditional forms becomes an artisan, often a miniaturist, like many of the nationalist composers or the numerous superb short story writers who emerge from almost every country except England. The grand formal problems all but vanish, and hitherto subordinate resources of nuance and tone color are featured, such as piquant chords and dialect words. Increasing formal ease and virtuosity mean that a whole piece may be generated out of a kernel phrase, as in the famous Maupassant story about a string of diamonds ("rivière de diamants") that is lost in the river, making martyrs out of the poor bourgeois of the nearby Rue des Martyrs.

Finally, as the charisma of the dialectic is routinized, all that matter are color and atmosphere – tone-painting or word-painting. From the other side of the great stylistic divide Schoenberg made merry over the minimal character of a language based on color: "When songs from the southern portion of West-Farinoxia," he writes in an essay on "Symphonies from Folksongs," "show Lydian

[10] Thomas Hardy, *The Life and Work of Thomas Hardy*, ed. Michael Millgate (Athens, Georgia, 1985), p. 154; Charles Dickens, *Bleak House* (1852), Preface; Henry James, "Guy de Maupassant" (1888), in *Partial Portraits* (Westport, Conn., 1970), p. 269.

[11] So, in connection with the "antinomy that everything should be at once understandable and striking ['verständlich und apart']," Adorno writes even of so complex a work as *Tristan* that "The socially conformist demand of comprehensibility and the artistic one of plasticity split asunder," Theodor W. Adorno, *Die musikalischen Monographien*, in *Gesammelte Schriften*, vol. 13, p. 51.

tendencies in a prevailing Phrygian, whereas dances from the neighboring northern part of Franquimonia show the opposite, namely traces of Phrygian in decidedly Lydian melodies, such differences may, to a specialist in the region, indicate signs of autochthonous originality."[12] But late in the nineteenth century such minimal originality was often a composer's or a short story writer's primary resource. The character piece is a distillate, the passion without the story of the passion, "not the tale, but the sketch of a tale," "only the point of departure and that of arrival," as Giovanni Verga says in the programmatic introduction to "Gramigna's Lover" (1880),[13] or, in other words, a beginning and an end with no middle. This type of colorful sketch, popular in both literature and music toward the end of the century – and the inspiration for verismo opera – ultimately became in its turn a commonplace convention.

When formal coherence of the old sort is abandoned in favor of such fragmentary evocation, larger structures become problematic, as most obviously in the monstrously episodic works of Bruckner, Mahler, and Zola. In longer works one solution – particularly associated with Wagner and his followers and, in literature, with Flaubert – was to sustain interest by refusing to come to rest: perpetual unresolved dissonance, a middle with very little end. This is, of course, signally the mode of Henry James's *The Turn of the Screw*, which seeks to turn the screws of intensity higher in each of its twenty-four chapters so as to maintain a constant frenzy of excitement, so different from the carefully paced, intermittent horror of romantic gothic. Alternatively, by the end of the century, impressionists like Debussy and Chekhov (exact contemporaries, though Chekhov wrote more quickly and died younger) preserve compositional depth by melancholy or ironic reminiscences of traditional motifs and forms, the sunken cathedrals of the past: think of all the unsent letters, untold stories, unnoticed crimes and cruelties of Chekhov's early tales.

Creators like these can now construct larger forms only as a

---

12 Arnold Schoenberg, "Symphonien aus Volksliedern," in *Stil und Gedanke: Aufsätze zur Musik*, ed. Ivan Vojtech (Frankfurt am Main, 1976), p. 134. I have retranslated this from Schoenberg's German version, which is a little more colorful than the original English, found in "Folkloristic Symphonies," *Style and Idea*, ed. Leonard Stein (New York, 1975), p. 161.
13 Giovanni Verga, *Tutte le novelle* (Verona, 1961), vol. 1, pp. 167–68. As late as 1942 we can find Katherine Anne Porter still feeling the need to defend color from the demands of plot; see the essay, "No Plot, My Dear, No Story," in *The Collected Essays and Occasional Writings of Katherine Anne Porter* (New York, 1970), pp. 460–63.

patchwork based on recognizable motifs but lacking a prevailing tonality. Chekhov's first longer story, "The Steppe," is a degenerate picaresque. The indifferent plain (the two words pun in Chekhov's text) through which Egorushka passes decomposes into contrasting story types, the idealized princess Dranitskaya and the mysterious Varlamov, but Egorushka remains equally untouched by the tonic stability of the one and the dominant excitement of the other: "Egorushka felt that, with these people disappeared for him, eternally, like smoke, all that had been lived through until now."[14] Such halting, uncertain cadences mark endings that are not culminations, but dissolutions. Debussy's composites are games ("Jeux"); for the gloomier Chekhov they constitute "A Dull Story," but for both the climactic, structuring elements of traditional forms remain but a hollow shell. The bang of excitement may resound, as it does, almost at the end of "A Dull Story" – "There are terrible nights with thunder, lightning, rain, and wind, that among the people are called sparrow's nights. One such sparrow's night occurred in my personal life . . . "[15] – but the end is at best a gloomy thud. The organization, though not the texture, of "A Dull Story" resembles that of Debussy's later Cello Sonata, where an excited climax of plucked dominant seventh chords on G, instead of resolving, is followed by a return of an earlier melancholy, wailing recitative, and then by a series of D minor chords, loud, to be sure, but ending low and abruptly muffled, with the marking "dry." Point and line come unglued, leaving structures that are heaps of fragments, not well shored up against ruin.[16]

By the early years of this century, post-Wagnerian continual modulation combined with the dissonant expressive leaps of Mahler's melodies and the rhythmic freedom of what Schoenberg

[14] A. P. Chekhov, *Izbrannye Sochinenia v Dvukh Tomakh* (Moscow, 1979), vol. 1, p. 334. The remainder of the close reads: "he descended in exhaustion into the shop and, with hot tears, greeted the new, unknown life, which was now beginning for him . . . How was this life to be?" (Chekhov's suspension points). The pun on "ravnodushno" (indifferently) and "ravnina" (plain) appears on p. 261, in the first chapter. For a more extended analysis, see the brilliant essay by Michael Finke, "Chekhov's 'Steppe': A Metapoetic Journey," *Russian Language Journal* 39 (1985), 79–120, where the "irreconcilable, disharmonious directions" of the anticlimactic plot (p. 91) are shown to be resolved in a "drama of motifs" and a musicality of structure (107–12) in which "Words more than characters are the story's actors" (p. 102).
[15] Chekhov, *Izbrannye Sochinenia*, vol. 1, p. 420 (Chekhov's suspension points).
[16] The emergence of modernist features in Debussy's style is well traced in Arthur B. Wenk, *Claude Debussy and Twentieth-Century Music* (Boston, 1983). There is a nice comparison of temporality in Debussy's *Canope* and in Proust in Claudia Zenck-Maurer, *Versuch über die wahre Art, Debussy zu analysieren* (Munich, 1974).

called "the progressive Brahms" to undermine totally the stability of the tonic, of the octave, and of the beat. If tension never relaxes, then tension also never builds, and the internal dramatic shape of the work is lost. There is no longer a progress from tonic to dominant, consonance to dissonance, the true to the interesting, and back again. Hence a work like Schoenberg's *Erwartung* becomes an extended, slow rhapsody of unfulfilled expectation, its texture pervaded by the disembodied sonority of the celesta, its epiphanic moment utterly subdued (see measure 390, text "Liebster, der Morgen kommt," marked "Ruhig, fast freundlich! ohne Leidenschaft!").

In the absence of an audible internal structure, music for a short period predominantly seeks its coherence from some external principle of reference. Ballet, program music, and song become the norm. Out of the heart of darkness there must emerge a voice, without which pure form retains only the briefest sustaining power: it is not by chance that Kurtz is the name of the mysterious central figure in the story that climaxes with the anguished cry, "A voice! a voice!" Or else music seeks a symbolic meaning, a fugitive vision that lies beyond words, the song of the nightingale perhaps. In some recently published program notes to his *Orchesterlieder*, Op. 22 (1915), Schoenberg speaks of this striving. Conventional program music, he says, had attempted to bring the represented object directly into the music; in semiotic terms, it had identified the musical sign with that which the verbal program signified. But Schoenberg envisioned a new music that could function like enactments, not like designations, and that would ultimately circumvent or surpass language in its meaningfulness. "If an actor will speak in a different cadence of a rough sea and of a calm one, my music will be no different: ... the music will not become agitated like the sea, but *differently*, like the actor ... A word describes the object and its condition; ... music ... *carries* the thing and its essence *up before the eye of the mind*."[17] A new semiosis is born that overcomes the disjunction between signifier and signified; the nature of meaning changes. To illustrate this transition from the literary side, I quote from the well-known "Letter to Lord Chandos" of 1902 by Hugo von Hofmannsthal: "Everything fell apart into pieces around me;

---

17 Schoenberg, *Stil und Gedanke*, p. 290. Cf. Vladimir Jankélévitch, *La Vie et la mort dans la musique de Debussy* (Neuchâtel, 1968), p. 93: "The voice of things is captured as closely as possible, and by so immediate an intuition that the human voice, that human presence, that the human person are finally effaced." This book also contains a sensitive appreciation of Debussy's temporality.

they coagulated into eyes which stared at me and into which I had
to stare back: they are whirlpools into which I gaze in giddiness,
which revolve incessantly and through which one reaches the void
... Since then I have led a life which you, I fear, can hardly grasp,
so spiritlessly, so thoughtlessly does it flow by ... A watering-can, a
harrow left in the field, a dog in the sun, a poor churchyard, a
cripple, a small farmhouse, any of these can become the vessel of
my revelation ... It is all a kind of feverish thought, but a thought
in a material which is more immediate, more fluid, more glowing
than words.''[18] Literature was striving toward the condition of
music, just as music was striving toward the condition of language,
and these apparently opposite strivings arose out of a single
impulse, to substitute embodiment for denotation in order to
restore expressivity where formal control had been lost.[19]

The limit case of the polarized forms of the nineteenth century is
thus a fragmentation of form. A curious passage in *Dr. Jekyll and
Mr. Hyde* seems to predict this development from polarized form to
fragmented form. It comes early in the concluding section of the
story, which contains Dr. Jekyll's coherent explanation of the
mystery, just before he loses all control over his identity.

I thus drew steadily nearer to that truth, by whose partial discovery I have been
doomed to such a dreadful shipwreck: that man is not truly one, but truly two. I
say two, because the state of my own knowledge does not pass beyond that point.
Others will follow, others will outstrip me on the same lines; and I hazard a guess
that man will be ultimately known for a mere polity of multifarious, incongruous,
and independent denizens.[20]

Those who outstrip nineteenth-century form arrive at the inco-
herence of what might well be called atonal literature. A reference
to Mallarmé's "Un Coup de dés" would seem to be called for at
this point, and that randomized flotsam of interwoven motifs is
surely one type of literary atonality, following a shipwreck like Dr.
Jekyll's. But even more revealing, because less flamboyant,
examples of what Schoenberg was to call the emancipation of
dissonance, may be found in the meandering inarticulacy of
Hardy's *Jude the Obscure* and the coolly dissonant, "uglified"

[18] Hugo von Hofmannsthal, "Ein Brief," in *Ausgewählte Werke*, ed. Rudolf Hirsch (Frankfurt am Main, 1957), vol. 2, pp. 342–43 and 347–48.
[19] There is a fine account of this development in both linguistics and poetics (Mallarmé,
Valéry, Sartre, and Jakobson) in Gérard Genette, *Mimologiques* (Paris, 1976), 257–314.
See esp. pp. 286–88 on the musicalization of language and pp. 298–99 on "signification
that has 'fallen into immanence,' [and] 'become a thing'."
[20] Robert Louis Stevenson, *The Complete Short Stories*, ed. Charles Neider (Garden City,
N.Y., 1969), p. 520.

romanticism of his later poetry. "So Various" is the programmatic title of a poem from the volume *Winter Words* that concerns the fragmentation of identity. Here is its discordant conclusion:

> Now ... All these specimens of man,
> So various in their pith and plan
>   Curious to say
>   Were *one* man. Yea
> I was all they.

Through the preceding twelve stanzas of contradictory self-portraits and all the way to the final, harshly fragmenting plural pronoun, the poem shows Hardy as precisely what Dr. Jekyll had predicted, "a mere polity of multifarious, incongruous, and independent denizens."[21]

Before the turn of the century, of course, large-scale dramatic structure was already often tending to yield to motivic consistency as a shaping force, as in Tchaikovsky's *Symphonie Pathétique*, an episodic work that is almost entirely generated by the four-note motif heard at the very start. And many works of the period seem to enact the struggle between opposing forms of organization. Thus in the last song of Mahler's *Das Lied von der Erde* the dissonant final chord, C–E–G–A, synopsizes one of the two leading motifs of the movement while refusing to come to rest harmonically and while the text likewise refuses closure through its repetitions of the word, "ewig" ("eternal"). James's *Turn of the Screw* is a work similarly in transition; a few years ago we were treated to the spectacle of an elegant, intricately knit essay concerning the fragmentation of identity in the story, published simultaneously with an equally brilliant, if disheveled structuralist reading that demonstrated how it is permeated by a systematic symmetry of motivic relationships.[22]

---

[21] The same program is enacted in Luigi Pirandello's novel, *Uno, nessuno e centomila* (1926; Mondadori edn., Milan, 1971); see the analysis in Gregory Lucente, *Beautiful Fables* (Baltimore, 1986), 116–55.

[22] Shoshana Felman, "Turning the Screws of Interpretation," *Yale French Studies* 55/56 (1977), 94–207; Christine Brooke-Rose, "The Squirm of the True: An Essay in Non-Methodology," "The Squirm of the True: A Structural Analysis of Henry James's *The Turn of the Screw*," and "Surface Structure in Narrative: The Squirm of the True, Part III," *PTL: A Journal for Descriptive Poetics and Theory* 1 (1976), 265–94, 513–46, and 2 (1977), 517–62. Christopher Lewis speaks of "a general trend in the arts away from a linear perception toward the idea of a multi-dimensional network of implications and cross-relations in all directions," ("Mirrors and Metaphor: Reflections on Schoenberg and Nineteenth-Century Tonality," *19th-Century Music* 10 [1987], 229–42). The term "trend" does not adequately capture the conflict between opposing modes reenacted so often in works of the period and well illustrated by the article's own examples of interference between Schenkerian monotonality and post-Wagnerian dual tonality.

Ultimately Schoenberg developed the twelve-tone system as a means for integrating larger works. He systematically subordinated dramatic modulations of intensity to the continuous fabric of intervallic relationships dispersed throughout the work. The local intelligibility of a melodic curve is replaced by long-range relationships that confer a meaning on each interval only in terms of its place in the tone-row and its employment elsewhere in the piece. The ecstatic semiosis of atonality thus eventually leads to a style where meaning is felt to arise from outside the local phrase.[23] Musical expression no longer seems natural and immediate. Stravinsky, Bartók, and even, to a considerable extent, the greatest of the traditionalists, such as Ravel and Prokofiev, are less schematic in their procedures, but fundamentally they share the same formal sensibility. The manner of proceeding common to all these composers derives from the breakdown of the polarizations that had structured music for the preceding 150 years.

Whereas each subsystem of nineteenth-century musical language (harmony, rhythm, and so forth) is divided into an unmarked and one or more marked components, in twentieth-century musical style these internal subdivisions no longer exist or – in more traditional composers who partially preserve them – their force is reduced. As Schoenberg says in the essay "Composition with Twelve Tones," "In this space ... there is no absolute down, no right or left, no forward or backward."[24] Thus, for instance, dissonance is no longer expressively marked with respect to consonance. The dominant, similarly, is no longer marked with respect to the tonic, so that though polytonal music continues to use triads, movement away from a given triad loses its significance. And melody loses its primacy through being fragmented in early twelve-tone music, demonized by pulsing ostinatos in Bartók, skeletonized by rhythmic displacement and pointillist instrumentation in Stravinsky.

As a result of these changes and others that need not be enumerated, formal unity and totality can no longer be generated "organically" through tension (internal division) and relaxation (reconciliation). The work is no longer an organism, self-defining and self-limiting. Instead, most often composers adopted historical

---

[23] In Schoenberg's atonality, as Carl Dahlhaus well expresses it in the essay "Emanzipation der Dissonanz," "consequentiality is taken away from the chord, but not comprehensibility"; see Dahlhaus, *Schönberg und andere* (Mainz, 1978), p. 148.

[24] Schoenberg, *Style and Idea*, p. 223.

forms to impose an arbitrary recognizable shape on their works.
The forms of music in this period were therefore not a product of
the musical language, as they had been earlier; the language
generates only fragments, and the larger forms actually employed
are alien to the language.[25] And this contradiction between form
and language leads in turn to the second main result of the stylistic
transformation, namely that a division between internal and
external components replaces a series of internal divisions as the
semiotic foundation of musical expression. The style has no internal limits – anything goes, so to speak – and only the bounded
forms of the past that lie outside the modern style carry any special
charge. Where dissonance is the norm, for instance, consonance
becomes an expressive device, but always, in music of this type, as
an untimely sonority, forbidden by some composers, archaic for the
others.[26] Consequently, expressivity is always attached to devices
that break the stylistic conventions of the form. And these devices –
semiotically marked, expressive, disruptive – are precisely those
features of melody, harmony, form, and so forth, that are the
familiar elements of the older style.

Thus we arrive at the law for music of this period, which is that
the familiar is always destabilizing, while the stable elements are
always estranged. Coherence and shape are at odds: the former,
the unity of the piece, comes from the modern style, most often
from the dense texture of microscopic motifs that permeate the
whole, while the latter, the expressive totality, comes from the
larger units like melody and structure that are borrowed wholesale
from the past. From this permanent division arises the unstably
ironic or elegiac character that seems inescapable in the period: the
music always seems to be saying one thing and meaning another, or
to be pointing toward a position it does not occupy. And yet the
irony rarely seems to arise from the kind of firm ground that

25 There is an excellent, nuanced description of the disjunction between style and form in
    Charles Rosen, *Schoenberg* (Glasgow, 1976), 79–116. He characterizes the aims as "a move
    to resurrect an old classicism" (p. 82) and "as much a defiant proclamation of freedom as
    an exercise in nostalgia" (p. 103), but the attribution of a mood is risky at best. Along
    similar lines, see the precise and eloquent analysis of musical structures in Thomas
    Mann's *Doktor Faustus* in Harry Redner, *In the Beginning Was the Deed: Reflections on the
    Passage of Faust* (Berkeley, 1982), 216–41, though Redner appears to understand Schoen-
    berg differently (pp. 236–37).
26 In Schoenberg's *Pierrot Lunaire*, for instance, consonances (never comfortably scored and
    in root position) always allude to the lost past. They appear at the opening of No. 4,
    "Eine blasse Wäscherin" ("A Pale Washerwoman"), in the nostalgic postlude of No. 5,
    "Valse de Chopin," and on occasion in the last song (No. 21), in connection with the
    text, "O alter Duft aus Märchenzeit" ("Old aroma from fairy tales of yore").

supports the puns of Haydn or the parody so frequent in late Beethoven. The great music of the twenties seems not to take a position; it rarely has the pronounced and unmistakable ideological character found in the music of powerful revolutionary composers like Mozart, Beethoven, and Wagner, or of powerful consolidators like Haydn and Brahms. It has no home base; even composers who preserve the notion of tonality use devices like a confusion of major and minor modes, or oblique tonal relations – the very key relationship that signals abnormality in Schubert or Chopin and madness in Smetana becomes unremarkable after 1900, and can be found in works like Kodály's Cello Sonata, Op. 4, Ravel's Sonata for Violin and Cello, and the first of Richard Strauss's *Four Last Songs* – in order to undermine the stability of the tonal system.

Music is not a referential art, and the homelessness of musical style in this period is a structural necessity, not a biographical or sociological one. This realization may offer us one way of understanding what Hardy once called "the ache of modernism" – the condition of homelessness or exile that besets the literature of the period.[27] The happy ending and the tragic but redemptive one have become equally obsolete; the inability of the citizens of Joyce's Dublin to get along with one another is an aesthetic precondition for the energy and movement required of a narrative. Thus Joyce's *Exiles* ends with Richard's confession of a wound "which can never be healed," a wound which consists of the "restless living wounding doubt" that makes love possible.[28] What is a law of musical form is merely a norm of literary expression. Joyce spoke, for instance, of the "scrupulous meanness" of his writing.[29] This does not mean that every sentence must be discordant, but it does mean that he wanted to emancipate dissonance, and that catachresis or category error becomes one of his most frequent and characteristic stylistic devices: "A bell clanged upon her heart" ("Eveline"); and "A light began to tremble on the horizon of his mind" ("A Little Cloud"). The old organic forms

---

[27] Thomas Hardy, *Tess of the D'Urbervilles*, Phase III. 19 (1891; New York, 1965), p. 105.

[28] James Joyce, *Exiles* (1918; New York, 1961), p. 112.

[29] Letter to Grant Richards, 13 March 1906, *Letters of James Joyce*, ed. Richard Ellmann, vol. 2, (London, 1966), p. 134. By "meanness" Joyce presumably understands parsimoniousness, but with an unpleasant affect, as in *Dubliners*, "A Little Cloud," p. 83 ("He found something mean in the petty furniture he had bought for his house on the hire system"), and "A Painful Case," p. 107 ("he found all the other suburbs of Dublin mean, modern and pretentious"). *Dubliners* is cited from the edition of Robert Scholes and A. Walton Litz (New York, 1969).

are reduced to a fragmentary residue; where there is a conflict and resolution, as in "The Boarding House," the climactic scene is omitted; where there is a plot, like the friends' scheme in "Grace" to get Kernan on the wagon, it seems to turn into a raucous imposition, parodied for instance by a millinery redemption in lieu of a genuine millenary one: "His hat, which had been rehabilitated by his wife, rested upon his knees."[30] Consistency comes from the web of motivic connections. There is no law, such as in the dodecaphonic system, requiring every note to be derived from the tone-row, but there is a principle that urges "scrupulous mean-ness" in the proper sense of concentration on a narrow repertoire of motifs. Totality or closure, on the other hand, comes from the archetypal patterns of aging, of the progression of the seasons, of the growth of social organization, that pervade the collection as a whole and that are entirely disjunct from the shape of the individual stories. And whereas tonal music is selective – some notes are in the scale, others are out – twelve-tone music substitutes what Rosen calls the saturation of the musical space: all notes must be represented equally.[31] Likewise, Joyce's encyclopedic impulse saturates the narrative space: all walks of life are represented, as are all ages of man, and the absence of spring from the cycle of seasons is the one significant structural irony in the collection: there is no pastoral and no regeneration.

At the very least, such parallels can confirm one's sense of what is truly general in the artistic culture of a period. No influence is in question here, no common heritage, no particular shared problematic, not even necessarily the same public – only a common sensibility. And I think, as well, that these parallels can aid those of us on the literary side with some of our interpretive problems and judgments. For the "laws" of musical structure offer firmer guidelines to interpretation than the more approximate principles of verbal expression. They can help guide our interpretive tact by clarifying for us what constitutes a message and what belongs to a cultural code and thus by indicating which features of the work we should decide to rely on or to stress. In Joyce's case, they can help us with the peculiar tonelessness of *Dubliners*, that deadpan succession of declarative sentences, poor in connectives, that characterizes his prose. There is a temptation to regard this feature as a savage irony, an Irishman's pitiless exposé of Dublin, as if Joyce might

---

30 The quotations come from *Dubliners*, pp. 41, 73, and 173.
31 Charles Rosen, *Schoenberg* (London, 1976), pp. 69–70.

have written differently of London, Paris, or Trieste. But, of course, the great artists of this period hardly wrote differently of these other cities: "scrupulous meanness" could well describe the tone of Svevo's Trieste, Proust's Paris, to a considerable degree even Woolf's London. Svevo even makes one of the apparent villains in *The Confessions of Zeno* a musician, the sort of violinist who plays Bach's Chaconne smoothly and sweetly. According to the title character, by contrast, "mistuning is the path to unison."[32] Yet Zeno's paradox reminds us that unison – the point of rest or the perspective point – can never be reached, but only approached through the increasing acuteness of permanent mistuning. Thus does the modernist sense of structure differ radically from the nineteenth-century principle that dissonance is the road to consonance – or in the Hegelian language of dialectical musical aesthetics, "in the suspension [*Aufhebung*] of equilibrium lies the tendency to return to a condition of equilibrium."[33] There is no implied superior position, ideological or utopian, from which the creator looks down on his creations; the disjunctions in the works are not a judgment, but the very form of modernism.

What are the consequences of the formalist history that the preceding pages sketch out? On one reading, they entail a fatalism or a Foucauldian power-play. I have invoked Debussy, Schoenberg, Stevenson, Hardy, Chekhov, and Hofmannsthal to suggest how the European spirit was Balkanized alongside the European polity. The fate of *Realpolitik*, this account would claim, was merely one expression of the fate of *Realismus*. A terrible beauty was born, with all the violence that we have come to associate with the term revolution. It happened to Hofmannsthal in 1902, to Schoenberg in 1911, and eventually to Europe in 1914.

There is a second reading of my argument that is closer to what I would like to believe. The second reading, like the first, claims a linkage between matters of the spirit and matters of history, for I hope that any reader of this volume feels that music matters to life.

---

[32] Italo Svevo, *La Coscienza di Zeno* (Milan, 1969), p. 101.

[33] Theodor Lipps, "Das Wesen der musikalischen Konsonanz und Dissonanz," in *Psychologische Studien* (Leipzig, 1905), p. 195. The key word is equilibrium, in contrast to the modernist sense of an ending that is illustrated by the work of D. A. Miller cited in note 7. Or, similarly, contrast the "resting place" in "The C Major of this life" at the end of Robert Browning's *Abt Vogler* with the conclusion of Thomas Pynchon's story, "Entropy," in *Slow Learner: Early Stories* (London, 1985), p. 98: "[Aubade] turned to ... wait with him until ... the hovering, curious dominant of their separate lives should resolve into a tonic of darkness and the final absence of all motion."

But the second reading would equate what I have called form not with fate but with what others would call ideology. A Marxist like Fredric Jameson has drawn powerful inspiration from the formalists Frye and Greimas, as well as from Adorno's musical writings. If we can take form as that which, in the sense of Edward Cone's *The Composer's Voice*, subconsciously regulates the possibilities of articulate thought, then I would like to think that formal analysis is the vehicle of self-reflexive ideology critique. Ruth Solie's defense of the indefensible in the present volume can serve as a touching example of such an ideologically aware formalism. Or one could invoke that other Marxist *malgré lui*, Charles Rosen, for his commitment – implicit throughout *The Classical Style* – to the view that music is the essential or inescapable carrier of our cultural determinants, precisely because it is free of the corrupting – or deconstructive – entanglements of words. On this second reading of my argument, we could say that formal analysis unveils the birth of ideology out of the spirit of music.[34]

[34] I want to thank Steven Hefling and Douglas Johnson for their thorough critiques of an ancient draft of this essay and Thomas Bauman for constructive objections to some passages in the penultimate version. I owe the Billings reference to Karl Kroeger.

6

Metaphorical modes in nineteenth-century music criticism: image, narrative, and idea

Thomas Grey

In the course of his famous treatise on *The Beautiful in Music*, Eduard Hanslick pointed to a perennial dilemma facing the critic of music: the fact that it "has no model in nature, it expresses no conceptual content." To gain verbal access to a composition, the critic is forced to choose between "dry technical designations" or else "poetic fictions," in Hanslick's words. Despite his reputation as a formalist, Hanslick clearly does not advocate here a purely technical discourse – which he accuses of dryness – over a more poeticizing style of interpretation. His point is merely that "poetic" discourse about music must be recognized for what it is, fiction rather than fact. "What is simply description in the other arts," he adds, "is already metaphor in music."[1]

Such metaphorical discourse has always been recognized as an indispensable, if troublesome, component of musical criticism. It is commonly called upon to moisten a bit those "dry technical designations," making them somewhat easier to swallow and perhaps enhancing their essential blandness – for wider audiences – with a certain piquancy of flavor. Conversely, a degree of analytical detail is generally thought necessary to provide some substantive base for the volatile nature of metaphorical impressions. That the two can and should be complementary is perfectly obvious, although it doesn't invalidate Hanslick's formulation of the critic's dilemma: the critic may not be faced with a choice between irreconcilable alternatives, but he still bears responsibility for striking a successful, convincing balance between them.

The struggle to achieve this delicate balance is one faced by nearly anyone writing about music in any way, from "serious" academic historical or analytical criticism to the everyday journalistic variety. A perceived tension or antagonism between descrip-

---

[1] E. Hanslick, *Vom Musikalisch-Schönen* (Leipzig, 1854; rpt. Darmstadt, 1981), p. 34. This and all subsequent translations are by the present author, unless otherwise indicated.

tive (objective) analysis and evocative (subjective) metaphor has doubtless become aggravated in our own time, when the claims of each often seem to be at odds (Joseph Kerman speaks of D. F. Tovey's "unabashed and frequently extravagant metaphors for the evocation of music's affect" as one of the traits of his criticism which most "exasperated" British analysts of the postwar era, who felt compelled to exorcise the lingering influence of such un-scientific dilettantism.)[2] The reliance of much nineteenth-century musical criticism on poeticizing, metaphorical modes of descrip-tion or interpretation is often assumed to stem from the unavailabi-lity of adequate analytical tools at that time, and from the proclivi-ties of Romantic critics themselves. It could be argued, however, that the more ambitious, serious examples of nineteenth-century criticism are precisely those which exploit such metaphorical means, while "objective" technical description is employed by reviewers whose principal aim is to make readers aware of the existence of new compositions (hence those who act merely as intermediary between composer, publisher, and public, and not really as critic at all).

The focus of the present essay is not, in any case, the dichotomy of metaphorical and technical discourse, but rather the role of metaphor itself in nineteenth-century criticism, particularly the implications of the categories or "modes" of metaphor commonly encountered and the manner in which they are applied. Broadly speaking, one can identify two predominant metaphorical modes in musical criticism since the late eighteenth century: a visual mode and a verbal, or more specifically, narrative mode. The sense of a composition might be sought in the images it seemed to evoke, or else in the events of which it seemed to speak – "events" which could themselves be construed either in strictly musical or in metaphorical terms. Analogies to the other (representational) arts could thus, by a transferral of properties, supply the representa-tional element which music lacked: music conceived, for instance, as "painting in tones" (*Tonmalerei*), or as a "language of feelings." Another visual analogy much favored by early aestheticians – that between music and architecture – circumvented the problem of representation and stressed perceived affinities of proportion, sym-metry, and hierarchical structure.

Of these various alternatives, the architectural metaphor proved to be of the least value for the criticism of individual works,

[2] Joseph Kerman, *Musicology* (London, 1985), p. 74.

however frequently it may be encountered in abstract aesthetic discussions. The affinities between music and architecture have to do with the nature of the media, but cannot easily be pursued on a meaningful, detailed level. The structural paradigms abstracted from the movements of a Mozart sonata or symphony might, according to the critic and historian A. W. Ambros, legitimately be compared to certain elements of classical architecture, but only at the level of abstract *schemata*, he admits, "without consideration of the musical content of the individual case."[3] Similarly, the analogy, popular during the early nineteenth century, between the intricate filigree of high gothic architecture and the polyphonic art of Bach, rests only on a broadly conceived set of affinities: both may display a rich, even seemingly chaotic profusion of surface ornament overlying a massive, tightly structured foundation. Yet the analogy will not tell us much about either the Strasbourg Minster or the St. Anne Fugue.[4]

Application of visual metaphor to music, of course, had to come to terms with the differences between spatial and temporal perception. Thus a much-cited aphorism – variously attributed to Goethe, Friedrich Schlegel, and Schelling – suggested a conception of music as "liquid" architecture and of architecture, conversely, as "frozen music." Disseminated by Mme. de Staël, among others, this version of the architectural metaphor soon attained the status of a cliché ("should one perhaps speak of ruins as a 'frozen cadenza?'" quipped Schopenhauer, some years later).[5] Even

---

[3] "Das allbekannte zweitheilige Schema [der Sonaten- oder Symphoniensatz] ... der Tonsatz mit unterbrechendem Alternativ ..., die verschiedenen Gestaltungen des Rondo, wie sie A. B. Marx aufzählt, alle diese Formen in ihrer abstrakten Allgemeinheit und ohne Rücksicht auf den musikalischen Inhalt in concreten Fällen betrachtet gleichen völlig dem allgemeinen Scheme eines nach dem Prinzip eines gewissen Baustyles gedachten Gebäudes." (Ambros, *Die Grenzen der Musik und Poesie* [Leipzig, 1855], p. 25).

[4] A classic instance of the analogy may be found in the essay, "Ideen über Baukunst und Musik," by C. J. Becker (*Neue Zeitschrift für Musik* 8 [1838], pp. 81–86), translated in *Music and Aesthetics in the Eighteenth and Early Nineteenth Centuries*, ed. P. le Huray and J. Day (Cambridge, 1981), pp. 493–97.

[5] Schopenhauer, *Die Welt als Wille und Vorstellung* II, ed. Arthur Hübscher (Zurich, 1977), ch. 39, p. 534. Writing in 1844, Schopenhauer speaks of the "*keckes Witzwort, so often repeated over the last thirty years, that architecture is a frozen music*," tracing the epigram to Goethe (J. P. Eckermann's *Gespräche mit Goethe in den letzten Jahren seines Lebens*, vol. 2 [1837], p. 88). Schopenhauer's skeptical attitude towards the analogy is conditioned by the nearly opposite positions of architecture and music with regard to the "Will" in his aesthetic theory. A. W. Ambros is among those who trace the epigram to Schlegel, in the *Athenäum*-fragments: see *Die Grenzen der Musik und Poesie*, p. 24, where he also refers to the likening of Bach's polyphony to gothic architecture ("Man hat in ähnlichem Sinne die tiefsinnig phantastischen Tongeflechte Sebastian Bachs mit den Wunderwerken germanischen Baustyles verglichen"). On the general background of

without invoking this conceit, the architectural image could (like Hanslick's infamous analogy of the decorative arabesque) suggest a rhythmic effect as the result of repeating visual patterns.[6] But the inadequacy of architectural and ornamental metaphor with regard to our "critical dilemma," however, is not so much a matter of their alleged static or schematic attributes. The problem lies, instead, precisely in those properties which music indisputably shares with architecture and ornament: as metaphor, they offer no means of penetrating the enigmatically nonrepresentational sounding surfaces of musical works. With respect to music, in other words, architecture and ornamentation are insufficiently metaphorical.

Two principal alternatives remain: what one could call a "pictorial" mode (appealing to a range of "natural," rather than abstract, imagery), and a "narrative" mode, which ascribes to a composition the teleological character of an interrelated series of events leading to a certain goal, or perhaps a number of intermittent goals that together make up a more or less coherent story. I will concentrate here on the second, narrative mode for several reasons: not only because of its closer relevance to the general topic of "music and text," but also because of its evident and increasing fascination for nineteenth-century critics, who often (perhaps unconsciously) adapt inherited concepts of imitation or "tone-painting" to newer narrative constructs.

Narrative metaphor may seem ideally suited to music because of the temporal, processive, and teleological characteristics shared by music and narrative. But narrative and visual or pictorial modes of metaphor are by no means distinct in nineteenth-century critical practice. The "story" conveyed by an instrumental work might, for some critics, have more in common with the kind of story conveyed by a series of images: a story expressed in mimetic rather than diegetic terms, in which levels of "discourse'" cannot be

---

these analogies, see also Hugh Honour, *Romanticism* (New York, 1979), ch. 3, and Eva Börsch-Supan, "Die Bedeutung der Musik im Werke Karl Friedrich Schinkels," *Zeitschrift für Kunstgeschichte* 34 (1971), pp. 276ff.

[6] Hanslick also went on to modify his analogy, recommending that one imagine an arabesque "emerging before our eyes, in a continual process of self-formation" (*Vom Musikalisch-Schönen*, p. 33). Hanslick himself dismisses the identification of "the musically beautiful" with an "architectonic" principle, which he seems to associate especially with Renaissance polyphony (" ... jene großartig düstern Stimmpyramiden der alten Italiener und Niederländer"). Likewise he notes the inadequacy of symmetry as an aesthetic criterion (the most "symmetrically" organized works being generally the most amateurish, pp. 46–47).

distinguished from the medium itself, and in which the events "depicted" resist verbal summary. Furthermore, the categories of "pictorial" or "descriptive" music – *malende Musik* – most often embraced concepts of musical narration as well, at least in the critical vocabulary of the earlier nineteenth century.

The ambiguity between narrative applications of visual and verbal metaphor is nicely exemplified by a dialogue published anonymously in 1827, whose title asked: "Should One Think of Anything While Listening to Instrumental Music?" The two inter-locutors have been listening to an unspecified Mozart Andante. The more poetically inclined speaker remarks that the piece made him think of "a story or a romance," although he failed to connect it to any one particular work among those that came to mind (which include "ballads of Goethe, Schiller, and Uhland, or one of Tieck's *Märchen*"). In the subsequent discussion, however, no distinction is made between "romantic stories" ("romantische Erzählungen") on the one hand and a "series of images" ("Folge von Bildern," "poetische Bilderreihe") on the other.[7] In his famous essay on Berlioz and the issue of program music (1855), Franz Liszt lumped together as a single phenomenon "those attempts, more and more common in the last fifteen years, to fix in the form of picturesque, poetic, or philosophical commentaries the images aroused in the listener's mind" by the symphonies, sonatas, and quartets of Beethoven (despite Liszt's own decidedly literary orien-tation, the unifying impulse noted here is that of "images").[8]

The notion of music that strove to imitate verbal narrative, of course, raised many familiar objections, analogous to those to literal or naive efforts at musical imitation. Schumann's defense of Mendelssohn is typical when he asserts that, in the *Schöne Melusine* overture, Mendelssohn eschews any "coarse narrative thread" ("groben historischen Faden").[9] In principle, the forms of narra-

---

[7] "Soll man bey der Instrumental-Musik Etwas denken?" (attributed to F. L. B. in index), *Allgemeine Musikalische Zeitung* 29 (1827), cols. 529–30.

[8] Franz Liszt, "Berlioz und seine Haroldsymphonie," *Neue Zeitschrift für Musik* 43 (1855), p. 39. When Liszt was contemplating a series of symphonic poems based on a cycle of historical frescos by Wilhelm von Kaulbach in Berlin (of which only *Hunnenschlacht* was ever realized), he commented to Princess Wittgenstein that he would first need to find a suitable poet to re-create the scenes for him in verse to help clarify the musical forms whose general outlines he had already "instinctively" conceived in his mind (see Peter Raabe, *Liszts Schaffen* [Tutzing, 1986], p. 101). The poetry Liszt has in mind is clearly of the epic–narrative genre rather than the lyric.

[9] Robert Schumann, *Gesammelte Schriften über Musik und Musiker*, vol. 1, ed. Martin Kreisig (Leipzig, 1914), p. 143.

tive prose or poetry appeared to be antithetical to the "architectural" symmetries and repetitions of "natural" musical discourse.
Yet this did not prevent many (even most) critics from freely
availing themselves of visual and narrative metaphor, when it
seemed appropriate. (Schumann himself admired the "novelistic"
character he identified in Schubert's C major Symphony, while
such a character did not, of course, presuppose the existence of any
"coarse narrative thread" in this case, either).

As Liszt suggested, Beethoven's works were among the first
music to attract such metaphorical interpretation on a large scale.
The major works inspired already in his own day the critical topos
of "idea" – often specified as a "fundamental" or unifying idea
(*Grundidee*) – which corresponded to the essential expressive
content of the individual work (Liszt himself, in the passage quoted
above, refers to the "leading idea behind the great instrumental
works"). German-language musical criticism remained very much
in the shadow of the prevailing idealistic philosophical and literary
discourse throughout the century, and the broader category of
"idea" readily subsumed both visual and narrative modes of metaphor. Metaphorical interpretation of music, whether couched in
terms of images or of actions, aimed to reveal the "idea," the true
spiritual–intellectual essence of which the "sounding forms" of a
composition were understood as the immediate sensual manifestation. Critical categories such as the "descriptive," the "pictorial," and the "characteristic" could all denote music that strove,
explicitly or implicitly, for the expression of an "idea." Beethoven's
two explicitly "characteristic" symphonies, for instance, carry
titles which might align them with principal genres of either
painting *or* poetry: the "heroic" and the "pastoral."[10] But let us

---

[10] In the case of the "Pastoral," where the connotation of landscape painting lies close at
hand, Beethoven seems to have been at pains to discourage a "visually" oriented reading
as well as any aesthetically pejorative associations of the category of *Tonmalerei*. In the
process of sketching the work, Beethoven ruminated on the matter of a generic rubric
("*Sinfonia caracteristica* – or recollection of country life," and further, "*Sinfonia pastorella*")
and on the problem of the "pictorial" metaphor: "All painting in instrumental music is
lost if it is pushed too far ... [W]ithout titles the whole will be recognized as a matter
more of feeling than of painting in sounds" (see Gustav Nottebohm, *Zweite Beethoveniana*
[Leipzig, 1887], p. 375, and A. W. Thayer and E. Forbes, *Life of Beethoven*, vol. 1
[Princeton, 1967], p. 436). The famous disclaimer entered at the beginning of a manuscript first violin part, "Mehr Ausdruck der Empfindung als Mahlerei," is an echo of
these same concerns. While they may represent, in large part, merely an acknowledge-
ment of conventional aesthetic doctrine, Beethoven's comments also have some bearing
on the question of metaphorical "mode": as "recollection" and "feeling," we are
encouraged to conceive the symphony in terms either of narrative or lyric genres, as
much as (or more than) that of landscape painting.

consider a case where such characteristic associations are not made explicit, and the critic is forced to choose for himself an appropriate metaphorical mode.

II

In a survey of the Beethoven symphonies according to their "ideal content" first published in 1854, the pseudonymous critic Ernst von Elterlein noted that less agreement existed as to the "characteristic ideal content" of the Seventh Symphony – "the fundamental idea of the work" – than about any of the other symphonies.[11] Underlying this diversity of opinion, however, was a general conviction that the Seventh *was* is some sense "characteristic," that it betrayed some potentially concrete expressive or "representational" impulse (in a way that the Fourth or Eighth Symphonies, for instance, did not). The notorious Parisian critic Fétis believed that much of the Seventh could only produce a "bizarre and forced" effect as long as one had no clue to its intended "idée principale." With reference to the "epoch of Beethoven's greatest compositions" in general, Fétis spoke of "a fundamental poetic or novelistic idea" behind these works ("une idée principale, poétique ou romanesque, qui devenait le cadre de toutes ses pensées et le but de tous ses moyens").[12]

In a Schumann-inspired critical vignette (published 1860), A. W. Ambros assembled a group of fictional enthusiasts to discuss the Seventh Symphony following a performance. His second-generation *Davidsbündler* adopt representative positions with regard to the interpretation of the piece and its critical history, some defending it as a piece of abstract "tone-poetry" in the early Romantic tradition, others embellishing fanciful programmatic accounts that had come to be attached to it.[13] Specifically, Ambros's vignette emerges as a trope on a similar scene imagined by Schumann in the third of his "Schwärmbriefe an Chiara" in

---

[11] "Gleichwohl herrscht über den besonderen Sinn der Symphonie, über den charakteristischen idealen Gehalt, die Grundidee der Schöpfung so wenig Übereinstimmung, so viel Verschiedenheit der Auffassung, wie rücksichtlich keiner der übrigen Symphonieen" (E. v. Elterlein [= Ernst Gottschald], *Beethovens Symphonieen nach ihrem idealen Gehalt* [Dresden, 1954; 3rd edn. 1870], p. 57).

[12] François-Joseph Fétis, "Ecole Royale de Musique: Société des Concerts" (concert review), *Revue musicale* 5 (1829), p. 131.

[13] A. W. Ambros, "Flaminiana. Phantasiestücke: I. Nach Beethovens A-dur-Symphonie," in *Culturhistorische Bilder aus dem Musikleben der Gegenwart* (Leipzig, 1860; 2nd edn. 1865), pp. 226–32. See Schumann, *Gesammelte Schriften*, vol. 1, pp. 121–22.

which Florestan claims to quote a still earlier account of the symphony "from an old issue of the journal, *Cäcilia*." (While this original model does indeed exist, Florestan's "quotation" turns out to be a thoroughly ironic transformation of it – a point that has often been overlooked by later commentators.) Florestan's "peasant-wedding" version of the original *Cäcilia* program is also alluded to in the course of Wagner's well-known story, "Ein glücklicher Abend" (1841), where it is criticized, paradoxically, from a very Schumannian perspective – a result of failing to register Schumann's critical irony. As this brief bit of critical genealogy suggests, the Seventh Symphony had acquired a fairly distinct hermeneutic tradition by the middle of the nineteenth century.

As one of the characters in Ambros's "Phantasiestück" remarks, there is an element of consistency among the various interpretations accrued by the Seventh Symphony, despite the whimsical variety and manifest foolishness of some of the details. In particular he notes the centrality of a ritual, ceremonial, or festival theme. Like Wagner's still-familiar characterization of the Seventh as the "apotheosis of the dance" in *The Artwork of the Future*,[14] such themes appear to be inspired by the role of persistent basic rhythmic figures in each of the movements. Wagner's friend, Theodor Uhlig, claimed that – due in part to the varied and complementary dance-like characters of the movements in the Seventh – the relation between movements here was "epic" rather than dramatic, as in the Fifth or Ninth.[15] In most interpretations, the movements are linked as a series of formalized, ritual "events" ranging from the solemnly hieratic (the Allegretto), to the celebratory (first and third movements), to the frenzied and orgiastic (the finale). Thus most accounts of the symphony invoke a series of "communal" events, as opposed to the individualized protagonist usually posited in the case of the "Eroica," the Fifth, and the Ninth. The ever-popular and highly evocative Allegretto seems to have formed the core of many interpretations, extrapolating from such features as the constant rhythmic tread and the influential dynamic shape of the movement, with its suggestion of a processional approach and departure.[16]

---

[14] Richard Wagner, *Gesammelte Schriften und Dichtungen*, vol. 3, ed. Richard Sternfeld (Leipzig, 1916), p. 94.
[15] Theodor Uhlig, "Die Instrumentalmusik" (1851), in *Musikalische Schriften*, ed. Ludwig Frankenstein (Regensburg, 1913), p. 147.
[16] The tendency toward slow tempos in the performance of this movement seems to have taken hold early in the century, to judge from its almost invariable citation as "Andante"

The early commentary referred to by Schumann, printed in *Cäcilia* in 1825 (signed C. F. Ebers), posits the representation of a wedding celebration through its various phases, from the gradual gathering of the guests in the introduction and first movement through a postnuptial bacchanale in the Finale, in which "all propriety is forgotten" and (by the final reprise) "tables, mirrors, and candlesticks" are all shattered by the intemperate revelers, and the whole affair ends in pandemonium.[17] A. B. Marx's account of the symphony imagines a series of loftier *tableaux* representing scenes from an imaginary Romantic moorish epic, but culminating again in a scene of "bacchic frenzy" (". . . das Südvolk im bacchischen Taumel").[18] Ludwig Nohl, a generally sober historian of the next generation, approved of Marx's moorish fantasies, and added that the Seventh was not only "the first significant [musical] work of truly Romantic character," but also "the first attempt to represent history in music" (perhaps a reference to the work's Napoleonic associations, but Nohl resists any detailed substantiation of his claim).[19] And although an "apotheosis of the dance" signified in Wagner's critical vocabulary of 1849 an apotheosis of "absolute music," he later confided to Cosima that "for me this work is a complete portrait of a Dionysian festival" and proceeded to sketch for her a series of ritual episodes, culminating, of course, in a bacchanale.[20]

This "bacchanale" association of the Finale, incidentally, is perhaps the most constant feature in the interpretive history of the work. An anonymous Viennese review of the new published score

(in at least one instance, even "Adagio"!). A typical image of the movement is expressed by Liszt, describing a kind of "vision" experienced in the Sistine Chapel: Liszt refers to "le mystérieux *Convito* de spectres et d'anges de l'Andante de la 7me Symphonie," and connects the "dominant ostinato" in this movement, in the funeral march of the "Eroica," and in the first movement of the "Moonlight" Sonata with Allegri's *Miserere* (*Briefwechsel zwischen Franz Liszt und Carl Alexander, Großherzog von Sachsen*, ed. La Mara [Leipzig, 1909], p. 116).

[17] C. F. Ebers, "Reflexionen," *Cäcilia* 2 (1825), pp. 271–72.

[18] A. B. Marx, *Ludwig van Beethoven: Leben und Schaffen*, vol. 2 (1859; Stuttgart, 1902), pp. 163–75.

[19] L. Nohl, *Der Geist der Tonkunst* (Frankfurt, 1861), p. 215 and p. 218 ("Es ist der erste Versuch, in Musik Geschichte darzustellen").

[20] *Cosima Wagner's Diaries*, ed. Martin Gregor-Dellin and Dietrich Mack, trans. Geoffrey Skelton, vol. 1 (New York, 1978), pp. 604–5. In a later reference to the Seventh Symphony, Cosima reports that Wagner "tells us his ideas about it (Dionysian celebrations), as he has often done before ..." (31 December 1880, vol. 2, p. 587). See also "Über das Dichten und Komponieren" of 1879 (Richard Wagner, *Gesammelte Schriften und Dichtungen*, vol. 10, ed. W. Golther [Leipzig, n.d.], pp. 147–48), where Wagner also scornfully alludes to a "masked ball" scenario for the symphony put forth by Alexander Ulybyshev (see note 29).

(1817) offers the following slightly cryptic view of the finale (without, however, attempting to trace any "narrative" connections to the preceding movements):

[The movement] divides into two main portions, within which we again encounter numerous repetitions of eight-measure [phrases], and which – in its general outline, bearing, and character – resembles the wild and dissolute activities of a young wastrel who seeks to drown away the first prickings of his bad conscience in a sea of intoxicating pleasures.[21]

Arnold Schering supposed the Finale to represent the episode from *Wilhelm Meisters Lehrjahre* in which a dramatic reading in Wilhelm's quarters degenerates into drunken revelry, ending with the mock-ritual destruction of the empty glasses and punch bowl, hurled from the window.[22] And D. F. Tovey maintained that "the Finale is and remains unapproached in music as a triumph of Bacchic fury."[23] Thus there has long prevailed a consensus that the character of the movement is one not only of intoxication, but even of violent and destructive abandon. This view is given fairly drastic expression in a remark made by Wagner to Cosima on another occasion, that the finale is "in a certain sense ... no longer music – but only [Beethoven] could do it." To which he added the intriguing observation that "last movements are the precipices; I shall take good care to write only single-movement symphonies".[24]

The problem of endings, noted by Wagner, was of course a problem symphonists shared with novelists. And one could say that the "problematic" status of the finale coincided with a new impulse to read the symphonic cycle in some kind of "narrative" terms, rather than as a pleasing aggregate of expressive–musical "pictures." Beginning with Beethoven, it seemed, the finale asked to be interpreted as the consequence of what precedes it. But in

[21] *Allgemeine musikalische Zeitung mit besonderer Rücksicht auf den österreichischen Kaiserstaat* 1 (1817), cols. 39–40 (cited from *Ludwig van Beethoven: Die Werke im Spiegel seiner Zeit*, ed. Stefan Kunze [Laaber, 1987], p. 308).

[22] Arnold Schering, *Beethoven und die Dichtung* (Berlin, 1936), ch. 7: 'Die 7. Symphonie op. 92, A-dur, nach Szenen aus Goethes Wilhelm Meisters Lehrjahre.' pp. 213–38.

[23] D. F. Tovey, *Essays in Musical Analysis*, vol. 1 (London, 1935), p. 60. A somewhat earlier commentary on the Seventh, by Otto Neitzell (1852–1920), concludes a fairly detailed, rather choreographic, account of the work (reminiscent of Marx) with the familiar bacchanale: "Another festival is celebrated here ... Bacchus himself rushes about with his wild, exuberant retinue (mm. 7–8); the wild company clash their cymbals, as all suffering is dissolved in a mighty rejoicing (mm. 26–29)" – and so on (*Beethoven's Symphonien nach ihrem Stimmungsgehalt erläutert* [2nd edn., Cologne, 1912], pp. 71–73).

[24] *Cosima Wagner's Diaries*, 17 November 1881 (vol. 2 [New York, 1980], pp. 749–50).

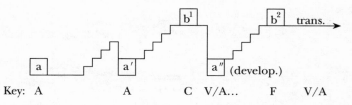

Figure 6.1 Beethoven, Symphony No. 7, first movement, poco sostenuto

Example 6.1 Beethoven, Symphony No. 7, first movement,
(a) mm. 1–4
(b) mm. 23–26

reflecting on the applications of narrative metaphor to this work, let us pause here to begin at the beginning, the introduction.

III

The introduction (*poco sostenuto*) to the first movement of the Seventh Symphony is imposing in its unusual breadth. It is somewhat more "architectural" in design than symphonic introductions tend to be, as a rule – especially due to a full restatement of a contrasting phrase (b) following a central development of the opening idea (a). (See Figure 6.1 and Example 6.1).

But what most intrigued early critics of the work, almost without exception, was an element that is *not* thematic, but accessory or accompanimental: the rising sixteenth-note scales introduced during the opening (a) group. (See Example 6.2).
In a passing reference to this introduction, Wilhelm von Lenz characterized these scales as great "staircases, built of thirds, and traversed by giants."[25] (On the inspiration of Lenz's architectural imagery, the blueprint of the introduction in Figure 6.1 attempts to

---

[25] "... escaliers dont les marches, construites en *tierces*, sont parcourues par des géants" (Wilhelm von Lenz, *Beethoven et ses trois styles* [1852; New York, 1980; rpt. Paris, 1909], p. 261).

Example 6.2 Beethoven, Symphony No. 7, first movement, mm. 7–15

indicate the role of this scalar figure by means of a stair-like symbol.)

C. F. Ebers's early "marriage" scenario begins with another architectural image: French doors of a large reception hall are thrown open, "the rising basses and violins are the respectable elder relations who walk about the room and set things in order. In the Vivace the guests gradually arrive. Various characters – alternately sedate, light-footed, comic, and sentimental figures – combine to form a whole, which becomes simply a colorful swirl ("buntes Farbengemisch").''[26] The narrative metaphor gives way to abstract imagery, a visual arabesque. Schumann and Ambros also elaborated on the idea of a gathering assembly.[27] Likewise Wagner, in his "Dionysian" gloss to Cosima: "At the start, the herald and tibia players, then the gathering people (the scale), after that the charming theme, whose swinging movement gives the idea of a procession, and so on.''[28]

Nearly all commentators remark on the vivid sense of expectations aroused, which is, after all, a natural function of introductions. A. B. Marx drew a parallel to the epic invocation, alluding to the opening verses of Wieland's *Oberon* ("Noch einmal sattelt mir den Hyppogriphen/Zum Ritt ins alte romantische Land").[29] Like the epic exordium, the introduction serves to gather the listeners' attention, but at the same time directs attention to the magnitude of things to come, of the story to follow. In particular, Marx draws attention to the effect of the rising string scales as they are gradually led away from the tonic by modulatory reiterations of the wide intervals of (a) over a descending bass line. "It seems to point us to something far away," he remarks, and indeed, this scale figure twice leads to relatively distant tonal realms, to C♮ and F♮ in each of the (b) phrases: march-like, but heard "as if from far away," as a gesture of "mysterious annunciation.''[30]

The specific relation of the (b) phrases to the rest of the introduction poses difficulties for a purely "architectural" reading of the form. The consequents of the (b) phrases, for instance, are not

---

[26] *Cäcilia* 2 (1825), 271.

[27] In Schumann's *Schwärmbrief*, for instance, Florestan remarks (paraphrasing Ebers): "Ich müßte mich irren, wenn nicht in der Einleitung die Gäste zusammenkämen, sich sehr begrüßten mit Rückenkommas ..."(*Gesammelte Schriften*, vol. 1, p. 122).

[28] *Cosima Wagner's Diaries*, vol. 1, p. 604. Wagner's programmatic sketch continues: "The Andante [*sic*] is the tragedy, the sacrifice of the god, memories of Zagreus, 'you, too, have suffered,' then the rustic celebrations, the vinegrowers and other country people with their thyrsi, and to end with, the bacchanale. But the music is, of course, very much more idealistic than any of that ..." (*ibid.*, pp. 604–5).

   Antony Hopkins remarks on mm. 1–10ff. of the introduction "The gradual accumulation of the various strands, each with its individual tone-color, suggests a literal gathering together of the available sources" (*The Nine Symphonies of Beethoven* [London, 1981], p. 198).

[29] *Berliner Allgemeine musikalische Zeitung* 1 (1824), p. 182. In the later Beethoven biography, Marx cites only the second line, but further elaborates on the rest of his "epic" metaphor originally sketched in 1824.

[30] Marx, *Ludwig van Beethoven*, vol. 2, p. 163. He describes the very end of the introduction (transition) in similar terms: "Es klingt das hohe e' '/e' ' ' *märchenhaft und weit hinaus*" (p. 164, original emphasis).

properly completed in either case, but gradually ousted by a
swelling sixteenth-note pulsation introduced in the woodwinds
(mm. 29ff. and 48ff.). The quality of the (b) contrast itself is
perplexing. The rather eccentric Russian critic, Alexander
Ulybyshev, registered *his* perplexity at this contrast in an allusion
to Lenz's image of the "staircase." "Where does it lead?" asks
Ulybyshev. "This 'staircase of giants' leads, in fact, to something
very shabby, which gives itself the airs of a triumphal march" (i.e.
phrase [b]). "It is indeed a march," he admits, "but executed by
the Krähwinkel garrison, consisting of twenty invalid soldiers and
three asthmatic oboists." Ulybyshev concludes that it must represent a misguided attempt at musical irony: "For a composer of such
eminent originality, who above all others might have taken for his
device 'odi profanum vulgus,' such things can only be taken in the
sense of the bitterest irony." Unfortunately, Ulybyshev adds, Beethoven "forgot that sarcasm in music is impossible," at least without
the aid of verbal explications – "and, as we know, *bons mots* which
must be explained are of no value."[31]

These characteristically flippant remarks of Ulybyshev's raise a
valid point: by investing the architectural metaphor with a kind of
narrative import ("where do these stairs lead?") we are forced to
consider the matter of causal relations between musical events –
their functional significance – beyond matters of balance, proportion, and order in abstract terms. In this case, the stairs lead not to
a place, but to an event, a march.

A. B. Marx had equated these "shabby" (b)-phrases with the
"annunciation" of something as yet only dimly apprehended, from
a distance. Marx does not attempt to tie this in with the colorful
details of his moorish battle epic. But his description is nonetheless
suggestive of a possible narrative reading (or hearing) of the
contrast as a kind of foreshadowing or intimation of future events –
a "prolepsis" in Gerard Genette's terms.[32] For of course, both of
these keys (C and F) will play a prominent role in the remainder of
the symphony in the relation of flat III and flat VI to the tonic, A.
Given the "epic" associations generated by the Seventh, we might
also recall what Thomas Leitch claims to be characteristic of the
great epics of Homer, Virgil, and Dante: that "in each case the
organizing principle of the adventures (from the hero's point of
view) and the discourse (from the audience's) is fundamentally

[31] Alexandre Oulibicheff [Ulybyshev], *Beethoven, ses critiques et ses glossateurs* (Paris and
Leipzig, 1857), pp. 226–27. On Ulybyshev's notion of musical "irony," see p. 236.
[32] Gerard Genette, "Discours du récit" in *Figures III* (Paris, 1972).

projective, based on intimations of a future goal whose full nature and significance are only imperfectly grasped, but which serves, through the heroes' guesses and doubts and half-formed interpretations about its problematic nature, to inform all their actions".[33] One might indeed claim that the "foreshadowing" of the key areas F and C continues to inform many of the tonal actions of the subsequent movements.

Such tonal foreshadowing is naturally not uncommon in Beethoven (see the introductions of the *Leonore* Overtures No. 2 and No. 3, for example). But the possible analogy to narrative functions underscores a crucial difference between visual and "narrative" metaphor, for music. Visual metaphor, whether static or animated, lacks the ability of narrative metaphor (e.g. prolepsis or analepsis) to posit a series or system of relations across time. Indeed, the *thematic* foreshadowings that become a hallmark of later nineteenth-century symphonic introductions would appear to represent an attempt to exploit the "narrative" function of the introduction already dimly apprehended (or perhaps not so dimly) by Beethoven.

In pondering the narrative significance of Beethoven's *tonal* prolepses, let us follow Marx into the main portion of the movement. The Vivace begins, Marx suggests, with a kind of reversal. It begins in a pastoral mode, with the main theme in bucolic woodwind guise. But, from the beginning, the bellicose string contingent is waiting impatiently behind the scenes (mm. 63–88, during which the strings gradually assert their presence). When the strings are set loose, at the counterstatement of the main theme (mm. 89ff.), the orchestra as a whole is alerted to an unexpected critical situation, and the mode becomes heroic (to paraphrase Marx).[34] The normally peaceable, agrarian populace is suddenly roused to glorious battle. (In a sense, this is hardly "unexpected." The loud, tutti counterstatement is, of course, a typical ploy of the later Viennese symphonic style. But what matters here, as Marx suggests, is how the relationship is dramatized, or seemingly motivated, by the role of the strings, in addition to the characteristic, strident orchestration of the counterstatement.)

What makes the epic recitation of such a scene compelling are the temporary setbacks, the moments of indecision. And although the dactylic fervor of Beethoven's Vivace rarely dissipates, such

[33] Thomas M. Leitch, *What Stories Are: Narrative Theory and Interpretation* (University Park, Penn. and London, 1986), p. 107.
[34] See Marx, *Ludwig van Beethoven*, vol. 2, pp. 243–45.

Example 6.3 Beethoven, Symphony No. 7, first movement, mm. 391–402

moments do occur. They occur, moreover, in the key areas and key relations intimated in the "tonal prolepses" of the introduction. For instance, as soon as the proper second key area (the dominant) has been established in the course of the exposition, the music plunges boldly ahead into C major. This "false move" is immediately recognized as a tactical error, and causes a moment of distinct unease (the textural and dynamic *diminuendo* to a hushed *pianissimo*, mm. 138–41).[35] A strenuous concerted effort to recover lost ground quickly leads back to the proper dominant and reattainment of full confidence (mm. 142–52) – only to be followed by another lapse, the striking Neapolitan (F^6) interpolation of m. 156 and m. 162.

Similar attempts to master the unfamiliar territory of C and F occur in the development. Of paramount importance, however, is not the existence of C and F as abstract tonalities, but a tonal progression C–F–E in which F functions as the flatted supertonic of the dominant. This progression is twice intimated in the introduction (for instance mm. 8–10: see Example 6.2). The same progression eventually shows the way out of the last "crisis" of the movement, at the beginning of the coda, following a sudden dip to A♭ (see Example 6.3).

One might go on to suggest that the problematic associations of these key areas (C, F) are worked out in the course of the following movements, particularly in the finale, where the center of what ought to be the "development" is occupied by a full-scale transposition of the opening group to C (mm. 146–61). The tonal traumas of the first movement are exorcised, as it were, in the bacchic frenzy of the finale. But I hesitate to pursue this particular line of interpretation any further, at least in this context, since few nineteenth-century critics show much interest in attaching metaphorical significance to such abstract or long-range tonal relations.[36] This is not to suggest, of course, that we need limit our own

---

[35] The effect of this passage is similarly described by Janet Levy in "Texture as a Sign in Classic and Early Romantic Music," *Journal of the American Musicological Society* 35 (1982), pp. 529–30: "The example from Beethoven's Symphony No. 7 [first movement, mm. 134–42] illustrates one way in which a unison may threaten or disrupt the world that we inhabit as imaginary participants in the unfolding of a musical drama or discourse."

[36] Leo Treitler's analysis of the "tonal narrative" in Beethoven's Ninth Symphony (he also speaks of "the phenomenology of key relationships, regarded in the sense of a narrative") – although offered as a historically oriented alternative to current formalist analytical methodologies – cannot properly be said to reflect nineteenth-century perceptions (the citation of Beethoven's scattered and cryptic remarks on key characteristics notwithstanding). See Treitler, "'To Worship that Celestial Sound': Motives for Analysis," *Journal of Musicology* 1 (1982), pp. 153–70.

applications of metaphorical discourse to music according to apparent practices contemporary with it, any more than we should feel compelled to analyze music solely by means of the theoretical vocabulary and constructs of the time. But my purpose here is simply to elucidate and amplify, slightly, the manner in which earlier critics do seem to have "heard" narrative or quasi-narrative implications composited from the kinds of images and gestures they perceived in certain musical works. Such practices may also serve to remind us of the extent to which almost any analysis or critical interpretation that takes account of temporality and causality in musical works will appeal to a narrative mode of understanding.[37] By way of considering further both the insights and dilemmas generated by such narrative metaphors, let us turn in closing to another introduction.

IV

The introduction to Mozart's *Don Giovanni* Overture functions in a very obvious sense as a "prolepsis" of the dramatic catastrophe. The music conjures a variety of vivid associations – demonic, ghostly, oracular. Unlike Beethoven's (somewhat atypical) introduction, Mozart's establishes no "architectural" pattern of contrasts and returns, remaining closer to the introductory paradigm of the extended half-cadence. It suggests a single moment rather than a series of events, and for most listeners the moment is defined by the image of a scene already familiar to them.

The relation of the introduction to the Allegro might normally be construed in terms of the two generic realms of Mozart's *dramma giocoso*, contrasting pictures of the tragic and the comic. The overwhelming intensity of the introduction, however, seems to have led not a few nineteenth-century critics to seek something more in the Allegro, a narrative or dramatic musical précis of the central "idea" of the opera. Prefacing an extended musical–semantic exegesis of the overture (1847), the critic–theorist–

---

[37] Carolyn Abbate, citing Nattiez, has suggested that "music analysis is itself [perhaps] born of a narrative impulse, that we create fictions about music to explain where no other form of explanation works" ("What the Sorcerer Said," *19th-Century Music* 12 [1989], p. 228). This statement, however, obscures the fact that not all narratives are necessarily meant as "fictions" – indeed, the larger number of narratives we encounter on a daily basis are presented as factual accounts. Of course, the "truth-value" (or conversely, the "fictional" or metaphorical element) of a given analysis can be the point of endless debate.

composer J. C. Lobe stated that "[the Allegro] depicts the course of Don Juan's licentious and debauched career – on that point all are agreed."[38] In his widely-read biographical and critical study of Mozart, Alexander Ulybyshev exercised his ever-fertile imagination in a detailed and explicitly "narrative" interpretation, which also incorporated the introduction:

In a legend or a poetic tale such as *Don Juan*, what most strikes the imagination is the catastrophe. Thus it is both natural and quite common to recall it at the very beginning of the narration [*récit*]: "I shall tell you of the adventures and of the terrible end of that audacious sinner who, fearing neither God nor man, was finally confronted by the shade of the old man he had murdered, and was thrown by demons into a fiery sepulchre." The tale could very well begin thus, and it is precisely such an exordium that Mozart chooses to begin with. "Listen well!" cry the opening chords ...[39]

Ulybyshev goes on to interpret the introduction partly as narrative, partly as a visual phantasmagoria on Don Giovanni's final moments: "After this sublime exordium, evoking the [impending] death of Don Juan, follows the narrative itself, properly speaking, in the Allegro. Here we have an exposition of the *avant-scène*, that is, how the hero of the piece has lived his life."[40] In the ensuing account of the musical "narrative," Ulybyshev gives free rein to his interpretive fancy. In mm. 1–9 of the Allegro, for instance, he imagines Don Giovanni in the guise of a stealthy wolf, approaching its unsuspecting prey: he leaps, seizes the helpless victim, and a little fanfare signals his success.

Of particular interest is Ulybyshev's reading of the internally contrasting second group, which is the starting-point for a number of similar "narrative" interpretations by other critics as well. He identifies the two constituent musical ideas here as "figures 1 and 2" (see Example 6.4).

"Figure 1, sounded by the whole orchestra in unison [i.e. octaves], has something peremptory and menacing about it. Figure 2 is light ("badine et railleuse"), played by first violins alone." The second figure he identifies with Don Giovanni, insolent and frivolous; figure 1 represents the outraged "fathers, brothers, husbands,

[38] Johann Christian Lobe, "Das Gehaltvolle in der Musik" [part 2], *Allgemeine musikalische Zeitung* 49 (1847), col. 369.

[39] Alexander Ulybyshev, *Nouvelle biographie de Mozart, suivie d'une aperçu* ..., vol. 3 (Moscow, 1843), p. 105.

[40] "Après cette exorde sublime, qui rapelle la mort de Don Juan, vient la narration proprement dite, l'Allegro de l'overture, qui expose les événemens [*sic*] de l'avant-scène, c'est-à-dire comme quoi le hèros de la pièce a vécu". *Ibid.*, p. 106.

Example 6.4 Mozart, Overture to Don Giovanni, *mm. 77–98*

lovers, cousins," etc. of his various conquests. The outraged group twice approaches threateningly, but Don Giovanni merely mocks them, and disappears. The group deems it advisable to divide forces [mm. 85–90]. With the modulation to C [m. 91], "the violins quit the search; thus abandoned by their leaders, the rest observe neither order nor discipline."[41]

[41] *Ibid.*, pp. 106–7. These fanciful readings excited the ire of Hanslick, who later cited them in arguing that the particular genius of musical ideas lies in their inherent musical value

Much the same reading is suggested by J. C. Lobe. For Lobe, "figure 1" represents the public demand that Don Giovanni repent; the subsequent dissipation of canonic activity (in C major) represents the milder entreaties of Elvira and Zerlina, ending in a sigh of despair (the A-minor cadence, m. 98).[42] For yet another critic of the 1840s, Eduard Krüger, figure 1 represents the "intrusion of foreign, demonic forces."[43] None of these "narrative" accounts, however, is carried out beyond the development section. The (quite literal) recapitulation may provide the requisite tonal resolution of musical events, but that resolution has nothing to do with the elements of narrative or drama perceived by these critics – its impulse is purely "architectural." (And in this sense the musical narrative of the overture may resemble more closely a narrative told in pictures, such as a fresco cycle, where the arrangement of frames may be dictated as much by an architectural context as by strictly narrative logic.)[44]

Søren Kierkegaard, in his encomiastic meditation on Mozart's opera (also from the 1840s), suggests that the overture "is related to the opera as a prophecy." Kierkegaard claims to abjure the aid of metaphor in his account of the overture: "I shall not ... attempt to translate the energetic and pithy brevity of the overture into long-winded and meaningless figurative language." He nonetheless permits himself a single exception, which grows to extensive proportions. As with other critics, the conjunction of introduction and Allegro occasions reflections on Don Juan's life: "... it is the whole power of sensuousness, which is born in dread ... but this dread is precisely the daemonic joy of life." The metaphor culminates in an apparent reference to the second theme group:

[Don Juan's] life is developed for us in the dancing tones of the violin in which he

rather than in their capacity to represent anything: "It would be perfectly correct, in our opinion, to classify the famous D♯ in the [first phrase] of the Allegro of the *Don Giovanni* Overture or the descending unison figure in the same piece as instances of genuine inspiration – but it is merely preposterous to maintain (as does Ulybyshev) that the former represents 'Don Juan's inimical stance against the entire male portion of humanity' or the latter 'the fathers, husbands, brothers, and lovers of the women seduced by him'" (*Vom Musikalisch-Schönen*, p. 42).

[42] Lobe, "Das Gehaltvolle in der Musik," col. 373.
[43] Eduard Krüger, *Beiträge für Leben und Wissenschaft der Tonkunst* (Leipzig, 1847), pp. 160–61.
[44] A. W. Ambros suggested something similar in an essay comparing Mendelssohn's *Schöne Melusine* Overture to a (later) fresco cycle on the same subject by Moritz von Schwind, surmising that the quasi-symmetrical narrative structure of Schwind's cycle was influ-

lightly, casually hastens forward over the abyss. When one skims a stone over the surface of the water, it skips lightly for a time, but as soon as it ceases to skip, it instantly sinks down into the depths; so Don Juan dances over the abyss, jubilant in his brief respite.[45]

For Kierkegaard, as for other commentators (E. T. A. Hoffmann and Wagner among them), the overture provides a *musical* metaphor, as it were, for the dramatic configuration governing the action of the opera as a whole: Don Giovanni in perpetual defiance of the social forces that condemn him, in perpetual flight from their pursuit.[46] The same "idea" informs the more explicit narratives of Ulybyshev and Lobe. But, as Kierkegaard seems to sense, the musical account of this idea operates within its own systems of logical development and causality – not those of narrative prose or drama. Mozart's overture has, indeed, a prologue, a beginning, a middle, and an end: but the "story" heard in it by these critics does not correspond to the division of exposition–development–recapitulation. Instead, the story emerges from a configuration of musical gestures. This configuration is elaborated and "reconfigured" in the middle, restated and *musically* resolved in the end. The elaboration and restatement are dictated by principles more architectural than narrative, and the "idea" of the gestural

enced not only by "the epic-narrative manner of the Old Florentine masters," but by even the *musical* design of Mendelssohn's overture ("Schwinds und Mendelssohns *Melusina*," in A. W. Ambros, *Bunte Blätter*, vol. 1 [Leipzig, 1872], pp. 119–26).

[45] Søren Kierkegaard, "The Immediate Stages of the Erotic or the Musical Erotic," in *Either/Or* (Copenhagen, 1843; trans. D. F. and L. M. Swenson, Princeton, 1971), p. 129. Kierkegaard's image might well have been inspired by the (visual) impressions of the overture related near the opening of E. T. A. Hoffmann's novella, *Don Juan*: "Wie ein jauchzender Frevel klang mir die jubelnde Fanfare im siebenten Takte des Allegro; ich sah aus tiefer Nacht feurige Dämonen ihre glühende Krallen ausstrecken – nach dem Leben froher Menschen, die auf des bodenlosen Abgrunds dünner Decke lustig tanzten." (E. T. A. Hoffmann, *Fantasie- und Nachtstücke*, ed. Walter Müller-Seidel [Munich, 1960], p. 68). Wagner's account of the overture, which accords well with other contemporary readings of the contrasting second group, is to be found in the 1841 essay "Über die Ouvertüre" (*Gesammelte Schriften und Dichtungen* vol. 1, pp. 199–200). Some residue from all of these interpretations is to be found in Charles Gounod's later "Commentary" on Mozart's opera. Following a typical, image-laden account of the "terrifying" introduction, Gounod, too, treats the Allegro as a kind of "character sketch" of Don Giovanni, noting among other things a characteristic "dwelling upon the second beat of the bar" (in the main theme). "This gives to the rhythm ... an air of eagerness, of impatience, of breathlessness, which well expresses the dissolute career of Don Giovanni among those pleasures so quickly forgotten, so constantly renewed" (Gounod, *Mozart's "Don Giovanni": A Commentary*, trans. W. Clark and J. T. Hutchinson [London, 1895], pp. 3–4).

[46] "... the overture, which most nearly gives the keynote of the opera in a condensed concentration" (*ibid.*, p. 125). See also Wagner, "Über die Ouvertüre" (1841), in *Gesammelte Schriften und Dichtungen*, vol. 1, pp. 199–200.

configurations might equally well be conveyed through a visual
metaphor, as Kierkegaard has shown.[47]

The tendency to mix metaphorical modes may reflect a critical
perception that most music partakes of certain qualities of these
other media, while of none exclusively. To some extent the narrative tendencies of these critics undeniably represent an imposition
of later nineteenth-century preoccupations on the music of Mozart
and Beethoven. Furthermore, the attempts of Marx and
Ulybyshev to view classical sonata-form movements in terms of a
literal narrative story-line inevitably highlight certain drawbacks
of this enterprise. While some details of Marx's account of the
Seventh Symphony are genuinely evocative and musically sensitive, the narrative trope to which he appeals in the first movement
(the epic battle scene) is one whose generality and all-too-easy
suitability to conventional musical–descriptive discourse – in terms
of polarity, conflict, interaction, and resolution – often tend to lack
metaphorical bite; the metaphor degenerates into figurative
cliché.[48] In the case of Ulybyshev, as we have seen, the narrative is
simply abandoned as soon as the musical form seems to resist its
logical continuation.

All the same, such criticism still constitutes a legitimate response
to the "critical dilemma" as formulated by Hanslick – an attempt
to illuminate certain musical works by means of "poetic fictions"
devised on their behalf. A misapprehension about the supposed
truth-value of such poetic fictions has often posed a stumbling-
block to their reception. On the other hand, the truth-value of any
analyses attempting to go beyond mere "technical designations"

[47] One might, on the other hand, attach some narrative–symbolic significance (in the vein
of these other critics) to the manner in which Mozart effects the transition to the first
scene of the opera by the unexpected intrusion of "figure 1," which arrives on the flatted
seventh degree (m. 278) in place of the tonic resolution of the closing phrase.

[48] This charge could be leveled, for instance, against Marx's application of the "battle"
metaphor across his extensive discussion of the first movement of the "Eroica" in *Ludwig
van Beethoven*, vol. 1, pp. 188–99. While not musically insensitive, the metaphorical
application becomes so attenuated as to lose any narrative force, and suggests a mere
dressing-up of descriptive prose. Another typical instance may be found in the account of
the "Große Fuge" by Ludwig Misch, included in the *Beethoven Companion*, ed. Thomas
K. Scherman and Louis Biancolli (New York, 1972), pp. 1013–16. "We know what
marching airs mean in Beethoven," writes Misch of the first *Allegro molto e con brio* (6/8,
mm. 233ff.): "a battle is in the offing. There is an energetic shift from B flat major to A flat
major and then the fugue theme in its mightiest form ... enters threateningly in the bass.
Desperate cries ... answer it. After the first development, the fugue theme breaks to
pieces in the battle. Its members continue to fight on independently ..."

has long since been called into question.[49] The interest of these earlier critical practices may remain, up to a point, historical. But, like any analytical methodology, their metaphorical procedures are always susceptible to refinement (one might recall, for example, the sophisticated application of metaphor in much of Adorno's criticism). Carl Dahlhaus comments, with reference to the poeticizing practices of nineteenth-century critics and musicians, that "hidden behind those extravagant metaphors, which easily provoke an ironic response, one may frequently discover an intuition of formal problems."[50] An attempt to analyze these poetic images and the manner in which they are generated could, according to Dahlhaus, provide insight into the formal musical processes that have inspired them. And, as I have attempted to demonstrate here, the significance of such practices as "history" and as "criticism" may productively converge.

[49] See note 37 above.
[50] Dahlhaus, "Liszts Faust-Symphonie und die Krise der symphonischen Form," in *Über Symphonien: Beiträge zu einer musikalischen Gattung* (Festschrift für Walter Wiora), ed. Christoph-Hellmut Mahling (Tutzing, 1979), p. 138.

7

Narrative archetypes and Mahler's
Ninth Symphony

Anthony Newcomb

Adorno, in the chapter titled "Roman" from his book on Mahler,
at once justifies and qualifies his assertion that Mahler's music is
narrative by saying that it is "not that music wants to recount
something, but that the composer wants to make something in the
same way that one tells a story".[1] He goes on to explain: at the basis
of what he calls the musical novel lies a certain kind of formal
freedom – freedom of the succession of events in a functional sense.
He speaks of "an idiosyncrasy that must have been felt long before
Mahler, who was, however, the first not to suppress it. This
idiosyncrasy hates to know in advance how the music is going to
continue. Such an 'I know already' insults musical intelligence,
spiritual nervosity, Mahlerian impatience."[2] In Adorno's view, this
loosening of control "from the outside" by a loosening of standard
formal schemata or successions is one of the primary elements
giving Mahler's music its narrative character. Various recent theorists of narrative would agree, at least in the point of distinction.
Todorov's opposition between ritual logic and narrative logic uses
the same distinction.[3] Paul Ricoeur would say that such freedom of
succession makes the listener engage in what Ricoeur calls the
"narrative activity" by forcing the listener to interpret at every
moment where he/she is in what kind of a paradigmatic series of
events – forcing the listener to elicit, if only temporarily, a coherent
configuration from a mere series of events.[4] Clearly this does not
mean complete freedom from formal paradigms.[5] It means the

---

[1] Theodor W. Adorno, *Mahler. Eine musikalische Physiognomik.* (Frankfurt, 1960), p. 86.
[2] *Ibid.*
[3] Tzvetan Todorov, *The Poetics of Prose*, trans. Richard Howard (Ithaca, 1977), pp. 130–37.
[4] See Paul Ricoeur, "Narrative Time," *Critical Inquiry* 6 (1980), 169–90, esp. p. 174. A more
detailed exposition of these ideas is found in Ricoeur, *Time and Narrative*, trans. Kathleen
McLaughlin and David Pellauer, vol. 1 (Chicago, 1983), ch. 2.
[5] "Dadurch wird die compositorische Situation, aus der Mahler spricht, prekär. Denn
weder ist die Musiksprache schon so entqualifiziert, daß das kompositorische Subjekt rein
darüber verfügen könnte, aller vorausgesetzten musiksprachlichen Formen u. Elemente

deflection and interaction of these formal paradigms for communicative purpose.

The narrative quality in Mahler's music also involves for Adorno a particular attitude toward thematic material. The themes are not only highly differentiated and highly characteristic, they are also constantly and explicitly changing, constantly being transformed into something new. "These Mahler themes remain recognizable like characters in a novel – as beings that are constantly evolving and yet constantly identifiable with themselves. Impulses drive them forward. Still the same, they become different; they shrink, expand, even grow old ... Nothing in them is totally consumed by this process, but nothing remains what it was. Time enters into these characters and changes them, as empirical time changes faces."[6]

I would go on to say that the narrative quality in Mahler's music comes most powerfully from the intersection of formal paradigm, thematic recurrence and transformation, and a third element, which I have gropingly called plot archetype – that is to say, various standard configurations of actions or intentions, configurations that are a fundamental part of our vocabulary for interpreting the design and intention of human action and its simulacrum, narrative.[7] These archetypes are not texts. They are by no means exclusively verbal. They are more generally conceptual, and they inform our understanding of liturgies, of paintings (nowadays) of films – indeed, of all human actions, symbolic or other, wherever we confront them. And they are often better thought of not as paradigmatic spatial structures but as paradigmatic temporal procedures, operations, or transformational sequences. The comprehension of these standard configurations is part of a person's narrative competence in a given culture. Mastery of this (culture-specific) typology of plots is part of any narrative understanding.[8]

ledig; noch sind diese umgekehrt noch so intakt, daß sie von sich aus das Ganze zu organisieren vermöchten." (Adorno, *Mahler*, pp 94).

[6] "Dabei bleiben die Mahlerischen Themen insgesamt wie Romanfiguren kennbar, noch als sich entwickelnde mit sich selbst identischen Wesens ... Impulse treiben sie an, als gleiche werden sie zu anderen, schrumpfen, erweitern sich, altern wohl gar ... Nichts darin wird von der Dynamik ganz verzehrt, nichts aber bleibt je, was es war. Zeit wandert ein in die Charaktere und verändert sie wie die empirische die Gesichter." (*Ibid.*, ppp 100–101).

[7] Anthony Newcomb, "Once More Between Absolute and Program Music: Schumann's Second Symphony," *19th-Century Music* 7 (1984), 233–50, esp. pp 234. Compare the tendency by nineteenth-century writers about Beethoven to fit his symphonies into such configurations, as reported in Thomas Grey's essay in the present volume.

[8] See Peter Brooks, *Reading for the Plot* (New York, 1984), pp 19.

I must stress that this interaction of formal paradigm, thematic character and recurrence, and plot archetype is in no sense an "extramusical" matter, something external to the musical happenings themselves. Rather it is *produced* by these musical happenings, in interaction with those conceptual paradigms I have called archetypical plots, just as literary meaning is produced by the interaction of verbal happenings with those conceptual paradigms.

As a first step in interpreting Mahler's Ninth as narrative we must, I believe, back away from the temptation to interpret it as autobiography. To interpret it that way inappropriately limits the variety and breadth of significance that is one of the glories of musical narrative. In addition, the recent biography of Mahler by Henry-Louis de La Grange presents considerable evidence contradicting the particular autobiographical interpretation to which many of those closest to Mahler were driven by the highly charged emotional circumstances of the premiere of the Ninth. De La Grange shows that at the time of the composition of the Ninth, Mahler repeatedly expressed himself as full of vitality and optimism about the future, even about his hopes for a long life.[9] Thus the apocryphal view of the Ninth as the death-obsessed swansong of a dying man seems on the evidence to be inaccurate. It should in any case be rejected as irrelevant to our narrative analysis.

In place of this particular autobiographical paradigm I should like to suggest a more general one, which Mp H. Abrams identifies as basic to English and German Romantic literature: what he calls the Romantic plot of "the circular or spiral quest".[10] One of the forms of this plot most common in the nineteenth century was the *Bildungsroman*, or education of X – with protagonists such as Siegfried, Becky Sharp, Parsifal, or Pip.

In defending this interpretation, I shall both sketch the ways in which this conceptual paradigm affects the four movements of the typical sonata cycle and look in closer detail at the way this particular instance of the educative plot emerges from the musical detail of individual movements. The focus of my attention will be not so much what follows what – the pattern or sequence of functional sections or themes – but rather *how* one thing becomes, leads to, interrupts, distorts, or replaces another; its solidity, its

---

9 See Henry-Louis de La Grange, *Gustav Mahler: Chronique d'une vie*, 3 vols. (Paris, 1979–1984), ch. 55, esp. vol. 3, ppp 537–41.

10 Mp H. Abrams, *Natural Supernaturalism* (New York, 1971), pp 193. The idea is elaborated in chs. 4 and 5.

fate, once it has done so; and the relation of its actual formal function to that implied by its preparation and by the characteristic style to which it appeals. This focus of attention is the distinctive element that narrative analysis can bring to our understanding of (certain pieces of) music. Neither pitch analysis nor motivic analysis nor standard *Formenlehre* have anything to say about these matters, which are crucial to an understanding of Mahler's music as I hear it. Finally, at the close of this essay, I want to raise some questions about the particular nature and meaning of repetition in the opening and closing movements of Mahler's Ninth.

A clear sign of the conceptual paradigm appealed to by this four-movement symphony as a whole is given by the nature of the contrast laid out in the first five pages of the score. It is a musical contrast whose meaning was well established at least since Wagner's *Ring*: that of diatonic purity with a subverting, corrupting chromatism. The first page of the score, the first thematic presentation, uses no pitches outside the diatonic scale of D major, until a B♭ is slipped in (*pp sempre*, cautions Mahler) on the last beat of the page. The ensuing, song-like variant of this first thematic material on the second page is similarly pure, until a B♭ and an F♮ enter in the echoing after-measures of the theme (mm. 26–27, ppp 4–5 of the Universal-Edition score). These foreign tones then bring about a rapid slippage into an agitated, unstable contrasting idea full of chromatic tones and local leading-tone tensions. The contrast of mood implied by the pitch vocabulary is reinforced by virtually all musical elements: *rhythm* (movement in eighth-notes or slower in the first material replaced by movement in triplet eighths and sixteenths in the second, accompanied by nervous, fragmentary figuration beginning after one downbeat and not reaching the next); *melodic vocabulary* (diatonic intervals in the first material replaced by half-steps, augmented seconds, diminished fourths and sevenths) and *harmony* (diatonic major mode replaced by minor mode and a pervasive use of alteration chords, including a cadence by augmented sixth around the tonic in mm. 38–39, pp 6 of the score). The effect of these first forty measures of the score is one of a placid stability undermined.[11]

---

[11] As Abrams (*ibid.*, pp 193) says about his "spiral quest" plot archetype: "the journey is a spiritual way through evil and suffering which is justified as a necessary means to the achievement of a greater good; and usually, although with greater or less explicitness, this process is conceived as a fall from unity into division and into a conflict of contraries which in turn compel the movement back toward a higher integration." Throughout this essay "the score" refers to the edition first published in 1912 by Universal-Edition,

The result of this slippage is immediate: with a violent and heroic gesture (sweeping ninths in the strings replace the falling seconds of the opening, emphatic downbeats replace the empty ones of the previous section) the diatonic purity of the opening is reasserted (mm. 47 ff., pp 8 of the score). But within eight measures it slips again (mm. 54 ff., pp 9 of the score – note that the contrasting thematic element is again introduced not by confrontation but by quiet, almost inadvertent slippage). The slippage is first into B♭ (the key of the flatted sixth degree), then ever so gently into G♭ (the flatted sixth of the flatted sixth). This style of movement – down by a major third – will be the primary symbol of alienation, of loss of center, in most of the piece. Soon the music will pull out of this problem zone by another willful, slightly desperate gesture, reasserting rather than modulating back to D (cf. mm. 63–64, ppp 10–11 of the score – more a sudden leap than a modulation). The pattern of the piece has been set: the quiet subversion of the diatonic purity of D major by chromatic notes outside the scale – especially by introducing notes from keys a major third below, which rapidly takes one into the flat keys, traditionally regarded as "dark."

Each of the ensuing slippages will cause a crisis, a confrontation, and, most characteristically, a collapse – a way of ending a section that, as Adorno has reminded us, is typically Mahlerian. Out of the ruins caused by these confrontations and collapses the music moves by a kind of transition that is so unusual and full of character as to force a narrative (or at least a referential) explanation: the conceptual topos embodied in these transitions is that of the protagonist rebuilding a life undone by ruinous experience.

In mm. 234–67 (ppp 35–38 of the score), for example, one hears: a collapse; a descent from D minor through B♭ to G♭ major, and finally to the relative minor of G♭, E♭ minor; then the gradual rebuilding of diatonic D major, presented most clearly by physically pushing the pitch B♭ (in the violins) half-step by half-step up to F♯, whence it can rebegin the opening theme in D major. (The passage is headed "Allmählich an Ton gewinnend" in the score.)

It was at this return of D major that Mahler wrote in his draft score "O Jugendzeit! Entschwundene! O Liebe! Verwehte!", which is often cited as evidence of his fearful preoccupation here

---

Vienna, and reprinted several times under various imprints. The first 40 measures reach nearly through pp 6 of this score.

with his own death. I shall later want to dispute that meaning. I want now only to point out that we get here our last glimpse of diatonic D major (however pale and frail) until the last page of the movement.

After the next, most extended and violent of the confrontations, crises, and collapses characteristic of the progress of the movement, the key of D major is gradually rebuilt across an extended retransition (mm. 318–45, ppp 48–51 of the score), in order to arrive at a recapitulation-like moment (marked "Wie von Anfang"). This moves with rapid assurance to a rhythmically vigorous, texturally full-bodied, emphatic version of the opening material, a version recalling the first return of D major on pp 5 of the score. But this new D major is a different one from all the earlier instances. It is a D major saturated with F♮s, B♭s, and E♭s. These pitches, which had caused crisis and collapse before, are now confidently integrated as local appoggiaturas to tonal degrees, in the context of a stable and sustained D major. The musical metaphor is one of sophistication – the replacement of the first D major by one more able to incorporate external shocks, but also one less pure, open, and innocent.

As I just observed, a last, extremely fragile glimpse of the original, innocent D major comes on the last page of the movement (mm. 433ff., pp 60 of the score), where dissolving fragments of the opening material reappear and do not so much cadence as evaporate in a disembodied high note of piccolo plus harp and cello harmonics. On this last page of his draft score, Mahler wrote "Leb! wol, Leb! wol!" [*sic*].[12]

From the early exegeses of Bruno Walter and Alban Berg onward, most commentators have seen this movement as Mahler's own death song, his farewell to life.[13] This interpretation poses some problems for an understanding of the remaining three movements. What is left for them? (It is typical of such exegeses that they lay their weight on the first movement, long the most admired of this symphony.) This interpretation also ignores, probably under

[12] The two notations in the draft score are documented in Peter Andraschke, *Gustav Mahlers IX. Symphonie*. Beihefte zum Archiv für Musikwissenschaft, 14 (Wiesbaden, 1976), ppp 49–54. They can be seen in the facsimile of the *Partiturentwurf*, ed. Erwin Ratz (Vienna, 1971), ppp 29 and 52.

[13] Bruno Walter, *Gustav Mahler* (Vienna, 1936), cited from the reprint (Wilhelmshaven, 1981), pp. 94–95. Alban Berg, undated letter to his wife, apparently written in the summer or autumn of 1912; see Alban Berg, *Briefe an seine Frau* (Munich and Vienna, 1965), no. 165, p. 238.

the pressure of biographical event, some of the musical evidence. I hope that even my quick sketch of the movement has suggested that the musical occurrences map out not so much a farewell to life as a farewell to childhood and to primal innocence. The musical metaphor is of growth through to young adulthood – and of the inevitable hardening and toughening that comes with this process, the inevitable loss of gentle innocence and openness to love and the learning of self-protective strategies that come with its storms and crises.

Seen against the conceptual paradigm of this particular "spiral quest," the place of the second movement in the narrative whole poses no more riddles. Here our protagonist, "bold, plucky, some- what clumsy, and very square of build" ("etwas täppisch und sehr derb", and "keck" are markings on the first page of the move- ment), throws himself into the physical sensuality and distractions of the modern urban world. The movement begins with rough- hewn, rustic musical images (rusticity is, after all, innocence made inappropriate by a change in viewpoint – innocence as viewed from the sophisticated world). But it soon plunges deeper and deeper into musical images of the sometimes desperate search for outside diversion characteristic of the modern world – of our search for forces outside ourselves to modify and control our own moods. The primary images in this movement are called up by the use of what Maynard Solomon, in his article on Beethoven's Ninth Sym- phony, has called characteristic styles.[14] We get Ländler of various kinds, merry-go-round music, even the waltz of the sophisticated beau-monde. All of these styles fit easily into the traditional musical paradigm of the series of alternating dances in the Scherzo–Trio–Scherzo movement. The threat of triviality or bana- lity inherent in these styles is avoided only by the subtlety with which Mahler handles the interaction of musical paradigm (the alternating dance types) and conceptual paradigm (the young personality buffeted by various types of external distractions). The crux of the movement lies in the referential potential both of the characteristic styles and of the way in which these styles succeed or displace each other.

The rustic, heavy-footed initial Ländler (literally a point of

[14] Maynard Solomon, "Beethoven's Ninth Symphony: A Search for Order," *19th-Century Music* 10 (1986), 3–24, esp. pp. 5 and 18–19 ("Beethoven's modernist contribution, then, was to symbolize extreme states by means of a host of new musical images and image clusters that we may collectively designate as authentic characteristic styles, prototypical styles which have yet to be named, let alone fully analysed").

departure for our protagonist) is replaced first by an urbane waltz (mm. 90ff., pp. 66ff. of the score). This new dance has its own contrasting, faster tempo. The battling intercutting of tempos in this movement will be one of its strongest ways of projecting its content. It is as part of this second dance, the waltz, that the corrupting harmonic motto of descent by a major third, established in the first movement, is gradually reintroduced (now by downward-spinning deceptive cadences to the flatted sixth degree). Against this waltz, the first Ländler tries to reassert itself (mm. 168ff., p. 72), but it cannot break the hold of the tempo of the waltz, which runs increasingly out of control before collapsing in giddy exhaustion. Out of this collapse (p. 75) comes the third dance (and the third tempo – *ganz langsam*) of the movement: a gentle slow Ländler explicitly recalling the falling seconds and the diatonic purity of the first movement, in a version closest to the fragments over which Mahler had written "O Jugendzeit! Entsch- wundene! O Liebe! Verwehte!"

The fate of this slow, gentle Ländler exemplifies particularly clearly the narrative potential in the way sections replace or succeed each other in Mahler's music. The section initially seems to conform to the ABA formal scheme conventional for such small dances, but its gentle A section is tiny and cannot find a cadence. It is instead brusquely interrupted (m. 229, p. 76) by a B section made of the first Ländler (with its faster tempo). The slower A section then finds its way back (m. 251, p. 77) to round off the ABA design, but once more it does not have the force or direction to reach its own cadence. Instead it winds down, drooping and loosing speed, until it is brusquely cut off by the waltz with its tumbling downward major thirds (mm. 260ff., p. 78), now running in longer and longer cycles, like a large musical machine out of control. On the scale of the movement as a whole, it is also the style and nature of the replacement/successions that are the point here. The third dance (the slow Ländler) nostalgically evokes the material of the first movement after a collapse of out-of-control sensuality in the second dance (the waltz). But the third dance loses direction and cannot complete its own phrase, let alone its section. By its own weakness, it opens itself up to the near rape done by the second dance (and tempo), which brusquely sweeps it aside, and proceeds to run more out of control than ever, tumbling down its chains of deceptive cadences under increasingly intoxicated waltz figurations (mm. 260–330, pp. 78–84).

Later in the movement, the opening rustic Ländler tries to reassert itself, but it, too, cannot put itself together and is soon infected by phrases of the waltz (mm. 368ff., pp. 87–89). The Ländler appears in faded timbres of solo violin instead of its original "bold" orchestration (mm. 389ff., p. 88), and is rapidly subverted by the waltz, which now takes on some shriekingly banal merry-go-round, fairground music.[15] The tempo of the waltz gets faster and faster. The slow Ländler (dance 3) tries once more to intervene (m. 515, p. 99), but survives for only four measures, without being able to break the hold of the fast waltz tempo. At this point, the material of the first, rustic Ländler brusquely intervenes in a sectional joint that is not a transition but an almost desperate interruption of the waltz. But now the first Ländler, like the slow Ländler before it, cannot bring even a single thematic statement to a correct cadence. Its material is thoroughly mixed with motivic material from the waltz. Soon the movement evaporates in a hollow cadence of piccolo and contrabassoon five octaves apart, on a note of dissolution and fragmentation.

Tempo contrasts were a major structural and expressive element in the second movement. Tempos engaged in open confrontations: one brusquely overrode another, or failed to withstand the momentum of another. In the third movement there is nothing so emotional, so indecorous as an open fight. Here is the bright, competent, hard adult. Three tempos are magisterially unified under a single pulse. Everything projects unity of purpose, assurance, mastery.[16] The characteristic style of this movement is dense, highly worked, motivic counterpoint, often without the explanatory and uniting control of a firm diatonic bass line. The third movement as it proceeds gives the impression of another mechanism running out of control, this time the machinery of counterpoint. The musical–formal schema invoked (here explicitly, by a title) is the Rondo, the form of the conventional happy-ending finale. The first episode of the Rondo gives a new embodiment to the harmonic motto of progression by a descending

---

[15] See mm. 444ff., p. 92, for high woodwinds, including piccolo and E♭ clarinet. The material is developed from an accompanimental voice at a structurally analogous earlier spot – trumpet, mm. 187–90.

[16] The inscription that Guido Adler claimed to have seen "on the manuscript" of this movement – "Meinen Brüdern in Apoll", to my brothers in Apollo, or to my fellow musicians guild members – certainly seems to the point. Though it is widely cited, it has been found, to my knowledge, on no surviving manuscript. See Guido Adler, *Gustav Mahler* (Vienna, 1916), pp. 66 and 73.

third (this instance recalling, at least to Adorno's ears, another symbol of urbane sophistication, the "Weibchanson" from Lehár's *Merry Widow*).[17] Here there is no battle between the two sections, refrain and first episode. Their material and tempos combine and flow into one another.

To summarize the course of the movement somewhat drastically: its progression is toward ever stricter species–counterpoint sounds and characteristic styles. Especially in the episodes of mm. 209–61 (pp. 122–25) and from m. 311 to the interruption in m. 347 (pp. 132–34), long-note *cantus firmi* in solemnly spaced imitative entries are accompanied by fitful, rhythmically contrasting motivic countersubjects (most of them skillfully fashioned, of course, from the main theme of the Rondo). The result is, indeed, a symbol and embodiment of musical–professional skill, invoking perhaps the last movement of the "Jupiter" Symphony. But, increasingly as Mahler's movement proceeds, it is also hard, cold, even violent and ugly.

This progression is abruptly deflected by an interruption, a revelation, what Adorno would (and did) call a "Durchbruch."[18] The harsh motivic–intervallic counterpoint, fitful rhythms, and tonal instability that had become increasingly prominent throughout the movement are abruptly replaced by chordally based intertwining melodic lines over firm diatonic harmonies, by smooth rhythms, and by a stable D major. The *cantus firmus* and countersubject from the previous section are retained but transformed.[19] The metaphor is of a vision – a revelation that these same thematic and stylistic elements can lead somewhere radically different; this same network of characteristics, this same musical protagonist, can be reformed as something quite different. The melodic, rhythmic, and tonal language of the replacement refers clearly back to the initial material of the first movement.

The increasing prominence across movements 1 through 3 of a

---

[17] "Es schlenkert im Rhythmus des Weibchansons aus der Lustigen Witwe, das damals aus den Messingtrichtern der Grammophone quäkte" (Adorno, *Mahler*, p. 211). It is, indeed, only the rhythms that are similar. The passage could certainly not be called a quotation. It is not clear whether Adorno is even claiming that it is a reference. He may simply be saying that it reminds him of the Lehar.

[18] *Ibid.*, p. 212.

[19] My *cantus firmus* is the material found, for example, in clarinets, bassoons, cellos, and basses in mm. 320–23. The retained "countersubject" is the material found in oboes and violins in mm. 320–21 (p. 132, at the change of signature to four flats).

textural type consisting of dissonant, highly independent motivic lines, without firm diatonic bass and bound together by no clear harmonic foundation, is an important factor in setting up both the metaphorical–expressive and the structural meaning of this inter- ruption–revelation in the third movement and its continuation in the fourth. This textural type is thrown into prominence for the first time in the *misterioso* of movement 1 (mm. 375–90, p. 56). It becomes yet more prominent in movement 2, especially in the combination of motivic elements of dances 1 and 2 in the final section of the movement (mm. 368ff., pp. 87–105), before taking over entirely in movement 3. This unidirectional textural evolution makes the harmonically determined, chorale-like texture of the first theme of movement 1 particularly striking when it returns at the interruption in movement 3 (mm. 347ff., pp. 134ff.). A polarity is set up between the two textural types at this point that will be an important structural and expressive element in movement 4. In this case again, the ideas and their manipulation are strictly, "abstractly" musical. But a metaphorical interpretation lies close at hand – the highly independent, dissonant contrapuntal textures representing alienation, the harmonically controlled ones repre- senting integration.

This interruption–revelation in movement 3 is the crux, the Aristotelian moment of recognition, in Mahler's plot.[20] One of the subtlest points in Mahler's handling of this moment is that the transfigured mood of the revelation–recognition does not hold at first. Again, meaning arises here through an interaction of the conceptual plot and the musical paradigm. The musical paradigm (Rondo) entails a return of the principal musical element, a return of the refrain after this "episode." And in fact one gets this return, in what is musically one of the most difficult and wondrous pas- sages of the symphony.[21] For a narrative analysis, the essential matter is how this return happens. The revelation of the "episode" (according to the formal scheme) can come as a thunderstroke, by interruption. But how does one assimilate it, recover from it, move away from it? Here, it is gradually subverted in a violent (though texturally spare), Jekyll-and-Hyde-like, almost cinematic intercut- ting between the two guises of the same material – between the two

20 See Ricoeur, *Time and Narrative*, vol. 1, p. 43, for his discussion of this narrative device,
    called *anagnorisis*.
21 The surviving drafts of the symphony indicate that this section cost Mahler the most
    labor of revision. See Andraschke, *Gustav Mahlers IX. Symphonie*, pp. 71–72.

personalities, or the two possibilities revealed in the same personality (mm. 440–521, pp. 140–46).

In the Rondo, the revelation finally yields to a restatement of the main thematic material of the movement, picking up the fast, increasingly headlong elements that had run through the second dance of movement 2 and all of movement 3 up to the interruption. But whereas movement 2 had ended in exhaustion after repeated confrontations, movement 3 now rushes unrestrained to the ultimate tempo extreme and ends in explosion – what we might now call burn-out.

Out of these ashes the last movement arises, picking up the material of the revelation of the previous movement, but altering its implications in several subtle ways. First, into the firm chordal homophony with functional bass line of the revelation is incorporated the thoroughly saturated chromaticism that had been increasingly characteristic of what one might call the worldly sections of the previous movements. Second, the descending progression by a major third, which had always previously been a centrifugal, corrupting force, is now accepted as the opening gesture of a tonally stable, clearly structured, hymn-like theme.[22] Even the mocking version of the material of the revelation episode, whistled Berlioz-like by the E♭ clarinet in the subversion of the episode by the main theme at the end of the Rondo (mm. 444–45, p. 141), is incorporated literally into the ecstatic cadence of this main theme of the last movement (m. 24, violin II, p. 167).

All these things are clear by the completion of this cadence at the outset of the last movement. As the movement progresses, additional narrative transformations become clear. One involves the meaning of the motivic–contrapuntal textural type singled out above, and comes as part of the principal contrast of the last movement, proposed after the end of the main theme (mm. 28ff., p. 167). In the last movement, the textural polarity set up at the interruption in movement 3 is continued, but the roles of the two textural types are gradually reversed as the movement progresses. The lean, bass-less contrapuntal textures at first make up the fragile secondary idea (mm. 28ff.). When spare, empty, contrapuntal textures are introduced here (together with the minor

[22] The theme is so hymn-like as to cause Deryck Cooke, completely irrelevantly in my view, to connect it with the hymn "Abide with Me" (see Deryck Cooke, "Mahler's Melodic Thinking," in *Vindications: Essays in Romantic Music* (London, 1982), p. 103. This connection, of course, ruins the theme for Cooke.

mode), they sound once more, especially in conjunction with the
disappearance of independent functional bass lines and of periodic
four-measure phrase structure, like a metaphor for alienation or
loss of center. The introduction of this particular contrasting
material here seems to promise an ABABA slow-movement type,
alternating the emotional worlds of the hymn-like principal material with this secondary contrapuntal material in confrontation and
combination. The implied meaning of the textural contrast is
transformed, however, when it returns in its proper place (in the
musical paradigm) after the principal cadence of the second A
section (mm. 73ff., p. 172). Structurally, m. 73 corresponds to m.
24 of the original theme, but the tension-filled dominant of m. 24 is
here replaced with a tonic, and the contrasting texture now clothes
a stable closing section to the first theme. The texture now carries,
instead of the secondary material, fragments of the principal
theme, which float to near stasis over long, stable tonic and
dominant prolongations. Then fragments of the contrasting material itself return (mm. 88ff. p. 173), but transformed by the addition of rocking minor third oscillations (on F♯–A or C♯–E)
and by persistent allusions to A major and D major, which
combination recalls the opening ostinatos of the first movement
itself. This transformed contrasting material then fills out in
texture and flows easily and directly (in the middle of m. 107,
p. 174) into the midst (the third phrase) of the principal theme.
The process is one of assimilation rather than confrontation as
before.

The next and last time these spare textures return is as the
cadence and epilogue to the entire movement and piece (mm.
159ff., p. 182), carrying only an occasional flicker of movement
from the dissolving motivic material, now over a firm foundation of
low string triads. The context lacks all tension and implications of
alienation; the atmosphere is one of integration, serenity, stability,
and stasis. The spare textures and both the thematic material and
the expressive meaning associated with them gradually disappear
entirely in the course of the last movement, completely absorbed by
the lush, harmonically based, chorale-like texture of the first idea
of both first and last movements.

Thus the textural transformation. The allusions to the keys of D
and A in the penultimate appearance of this thin-textured, contrasting material in the last movement are part of the subtlest
transformation in this movement: that in the meaning of the key of

D. Here again meaning arises through the interaction of musical and conceptual plots or paradigms. The four-movement cycle will, according to the musical paradigm, return to its opening key at the end. This particular four-movement cycle had seemed to predict that outcome insistently, with the repeated returns to the key of D major as a source of solace and stability in the first movement and with the reiteration of that meaning in the "revelation" episode of the third movement, which was also in D major.[23] Although the fourth movement begins in D♭, repeatedly and at crucial moments it looks longingly toward D major (for example in three of the five phrases of its main theme, and in the ecstatic cadence to this theme and the transition to the B material that follows it – mm. 9, 19, 23–24, 27, pp. 166–67). Particularly striking instances of the yearning toward D (in addition to the already mentioned transformation of the B material, formerly in D♭ [C♯] minor, in D major and A major in mm. 88ff., p. 173) are the two climactic moments in the second and third statements of the main thematic material, when the D–F♯–A–B pitches fundamental to the first movement's diatonic–pentatonic D major hang for long periods suspended in acute tension high in the texture (mm. 62–63, p. 170 and mm. 122–25, p. 177). But these pitches always sink back into the key of D♭. The final cadence and epilogue of the movement definitively incorporate A and D as the flatted second and sixth degrees of the D♭ scale, and the movement fades out in D♭.

In his recent article on Beethoven's Ninth Symphony, Maynard Solomon points out that commentators since the late nineteenth century have suggested the conceptual paradigm put forth by Schiller in his essay, "Naive and Sentimental Poetry," as lying behind Beethoven's Ninth. According to this paradigm (which is one instance of Abrams's "spiral quest"), the role of the modern artist "is imaginatively to represent the possibility of a renewed harmony to heal the wounds inflicted by mankind's alienation from nature ... We cannot go backward to our biological or historical beginnings, as the pastoral poet desires, for this would place '*behind* us the end *toward which it ought to lead us.*' In Schiller's famous phrase, the task of the artist, therefore, is to lead us, 'who no

---

[23] This is not just a matter for those with perfect pitch – instruments sound distinctly different in D major than they do in D♭, because of the placement of the open strings in the stringed instruments and the fingerings in the winds.

longer can return to Arcadia, forward to Elysium.' "[24] The burden
of the present essay is that Mahler's Ninth works with the same
conceptual paradigm. Although one may long for the primary,
diatonic D major innocence of the opening of the symphony, one
can only recover it tarnished by chromaticism and in the darker,
perhaps richer hues of D♭. The original experience remains alive in
memory, but it is inevitably transformed by it.

The transformation of experience by memory is in fact one of the
essential messages of narrative and of Mahler's Ninth. The insistence in the flanking movements of the Ninth on repetition – or
more precisely on the return to the same material in order to
rebegin it and work it through again differently – has been to most
commentators one of the most notable, and most formally puzzling, features of the two movements. Indeed, the procedures of all
movements of the piece are marked by repeated transformed
thematic rebeginnings rather than by an opposition and alternation between motivic development and repetitions of intact
thematic blocks. Constant transformation of thematic material (as
opposed to fragmentation and development placed against repetition) is, in Adorno's analysis, one of the primary narrative
elements in Mahler's music.

Peter Brooks has pointed out in *Reading for the Plot* that such
transformed repetition is also one of the primary features of the
narrative middle (the little discussed space between the narrative
beginning and end, both of which are much discussed by Aristotle).[25] Brooks' concern with the narrative middle, with what
Barthes (*S/Z*) calls the dilatory space of narrative, is particularly
germane, for this middle is the locus of narrative activity, on both
the reader's and the creator's part – of the attempt to read design
and intention in a sequence of events. According to Brooks, this
"space of retard, postponement, error, and partial revelation is the
place of transformation: where the problems posed to and by
initiatory desire are worked out and worked through." In Brooks'
view, transformed repetition is a way to harness or bind experience
through memory for use in narrative form: "Repetition, recall,
symmetry, all these journeys back in the text, returns to and

---

[24] Solomon, "Beethoven's Ninth Symphony," 9. The internal quotations in Solomon's
   paraphrase of Schiller are from Schiller; the emphases are Schiller's.
[25] Brooks is to my knowledge the most detailed analyst of the narrative middle – see esp.
   chs. 4 and 5 in his *Reading for the Plot*. The position of Aristotle as a pioneering theorist of
   narrative is worked out in detail by Ricoeur in *Time and Narrative*.

returns of [previous material] ... allow us to bind one textual moment to another in terms of similarity or substitution rather than mere contiguity."[26]

Brooks draws his fundamental paradigm for narrative from Freud (*Beyond the Pleasure Principle*). For Freud, repetition is a way of mastering past experience by returning to it in order to work through it correctly. It follows from this that repetition has to do with finding the proper ending.[27] In Freud's and Brooks's textual psychology, this quest involves the balancing of two basic drives. On the one hand is what Brooks (quoting Freud) identifies as "an urge inherent in organic life to restore an earlier state of things,"[28] in this case an inorganic quiescence. Against this instinct fights Eros – the desire of narrative, the impulse of beginnings, stimulation into tension – in order to produce the narrative middle. What operates in the text through repetition is this drive toward the end-which-is-the-beginning, toward death and the quiescence of the origins, the pretextual. But the organism wants its *own* death – a proper death – and it must struggle against events that would help it to achieve its goal wrongly, too rapidly – by a kind of short circuit. One needs, in other words, Aristotle's (always undefined) appropriate length, a necessary distance between beginning and end.[29]

In his analysis of Dickens's *Great Expectations* (chapter 5), Brooks locates a primary experience (in this case, the opening confrontation in the graveyard), whose energy the ensuing plot works to master, to bind, and to discharge. Here the analogy to Mahler's Ninth becomes close, I think. The traumatic moment of the confrontation of the two thematic styles and the fearsome energy of the immediately ensuing struggle in the first five pages of the score is such a primary experience, and it releases a tremendous amount of energy. The first movement returns to this confrontation again and again, puzzling many who have attempted to understand the form. Is it a sonata? If so, why so many returns to the initial material and key? Is it a Rondo? If so, why is it made up of the manifold repetition of but one main alternation?

Once one thinks of the movement as an archetypical conceptual plot worked out in musical terms by a musician whom Freud

---

[26] Brooks, *Reading for the Plot*, pp. 92 and 101.
[27] *Ibid.*, pp. 97–98.
[28] *Ibid.*, p. 102.   [29] *Ibid.*, pp. 102–12.

himself was to compliment for his exceptional sensitivity to (Freud-ian) psychology, these questions become less difficult, even irrele-vant. The many returns, especially when prepared by the mimetic collapses and laborious rebuildings that precede them, are overt attempts to master the primary experience and work it through to a proper end – an end that does not cause crisis and collapse. The sophisticated transformation of this primary experience at the recapitulation-like moment of the first movement (mm. 355ff., pp. 52f.) may absorb the energies of the center of this movement. But the two places in the movement that were inscribed by Mahler is his draft score – the return, that is, to D major after the *schattenhaft* episode in E♭ minor (mm. 267ff., p. 38), and especially the fragile and artificial sound of the ending of the movement (evaporation into thin, high textures and disembodied harmonics) – suggest an inconclusiveness, an unresolved nostalgia for the primal innocence of the beginning. They suggest what Brooks's analysis might call an improper end at the close of the first move-ment – a short circuit at this point.

In this interpretation, the middle movements of the symphony become the large-scale "space of retard, postponement, error, and partial revelation" that is necessary to the determining plot of transfiguration and transformation – necessary to the revelation of movement 3, which breaks through to the repressed plot of that unresolved nostalgia and stimulates the large-scale summarizing return of the last movement.[30] The conceptual paradigm here is much like the one Brooks finds in the scene of Magwitch's return in *Great Expectations*: "The scene replays numerous details of their earlier encounter, and the central moment of recognition comes as a reenactment and revival of the novel's primal scene ... " and "Whereas the model of the *Bildungsroman* seems to imply progress, a leading forth, and developmental change, Pip's story – and this may be true of other nineteenth-century educative plots as well – becomes more and more as it nears its end the working through of past history, an attempted return to the origin as the motivation of all the rest ... The past needs to be incorporated *as past* within the present, mastered through the play of repetition in order for there to be an escape from repetition."[31]

---

[30] See *ibid.*, pp. 122 and 128–30 on the repressed or short-circuited plot in *Great Expectations*.
[31] *Ibid.*, pp. 128 and 134.

This incorporation of the past as past within the present through the play of repetition is an essential element in Mahler's last movement. Indeed, as the movement progresses, the issue of repetition becomes ever more prominent. It may not seem so central at the outset. There we are presented with a seemingly well-formed tune: five four-measure phrases, with a contrast in the central phrase (mm. 13–16, pp. 166–67) and a clear return at the beginning of the fourth phrase – a strong traditional shape articulated by a central contrast. The bald assertion of unresolved conflict made by the strange thin-textured interlude between the second and third phrases of the tune (mm. 11–12) is then picked up after the conclusion of the tune by the larger-scale contrast of the thin polyphony (mm. 28ff., p. 167) to which I have referred above. At this point the movement does not seem to lack well-defined contrast.

But, as we have seen, the larger contrast disappears as the movement progresses. The contrasting material is first replaced by a coda-like extension and repetition of the cadence to the main tune (mm. 73–87, pp. 172–73, which look forward to the coda to the movement as a whole); it then reappears in a much less highly contrasting, major-mode version that is gradually integrated with the material of the main tune, into which it is explicitly transformed in mid-measure (mm. 88–107, pp. 173–74).

Even the five-phrase main tune turns out not to be the ordered, well-shaped succession of phrases it had initially seemed – with an opening antecedent–consequent phrase pair, a central contrast, and a closing reprise of the antecedent–consequent pair. It is gradually revealed as a slight central contrast (in the third phrase) and four rebeginnings of the same material, which become increasingly difficult to distinguish from one another. The movement, as it unfolds, is reduced to a process either of minimal departures (via this central contrasting phrase) in order to set up rebeginnings with reworked continuations, or simply a process of rebeginnings themselves without departure. It becomes a constant turning-back-on-itself, in a vortex of rebeginnings searching for the proper end, for the "quiescence of the origins." To quote again Brooks's summary of Freud: "Repetition, remembering, reenactment are the ways in which we replay time so that it may not be lost. We are thus always trying to work back through time to the transcendent home, knowing, of course, that we cannot … Desire is the wish for the end, for fulfillment, but fulfillment must be delayed so that we can understand it in relation to origin and to desire itself."[32]

At the end of Mahler's last movement, the oscillation of forward and backward movement in time produced by return and new continuations rocks to a stasis. This ending has elicited many interpretations. Its representation of quiet and fulfillment may be understood as death; it may also be understood as a kind of quiet readiness that comes with maturity (an attitude characteristic of some Eastern religions). Some commentators have noted that, while the movement has indeed returned to what Brooks/Freud might call the original, inorganic quiescence, it also seems poised to rebegin.[33] The reasons for this curious paradox again lie in the musical material. The motivic fragments that float through the thin ether of the last page of the score are drawn from the upbeat to the large-scale contrast of the movement (compare m. 159, violin II, p. 182 and m. 28, cello, p. 167) and from the third, slightly contrasting phrase of the main tune itself (compare mm. 160–61 and mm. 13–14, p. 166). They are drawn, that is, from the bits of musical material that had themselves offered the points of departure and contrast in the movement, and thence the stimuli to return and rebegin. They are the faint flickerings of Eros – "the desire of narrative, the impulse of beginnings, the stimulation into tension" – that remain unextinguished in the texture.

Thus it seems not so much that Mahler's movement (and symphony) ends, as that its formative energy, always ready to be stirred again into life, passes out of hearing. The question as to whether the symphony presents the suspension of temporality or its triumph in death is left in a state of ambiguous uncertainty. It is the distinctive glory of music as a narrative art that it can embody such a question so concretely without having to imply an answer.

[32] *Ibid.*, p. 111.
[33] Kurt von Fischer, "Die Doppelschlagfigur in den zwei letzten Sätzen von G. Mahlers 9. Symphonie," *Archiv für Musikwissenschaft* 32 (1975), 105, cited in de La Grange, *Gustav Mahler*, vol. 3, p. 1218.

Part III
Representation, analysis, and semiotics

8

Music and representation: the instance of Haydn's *Creation*

Lawrence Kramer

Representation in music has a checkered critical history. To a certain temperament, the musical "painting" of a scene or a process is inevitably naive, best tolerated when it can be over-looked in favor of a self-sufficient musical structure. A hostile contemporary critic of Haydn's *Creation* had virtually the last word on this subject several years before Beethoven nervously insisted that the Pastoral Symphony is "more the expression of feeling than painting."[1] "What can one say," writes the semi-anonymous Herr Triest, "to a natural history or geogony set to music, where the objects pass before us as in a magic lantern; what to the perpetual pictorializing ...? Truly, the author of the old Mosaic story of the seven days of creation probably did not dream it would make such a great hit again at the end of the eighteenth century!"[2]

Triest's attitude is proto-formalist; it understands music as a hopelessly poor or ineffable bearer of meaning. First crystallized in Eduard Hanslick's *The Beautiful in Music* (*Vom Musikalisch-Schönen*, 1854), the formalist attitude has long – too long – set the terms for serious thinking about music.[3] Those terms embrace a number of skeptical assumptions: that music is radically inferior to language as a medium of discourse; that intelligibility in music rests on a purely "musical" foundation, the working-out of "musical ideas"; that any definite meaning attached to a composition is in principle detachable as "extramusical" – or, if not, that the music is somehow trifling. I want to take a new look at musical represen-tation in order to contest the formalist attitude on behalf of what

[1] The disclaimer was appended to the title of the symphony as it appeared in the program of the first performance; an earlier version appears in one of Beethoven's sketchbooks.

[2] *Joseph Haydn*, a translation by Vernon Gotwals of *Biographische Notizen über Joseph Haydn*, by Georg August Griesinger, and *Biographische Nachrichten von Joseph Haydn*, by Albert Christoph Dies (Madison, Wisc., 1963), p. 200.

[3] On the history of this problem, see Carl Dahlhaus, *Esthetics of Music*, trans. William W. Austin (Cambridge, 1982).

has come to be called musical hermeneutics.[4] My claim is that musical representation has significant, definite, interpretively rich ties both to musical processes and to cultural processes. Far from being a slightly embarrassing extra, musical representation is one of the basic techniques by which culture enters music, and music enters culture, as meaning, discourse, and even action.

To start with, a working definition of representation is in order. As I understand it, a representation is established to the extent that one thing is taken to resemble another, provided that the resemblance is also taken to be intentional.[5] In most cases, perhaps in all, this double understanding is only possible with the help of a feature that I will call the designator: an allusion, implicit or explicit, that tells the observer what is being represented. Virtually anything can act as a designator, from a forthright title to an almost subliminal detail. Whatever form it takes, however, the designator is never extraneous to the representation. It does not occupy an "outside" in relation to a representational "inside." If Edvard Munch's painting "The Scream" were entitled "The Toothache," it would be quite a different work. The role of the designator suggests that no advance criteria can be given for the constitution of a representation. Representations seem to be like performative utterances in J. L. Austin's theory of speech acts: they cannot be validated or invalidated.[6] Performatives are successful or unsuccessful; representations are accepted or refused.

In music, the most common designators consist of texts for vocal setting; titles, programs, and epigraphs; and musical allusions to sonorities, styles, or specific works.[7] Alerted by the designator, the

---

[4] For discussions of recent directions in this area, see Edward T. Cone, "Schubert's Promissory Note: An Exercise in Musical Hermeneutics," *19th-Century Music* 5 (1982), 233–41; Anthony Newcomb, "Sound and Feeling," *Critical Inquiry* 10 (1984), 614–43; and "Tropes and Windows: An Outline of Musical Hermeneutics," chapter 1 of my *Music as Cultural Practice, 1800–1900* (Berkeley, 1990). Peter Kivy's *Sound and Semblance: Reflections on Musical Representation* (Princeton, 1984) should also be cited here, though its taxonomic approach is far removed from the hermeneutic approach of the present essay.

[5] Nelson Goodman's critique of resemblance in *Languages of Art* (Indianapolis, 1976) suggests the need for two subsidiary points. Unlike Goodman, I use the term "representation" to mean, not signification in general, but a certain type of signification. Hence Goodman's argument that denotation, not resemblance, is "the core of representation" (p. 4) has no bearing on my definition. Unlike Goodman, again, I assume that resemblance is always a relationship between significantly different terms.

[6] See J. L. Austin, *How to Do Things with Words*, ed. J. O. Urmson and Marina Sbisa (Cambridge, Mass., 1962).

[7] A special class of instances is created when one work of music actually imitates the performance of another. Peter Rabinowitz calls the result "fictional music"; for discuss-

listener is empowered to find likenesses between the details, textures, or processes of the music and the designated object(s) of representation. Once such likenesses have crystallized, the same listener can go on to make interpretive connections between the music as likeness and the music as structure.

How would such an interpretive practice work? From a rhetorical standpoint, to posit a tacit resemblance between disparate terms is one way to form a metaphor. And to form a metaphor is to open up the possibility of two-way transfers of meaning, as the discourses in which each term of the metaphor is inscribed become available to the other term. This is essentially what happens with musical representation. If I take, say, the harmonically indefinite opening motive of Liszt's *Faust Symphony* as a representation of Faust's endlessly striving character, what I have done is not all that different from remarking, reasonably enough, that Goethe's Faust is like a half-formed melody that can't find its proper key.

The value of the representational metaphor lies in its ability to enable interpretation. Like most metaphors, this one is unlikely to be unique. It will be an instance of a metaphor common in certain discourses, found in certain exemplary texts, laden with what literary critics of various persuasions would call plural significance, intertextuality, heteroglossia, dissemination. The interpreter thus has the opportunity of investigating the discursive field in which the enabling metaphor is situated, and of trying to correlate what seem to be noteworthy features of the field to the musical processes of the composition. This correlation, like the internal structure of a metaphor based on resemblance, moves in two directions. It "condenses" the discursive field into the music, and at the same time reinterprets the discourse by means of the music. The music and the discourse do not enter into a text–context relationship, but rather into a relationship of dialogical exchange.[8]

For an illustration of musical representation and its interpretation, I turn to Haydn's *Creation*, and in particular to its Introduction: an instrumental movement that Haydn calls "Die Vorstellung des Chaos" (mm.1–59), followed by a choral setting of the

ion, see his "Fictional Music: Toward a Theory of Listening," *Bucknell Review* 26 (1981), 193–208.

[8] I use the term "dialogue" in the sense developed by Mikhail Bakhtin: a process in which different modes of expression at once presuppose, question, and interpret each other. For discussion, see Bakhtin's *The Dialogical Imagination*, trans. Caryl Emerson and Michael Holquist (Austin, Texas, 1981), especially the essay "Discourse in the Novel."

opening lines of Genesis (mm. 60–96).[9] Both Heinrich Schenker and Donald Tovey, from their different vantage points, found representational meaning in the structural processes of this music. Schenker identifies Haydn's Chaos with a series of orchestral "thrusts" (*Stöße*; dramatic *forte* attacks) that are gradually mollified (*gesänftigt*) by large-scale linear motion in association with a registral sinking (*Senkung*) in the foreground. Tovey connects similar thrusts and mollifications in the foreground alone to the evolutionary paradigms of eighteenth–century science. He specifically cites the nebular hypothesis of Kant and Laplace: the conjecture that the solar system evolved from a swirling cloud of gaseous matter.[10]

Tovey's suggestion, which can be said to historicize Schenker's, is the place to begin. Haydn's Chaos is unmistakably conceived as an incipient cosmos; the music begins in mystification and slowly explicates its underlying coherence. This conception, however, cannot merely rest on its scientific laurels; as an element of *The Creation*, it must also fit into a religious narrative. Haydn essays the fit by drawing on the ancient concept of *harmonia mundi*, which not only has historical links to astronomical and cosmological speculation, but also, more importantly, provides a model of creation founded on both biblical authority and something very ready to Haydn's hand: music.

The idea that cosmic order coincides with musical harmony derives from Pythagoras, enters Western literature in Book 10 of Plato's *Republic*, and passes into music theory through Boethius's concept of *musica mundana*.[11] As the concept of world-harmony becomes Christianized, creation narratives emerge that combine biblical creation imagery with the Pythagorean imagery of the

[9] Strictly speaking, Haydn's title for the instrumental movement is untranslatable. The term "Vorstellung," appearing in the place of the more straightforward "Darstellung" ("representation"), combines the meanings of "conception" and (theatrical) "presentation." Haydn's choice of "Vorstellung," I surmise, rests on a representational metaphor that is clearly pertinent to *The Creation* but beyond the scope of my discussion. This is the figure of *theatrum mundi* – of the world as a stage on which God watches (in some versions, manages) the drama of existence. For discussion see Ernst Robert Curtius, *European Literature and the Latin Middle Ages*, trans. Willard R. Trask (1953; rpt. Princeton, 1973), pp. 138–44.

[10] Heinrich Schenker, *Das Meisterwerk in der Musik*, (Munich, 1926), vol. 2, pp. 163–68; Donald Francis Tovey, *Essays in Musical Analysis: Concertos and Choral Works* (1935–39; rpt. London, 1981), p. 349.

[11] For full accounts, see John Hollander, *The Untuning of the Sky: Ideas of Music in English Poetry, 1500–1700* (New York, 1970), pp. 3–51; and James Anderson Winn, *Unsuspected Eloquence: A History of the Relations Between Poetry and Music* (New Haven, 1981), pp. 30–73.

music of the spheres. Both the creating Word and the created world come to be represented as forms of music. These representations were already commonplace by the time that Isidore of Seville compiled his highly popular encyclopedia in the seventh century. "Nothing exists," writes Isidore, "without music; for the universe itself is said to have been framed by a kind of harmony of sounds, and the heaven itself revolves under the tones of that harmony."[12] As early as the second century, Clement of Alexandria identifies "the heavenly Word . . . the divine beginning of all things" as "an all-harmonious instrument of God, melodious and holy." Even incarnate, the Word still echoes the music of creation: Christ himself is "a new Song."[13]

Later, I will have occasion to cite revivals of this complex of ideas by Milton and Dryden. Meanwhile, it is worth noting that the metaphor of *harmonia mundi* was very much alive for Haydn's audience. *The Creation* inspired several eulogistic poems, most of which are alert to the figurative tie between harmony and creation. Gabriela Batsanyi, for example, explicitly transfers the power of the Logos to Haydn's music, in which she hears a second creation emulating the first:

> Jüngst schuf *Dein* schöpferisches *Werde*!
> Den Tonner durch den Paukenschall
> Und Himmel Sonne Mond und Erde,
> Die Schöpfung ganz zum zweyten Mahl.[14]

[Lately *thy* creative *fiat*! / Made thunder through the kettledrums, / Made heaven, sun, and moon and earth / Compose Creation a second time.]

It is also worth noting that the idea of a musical creation lingered in scientific discourse at least into the seventeenth century. In his *Harmonice Mundi* (1619), Kepler argued that God gave the planets elliptical orbits because the concentric spheres imagined by Pythagorean cosmology would have yielded an esthetically defective monotone, whereas the elliptical orbits yield a polyphony. For Kepler, God the creator is God the composer.[15]

Haydn's "Vorstellung des Chaos" opens with a vehement thrust by the bulk of the orchestra on an unharmonized C. As Tovey

---

[12] Quoted in E. M. W. Tillyard, *The Elizabethan World Picture* (1943; rpt. New York, 1961), p. 100.

[13] Quoted in Winn, *Unsuspected Eloquence*, p. 40.

[14] Gotwals, *Joseph Haydn*, p. 258. Subsequent quotations of contemporary verse about *The Creation* are taken from this volume.

[15] For a fuller account of Kepler's argument, see Hollander, *Untuning of the Sky*, pp. 38–40.

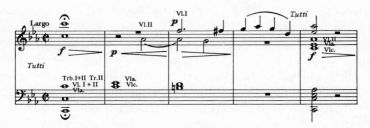

Example 8.1 Haydn, "Vorstellung des Chaos," mm. 1–5

observes,[16] this unison is strictly speaking the most chaotic element
in the movement. We would expect an unharmonized tone at the
beginning of a Classical composition to be a tonic or dominant, but
this tone opens a designated representation of chaos, so we must
hear it as raw material: an *Urklang*, not yet intelligible, not yet even
music. The vehicle of this primordial feeling is, famously, Haydn's
orchestration: mixed timbres, muted strings, unison brass on middle
C, a timpani roll. Writing on behalf of the first listeners to *The Creation*, Haydn's biographer Giuseppe Carpani described the opening
C as "a dull and indefinite surge of sound." The oppressive sensa-
tion was probably compounded, as A. Peter Brown has shown, by
the use of muted trumpets, horns, and timpani in performances
under Haydn's own direction – a practice not reflected in the
published score.[17] A further compounding comes from the only
fermata in the whole "Vorstellung des Chaos." Haydn's *Urklang* is
as indefinite in duration as it is in sonority (Example 8.1).

After the opening *forte* attack, the *Urklang* gradually fades to
black. What follows requires a detailed description.

Measure 2 quietly begins motion in tempo by adding tone to
tone, assembling the raw materials of harmony. The middle C at the
core of the *Urklang* reappears as a bass, first of a minor interval
(c^1–eb^1), then of a major chord (c^1–eb^1–ab^1). Neither tonic nor
dominant nor in root position, this first chord – call it the chaos
chord – is a model of instability. It progresses to dissonant polyphony around the dominant of C minor in measure 3, which in
turn leads to a linear unison statement in measure 4. The unison
rather grimly echoes the texture of the *Urklang*, but it also consoli-
dates the dominant of C minor. The next measure will bring

[16] Tovey, *Essays in Musical Analysis*, p. 350.
[17] A. Peter Brown, *Performing Haydn's Creation* (Bloomington, Ind., 1986), pp. 34–35.

Example 8.2 Reinterpretations of the chaos chord

disruption – a new orchestral thrust that fades into the chaos chord – but a horizon of consonance has been traced, a cadence promised. Tonal harmony has evolved from unharmonized tone.

With this gesture, Haydn forms the nucleus of everything to follow. He at once invokes the Classical/Christian metaphor of *harmonia mundi* and makes that metaphor evolutionary, scientific, modern, by deferring its realization in a cadence, projecting the cadence forward as the outcome of a more comprehensive process.

The movement unfolds by repeating the basic action of the opening (mm. 1–5^2) in expanded forms. Three large cycles fill out the whole, the end of each overlapping the beginning of the next (mm. 5–40^2, 40–50^2, 49^3–59). Each cycle begins as the chaos chord, which is fixed in pitch and tone-color, answers an orchestral thrust. Dissonant polyphony then leads to the dominant of C minor, from which cycles 1 and 2 close into their successors, and cycle 3 closes into the C minor cadence deferred since m. 5. A feeling of large-scale clarification emerges as the cycles progressively reinterpret the chaos chord in terms that subordinate it more fully to the

Example 8.3 Schenker's graphic analysis of the "Vorstellung des Chaos" (abridged)

ensuing dominant. An incipient IV/III in cycle 1 (mm. 5^3–9), the chord dwindles to an incipient German sixth in cycle 2 (mm. 40^3–44, recapitulating mm. 5^3–9), and to a mere chromatic auxiliary in cycle 3 (mm. 49–51) (Example 8.2).

The harmonic motion of the three cycles is matched by their linear motion. Each cycle coalesces with one of the three large-scale linear progressions that "mollify" Chaos in Schenker's analysis (Example 8.3). Chaos finally "expires" (*atmet aus*), in Schenker's phrase, when the registral descent allied with this chain of structural voices reaches the same middle C that resonates from the *Urklang* to the chaos chord. The tone coincides with the C minor cadence at the close of cycle 3.[18]

The harmonic and linear representations of chaos as incipient cosmos work in tandem with a more loosely framed melodic counterpart. The operative metaphor here is the traditional visualization of the cosmos as spatial/spiritual hierarchy, an ascending scale of being. Melody in the "Vorstellung des Chaos" is appropriately fragmentary, but what melody there is incessantly ascends. Uprushing scales and arpeggios that span more than an octave are recurrent; these tend to grow more mercurial as the music proceeds, as if to suggest a progressive "quickening" of vital forces. More constricted but even more pervasive is something we might call the chaos motive: three notes ascending a minor third in double-dotted rhythm.[19] On two emphatic occasions (mm. 22–24, 45–47), the chaos motive itself ascends sequentially through three steps, the second time decorated by a parallel group of ascending flute arpeggios.

This accumulation of ascending figures endows chaos with an urgent impetus, almost a desire, to be lifted into cosmos. The urgent feeling is partly a product of insistence, but even more of frustration: the most dramatic ascending gestures rush headlong to greet the cadences that fail to arrive at the end of cycles 1 and 2 (mm. 39, 49). The treatment of the chaos motive likewise both

[18] It should be added that the initial polyphony of cycle 1 relaxes into a harmonic elaboration of E♭ Major (the III to which the chaos chord stands as IV). The polyphonic impetus revives at m. 31, when an e♭^{3} both refers back to Schenker's primary tone (e♭^{3}, m. 9) and initiates the first of the cardinal linear progressions.

[19] Haydn all but explicitly associates this motive with the striving of formlessness after form. As H. C. Robbins Landon observes, the motive is later cited after the phrase, "Und die Erde war ohne Form und leer" (m. 69). Landon, *Haydn: Chronicle and Works, Volume IV, The Years of The Creation, 1796–1800* (Bloomington, Ind., 1977), pp. 414–15.

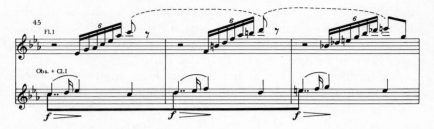

Example 8.4   Model/sequence contradiction, "Vorstellung," mm. 45–47

reveals and thwarts the aspiration to cosmos. In the chief polyphonic passage of cycle 1 (mm. 31–40), the motive rises through four
octaves in three overlapping entries, then shrinks back in registral
breadth and placement. In its subsequent sequential ascents, the
motive as model (spanning a minor third) is contradicted by the
linear melodic projection of the sequence (spanning a major third:
C–E♭ vs. C–E♮ at mm. 45–47 (Example 8.4).

The hierarchical model of the cosmos also aligns height and
depth with light and darkness. In *Paradise Lost*, Milton traces this
linkage to the original Word of creation:

> ... at the voice
> Of God, as with a mantle, did [light] invest
> The rising world of waters dark and deep,
> Won from the void and formless infinite.   (III. 10–13)[20]

On these terms, Haydn's failed ascending figures betoken a plea for
the voicing of the Word as the *lux fiat*. This plea assumes dramatic
impetus at the end of cycle 1, when the first flute sweeps through a
two-octave run to the registral apex of the movement, a brilliant
g^3, only to be contradicted by a brutal tattoo on the sonority of the
Urklang.

The registral gap thus opened is symbolically filled in, and a
transition to cosmos effected, in the closing measures of cycle 3.
Here a solo flute emerges *pianissimo* high above sustained string
harmonies and slowly descends by step to the cadence (mm.
55–58). I do not think it is fanciful to hear this phrase as a
representation of the descent of the unvoiced Word "[f]ar into
Chaos, and the world unborn" (Milton, *P. L.*, VII. 220). The

---

[20] All quotations from Milton are from *Complete Poems and Major Prose*, ed. Merritt Y.
Hughes (New York, 1957). *Paradise Lost* (*P. L.*) is, of course, the ultimate source of the
text of *The Creation*.

Example 8.5 Close of 1) flute descent ("Vorstellung," mm. 55f.), and 2) choral setting of "Und der Geist ... Wasser"

melodic descent by the flute answers and resolves the urgent rising figures that precede it; the chaos motive in particular is sublimated in the flute melody, which begins with an inversion of the motive in a dotted rhythm. When the chorus subsequently takes the text, "Und der Geist Gottes schwebte auf der Fläche der Wasser" (mm. 76–80), the setting of "Wasser" suggestively echoes the cadence to the flute solo (Example 8.5). Linked by a distinctive falling octave (c^2–c^1; recall Schenker's association between c^1 and the *Ausatmung* of chaos), the two passages effectively frame the interval of "brooding" – Milton's term[21] – that separates the divine descent from the creation of light.

The style assumed by the strings during the fluto solo bears a certain resemblance to Elevation music, the slow, soft polyphony improvised during the mass from the sixteenth to the late eighteenth century to accompany the Elevation of the Host. Beethoven would use a similar style, and a similar solo descent, to precede the Benedictus of his *Missa solemnis*.[22] Haydn's liturgical allusion draws a parallel between the descent of Christ to the altar at the close of the Consecration and the original descent of the creative but unvoiced Word. Suggestive enough in its own right, this link between communion and creation serves here primarily to mark a turning-point in the music. As chaos retreats, hints of Christian mystery emerge for the first time. Sacramental ritual

---

21 "[O]n the wat'ry calm / His brooding wings the Spirit of God outspread / And vital virtue infus'd and vital warmth," *P.L.*, VII. 234–36. The image ultimately derives from the Gospel accounts of Christ's baptism.

22 The connection between Beethoven's Benedictus and Elevation music is made by Warren Kirkendale, "New Roads to Old Ideas in Beethoven's *Missa solemnis*," in *The Creative World of Beethoven*, ed. Paul Henry Lang (New York, 1971), pp. 163–99.

supplements cosmological speculation; revelation supplements natural religion.

The reason for these supplements quickly becomes apparent. Haydn's flute solo is not set in high relief like its violin counterpart in Beethoven. As the flute completes its descent, it loses definition, gradually blending into the rest of the instrumental texture. When the long-awaited C minor cadence follows, the accompanying tone color is disconcertingly neutral. Worse, the cadence itself is neutral: Haydn attenuates it by dropping the fifth of the tonic chord, representing the tonic only by an expanded form of the C–E♭ interval that forms the germ of the chaos chord (m. 58, Example 8.3). A brief closing figure does add the missing tone after a rest, but the impression of a lacuna remains. The Word is still silent, and Chaos, evolve as it might, cannot transcend itself.

The consequent need for the voicing of the Word, to be represented by a perfect(ed) cadence, is also implicit in the formal plan of the "Vorstellung des Chaos." Agreement about the form of this music seems to be impossible to reach, and appropriately enough. Haydn, who ought to know, calls it an Introduction; Landon a "vague ternary form"; Brown a ricercar; and Charles Rosen a slow-movement sonata form.[23] Still, certain formal intentions are unmistakable here. The most important of these are recapitulation, as one might find it in a sonata form, and movement toward an extended dominant, the characteristic goal of a slow introduction. The two processes, however, cause more problems than they solve. Each of them contradicts itself, and the two contradict each other.

In establishing an extended dominant, the Classical slow introduction assumes the value of a large-scale upbeat. Something of this sort does happen in Haydn's chaos music – but then again it does not. At measure 44 a dominant pedal begins, but after only three measures the pedal tone shifts and the music embarks on a brief but emphatic turn to the subdominant. Measure 49 regains the dominant, but the passage that follows (mm. 50–54) imposes a degree of local harmonic obfuscation that has led more than one commentator to murmur "*Tristan.*" This is the sort of music with which a slow introduction is supposed to precede a dominant pedal, not to follow one.

Admittedly, from an analytical standpoint there is nothing

---

[23] Landon, *Haydn*, p. 414; Brown, *Performing*, p. 72; and Charles Rosen, *The Classical Style: Haydn, Mozart, Beethoven* (New York, 1972), p. 370. Brown develops the ricercar idea fully in his essay, "Haydn's Chaos: Genesis and Genre," *Musical Quarterly* 73 (1989), 18–59.

problematical about all this. The entire passage from the onset of
the pedal to the verge of the closing cadence unmistakably hinges
on prolongation of the dominant (Example 8.3). The tensions and
disruptions (even the whole of cycle 3) are no more than foreground complications, ripples in the surface. Yet the life of the
music lies precisely in these surface ripples, and I mean this in a
historical as well as a theoretical sense. The essential thing about
the dominant of a slow introduction is that it *is* a foreground effect,
a perfectly manifest dominant. Tonic, subdominant, and neighbor-
tone sonorities may all be involved, but the dominant is the focal
point; it commands immediate expectation. Eleven of Haydn's
twelve London symphonies have slow introductions; nine of them
follow this principle. As for the two that do not – No. 99 and No.
103 – they are the exceptions that prove the rule. Both of them
complicate expectation by juxtaposing the home dominant with
the dominant of the relative minor. In Mozart's 39th Symphony,
the last third of the introduction strongly digresses from the dominant, but the digression is amply compensated. The middle third of
the passage is devoted entirely to a dominant pedal, and on a time
scale that makes the dominant arrival almost premature. Haydn's
"Vorstellung des Chaos" effectively deconstructs the Classical slow
introduction by driving the intelligibility of the dominant into the
structural background. Where the digression in Mozart's 39th
extends a well-established expectation, the surface disruptions of
Haydn's chaos render expectation merely nebulous – or nebular,
confined to the realm of incipience that is the chosen territory of
the music.

The recapitulatory process in the "Vorstellung des Chaos" is no
less perplexed. Measures 40–48 plainly constitute a sort of recapitulation, though a notably constricted one. This episode treats the
chaos motive like the second theme of a sonata movement. Played
first off the tonic (mm. 22–24), the motive must, as Charles Rosen
insists, be repeated and resolved at the tonic.[24] The only trouble is
that the motive is never heard as part of a tonic chord! Its
recapitulation coincides with the emergence of the dominant
pedal, a passage that produces the tonic only as a dominant to its
own subdominant. By this means the essential function of the
Classical recapitulation, the resolution of large-scale dissonance, is
abrogated.

[24] Rosen, *Classical Style*, pp. 370–72.

More important – to repeat my last point with a difference in emphasis – the recapitulation and the dominant pedal are *one and the same*. In Classical practice, a dominant pedal often leads to a recapitulation, but the pedal is supposed to stop where the recapitulation starts. To displace a pedal into the recapitulation itself, as Beethoven made a point of showing in the "Appassionata" Sonata, is profoundly destabilizing. To do such a thing during a slow introduction, where no recapitulation belongs in the first place, is to form precisely what Haydn's contemporaries would have understood as chaos: a crazy mixture, a *Mischmasch*.[25] A sonata-style recapitulation discharges tension, recalls the past, precipitates a definite end; an introductory dominant pedal accumulates tension, delineates the present, precipitates a definite beginning. Superimposed, the two processes create a temporal snarl.

At the point of its greatest organization, then, Haydn's chaos music also reaches the point of its greatest perplexity. In rhetorical terms, the recapitulating pedal might be said to form an aporia: the figure of irreducible doubt, impassibility, being at a loss. As representation, this structural aporia gives the measure of the distance that divides a still incipient cosmos from God, particularly from the God of *Revelation* who affirms: "I am Alpha and Omega, the beginning and the end, the first and the last" (21: 6). In confounding the beginning and the end, the misshapen temporality of chaos amounts to a parody of the eternal present.

From another standpoint, the same aporia places the chaos music at the outer limit of representation as such. Haydn's contemporaries worried over the obvious but inescapable dilemma that the representation of chaos might itself have to court the chaotic, with results that are more muddle than metaphor.[26] Haydn's structural aporia explicitly accepts this dilemma, and more, compounds it, raises its stakes. The recapitulating pedal declares that the "Vorstellung des Chaos" does not rest on mere confusion but on a lucid and principled process of deformation. The music seeks to model what exceeds representation through a scrupulous logic of antinomy, imperfection, blockage. The full rigor of this logic may be gauged by the fact that the three principal measures of dominant pedal (mm. 45–47) coincide with the climactic contradiction of the chaos motive as model by its sequential projection.

25 On chaos and the *Mischmasch*, see Brown, "Haydn's Chaos," p. 59.
26 Brown, "Haydn's Chaos," pp. 18–19.

The negativity of the recapitulating pedal, in Kantian terms its "outrage on the imagination," is typical of what eighteenth-century aesthetics recognized as the sublime. Indeed, the "Vorstellung" shows a striking affinity throughout for the sublime as Kant, in particular, understood it. With its cyclical structure, the music continually approaches a closed totality that it never quite achieves. In that respect, it forms an exemplary provocation to the Kantian sublime: the mental state that occurs when one is forced to recognize a representation of limitlessness, but with a "superadded thought" of totality.[27]

If chaos, moreover, is represented as deformation, it follows that the creation must be represented as a re-formation. Haydn accepts this logic, which conforms both to the evolutionary paradigm and to a long hermeneutic tradition that associates divine wisdom with the "order[ing] and disposition of that chaos or mass" antedating the *lux fiat*.[28] The representation of the first day accordingly consists of a lucid ordering and disposition of the materials that make up the "Vorstellung des Chaos." The first-day music begins with an extended harmonic progression that retraces the broad outline of the "Vorstellung" without closing into a tonic cadence (mm. 60–80). The same progression amounts to a fourth structural cycle based on the opening measures. After the first phrase of recitative, unharmonized string octaves (starting on C) lead for the last time to the chaos chord. Episodes on iii and III follow, passing through V_3^4 to a pause on i. Missing here is the friction of dissonant polyphony, its absence part of a progressive emphasis on consonant sonority within the new cycle. As Haydn models it, the creation arises by repeating its own prehistory in "harmonious" form.

In keeping with this model, the climactic *lux fiat* (mm. 81–89) both repeats and revises the movement from unharmonized tone to tonal harmony traced at the opening. The passage forms yet a fifth structural cycle, but a cycle pared down to its essence, free not only of polyphonic distractions but also of the at last exhausted chaos

---

[27] Immanuel Kant, *Critique of Judgment* (1790), trans. J. C. Meredith (New York, 1973), pp. 91–92.

[28] The formulations here are from Francis Bacon, *The Advancement of Learning*, cited in Hughes's note to *P. L.*, VII. 176 (new edn., 1962). Both Lucretius and Ovid (drawing on Epicurus) can also be said to present creation as a re-formation, specifically a sorting-out of confused elements. The Christianized version of this idea is exemplified in Dryden's "A Song for St. Cecilia's Day" (1687), which describes how "cold, and hot, and moist, and dry, / In order to their stations leap" (9–10) in response to the "tuneful voice" of the Creator. Text modernized from Dryden's *Poetical Works*, ed. John Sergeaunt (Oxford, 1945).

chord. Unaccompanied, the chorus embarks on a series of three climactic phrases: "Und Gott sprach," "Es werde Licht," and "Und es ward Licht." Each phrase moves from unharmonized octaves to primary C minor harmonies. After the divine *fiat*, pizzicato strings interject a single soft V,^{7}, like a biblical "siehe!" The chorus then sings "Und es war" on three unharmonized Gs, consolidating the dominant on the model of the unison in m. 4. That earlier unison had been swept aside by the full orchestra with a mute-choked *forte* enclosing the chaos chord. This time, the chorus and orchestra join in an unmuted *forte* to proclaim the birth of light with a full cadence on the tonic – or rather on the brighter and more stable tonic major.

This sonority has nowhere been prefigured, and indeed has almost been interdicted. From Raphael's announcement of the beginning to the descent of the Holy Spirit, the music arches from i to iii; from the Spirit's hovering to the voicing of the Word, the music arches back from III to I. The modal shift from iii to III imparts a sense of impending brightness that the enveloping shift from i to I will confirm. Yet the shift to III also seems to anticipate the persistence of the tonic minor. The birth of light in the major, although a stabilizing gesture on the largest scale, *Urlicht* to *Urklang*, is in local terms a structural shock. The representation of the Logos thus appropriates but does not fully escape from the disconcerting logic of the sublime that governs the representation of chaos.

Not that any other outcome would be credible, either in mode or in key. In Haydn's frame of reference, to represent the dawn of creation is inevitably to stage a first sounding of the primal consonance, the C major triad: traditionally the chord of nature, the chord of light, and, for Haydn's Austrian audience, the tonic triad of the solemn mass.[29] The multiple shock of the Creation cadence in harmony, dynamics, and orchestration functions to defamiliarize the C major sonority so that it may be heard, with a sense of the miraculous, as if for the first time.

Considered as representation, the creation cadence seems to be modeled closely on a pair of thrice-famous biblical verses: "Make a joyful noise unto the Lord, all ye lands. ... Come before his presence with singing" (Psalm 100:1–2) and "Where wast thou when I laid the foundations of the earth. ... When the morning

---

[29] On C major and the mass, see Landon, *Haydn*, p. 400.

stars sang together, and all the sons of God shouted for joy?" (Job 38:4–7). These joyful noises are the prototypes of hymnody, and in the discourse of *harmonia mundi* they have a cosmological resonance. In the Christian cosmos, the music of the spheres inscribes hymnody in the order of nature; it constitutes a festive liturgy to guide the "mystic dance" of the planets and "Resound / His praise, who out of Darkness call'd up Light" (*P.L.*, V. 179). In their treatments of this topic, both Dryden and Milton conflate celestial motion with the primal hymn sung at the creation. Dryden alludes to the Platonic myth that the spheres are moved by Sirens, Christianized as hymning angels: [F]rom the power of sacred lays / The spheres began to move, / And sung the great Creator's praise / To all the blest above ("Song," 55–58). Milton condenses the parallel terms of Job 38:7, the morning stars singing together and the sons of God shouting for joy, into one packed phrase, "the sons of morning sung" ("Nativity Ode", 119). The metaphorical value of Haydn's creation cadence is similarly double. The awesome peal of C major invokes the dawn of the *harmonia mundi*, while the choral outburst on "Licht" praises the Creator by repeating the *lux fiat*, the musical Word, as both a song and a shout for joy.

The creation cadence also expresses an identity between light and harmonious sound, something implicit, too, when Milton calls on the "chrystall Spheres" to "Ring out" with their "silver chime" ("Nativity Ode", 125–28). In a celebratory poem that reportedly delighted Haydn, Christoph Martin Wieland mirrors this equation of light and harmony:

> Wie strömt dein wogender Gesang
> In unsre Herzen ein! wir sehen
> Der Schöpfung mächtgen Gang,
> Den Hauch des Herrn auf dem Gewasser wehen,
> Jetzt durch ein blitzend Wort das erste Licht
> entstehen.[30]

[How streams thy surging song / Into our hearts! We see / The Creation's mighty going-forth, / The breath of the Lord upon the waters breathe, / Now through a lightning Word first light arise.]

For Wieland, Haydn's song enables his audience not to hear but to *see* the process of creation. The creation cadence is a "lightning Word," a condensation of sound, light, and Logos, that makes primal light visible to the mind's eye. Behind this metaphor there

---

[30] Gotwals, *Joseph Haydn*, pp. 228–29.

may hover a long-standing iconographical tradition. As Warren
Kirkendale notes in relation to Beethoven's *Missa solemnis*, paint-
ings from the second to the sixteenth century often show the
Annunciation being carried to the Virgin's ear on rays of light.[31]

This mystical tradition of "hearing the light" has a significant
counterpart in the discourse of musical cosmology. The *musica
mundana* is normally inaudible to human ears, and there is a
Renaissance tradition that its inaudibility is a consequence of
fallen human nature. In a famous passage from *The Merchant of
Venice*, Shakespeare suggests that the corruptible body renders the
cosmic spirit mute:

> Such harmony is in immortal souls,
> But whilst this muddy vesture of decay
> Doth grossly close it in, we cannot hear it.   (V.i.63–65)

In *Pericles*, however, Shakespeare also makes the contrary suggestion that states of special blessedness or moral renovation may make
the music of the spheres briefly audible. This idea derives from an
extended family of metaphors in which the "well-tuned" soul is
said to be in harmony with the celestial music.[32] In a school
exercise on the subject, Milton writes: "If our hearts were as pure,
as chaste, as snowy as Pythagoras' was, our ears would resound
with that supremely lovely music of the wheeling stars" ("On the
Music of the Spheres"). This same utopian vision finds expression
in the "Nativity Ode" (126–27) when Milton calls on the "chrystall spheres" to "Once bless our human ears, / (If ye have power to
touch our senses so)."

Haydn's creation cadence makes the same invocation: or, more
ambitiously, it tries to touch our human senses with a metaphor
that figures, and to some degree confers, the blessing of hearing the
light. Certainly the music was received in these terms – among
others by Haydn himself, who was once so moved by his own
cadential outburst that he gestured heavenward and said, "It came
from there." One of the distinctive elements in the contemporary
reception of *The Creation* was the conviction that the work could
somehow form a ritual nucleus for the renewal of spiritual community. Gabriela Batsanyi, with the Creation cadence clearly in
mind, likens the effect of hearing Haydn's musical Word to a
renewal of prelapsarian bliss:

[31] Kirkendale, "New Roads," pp. 176–78 (see note 22).
[32] See Hollander, *Untuning of the Sky*, pp. 146–61 and 272–94.

Wie Adam einst in Paradies
Am Arm der Eva hingesunken
Zwar sprachlos den Erschaffer pries[,]
So hören wir entzückt die[se] Töne.

[As Adam once in Paradise / Into the arms of Eve sank down / Speechless in his Maker's praise, / So we in rapture hear these tones.]

Heinrich von Collin, with similar utopian fervor, assigns *The Creation* an explicitly liturgical power:

Wie nun in dieses Musentempels Hallen
Erwartungsvoll sich frohe Schaaren drängen;
So sieht man einst die späten Enkel wallen
Zu deiner Schöpfung hohen Himmelsklängen.[33]

[As to the Muse's temple of this hall / Expectant happy multitudes now throng, / Our grandchildren too will gather at the call / Of thy Creation's high and heavenly song.]

To put this in other terms, the creation cadence intertwines the tradition of hearing the light with eighteenth-century representations of spiritual harmony that speak of human perfectibility, the recovery of nature as unfallen and divinely ordered, the creation of amity through idealizing the work of civilization. The role of *The Creation* as a utopian ritual is the real significance of the bursts of applause that, in Haydn's day, regularly used to greet the annunciation of light.

Looking back over the musical processes that culminate in that annunciation, we can observe a tacit duality in the way Haydn relates chaos to cosmos. The turn from C minor to C major that accompanies the creation cadence is so abrupt, so startling, that the creation seems to be represented as a radical discontinuity, God's primal *fiat* as an unplumbable mystery. Haydn suggests as much when he sets the first appearance of the word "Gott," during an otherwise unaccompanied recitative, to an isolated diminished-seventh chord on the strings (m. 61). In its sublime aspect, the creation cadence presents light itself as a sacred mystery, a "quintessence pure / Sprung from the Deep," as Milton puts it (*P. L.*, VII. 244–45). Yet the representation of chaos as a germination, an evolution from incipient to imminent cosmos, is unmistakable. The evolution even continues right through the music for the first day, which, as we have seen, reenacts certain vital features of the "Vorstellung des Chaos." From this standpoint, creation is a

---

[33] Gotwals, *Joseph Haydn*, pp. 49, 258, and 255, respectively.

supremely intelligible process, and Haydn's creation cadence, which crystallizes the meaning of everything heard before it, can be taken to celebrate not only the light of what Milton called the "Birth-day of Heav'n and Earth" (*P. L.*, VII. 256), but also a much later conception: the Cartesian "natural light," the "light that lighteth ... understanding," the light of reason.[34]

This dual representation marks the confluence of the two metaphorical streams on which Haydn draws: one from traditional cosmology, with its discourse of music and mystery, and the other from eighteenth-century science, with its discourse of regularity and immanent world-order. Historically, these two models of the cosmos came into ever-increasing conflict with each other, and so helped to create the split between religious and scientific understanding that would haunt the nineteenth century. Haydn, however, brings the two models together as genially – as naively, if you like – as he combines Classical melody and Baroque recitative, Classical harmony and Fuxian polyphony. His unruffled attitude belongs as much to the seventeenth as to the eighteenth century. Like Sir Thomas Browne, Haydn finds the metaphor of the music of the spheres more revealing than the truth that the heavens are mute. "Thus far," writes Browne, "we may maintain the musick of the Sphears: for those well-ordered motions, and regular paces, though they give no sound to the ear, yet to the understanding they strike a note most full of harmony."[35] Browne's position is developed in a hymn by Joseph Addison, "This Spacious Firmament on High" (1712), that was later set in the Episcopal hymnal to some music from *The Creation*. Addison can plausibly be taken to speak for Haydn here:

> What though in solemn silence all
> Move round the dark terrestrial ball?
> What though no real voice nor sound
> Within their radiant orbs be found?
> In reason's ear they all rejoice,
> And utter forth a glorious voice,
> Forever singing as they shine,
> "The hand that made us is divine."

---

[34] On natural light (*lumen naturae*, the faculty of knowledge), see René Descartes, *Meditations on First Philosophy*, no. 3, and *Principles of Philosophy*, Book One, section 30, in *Philosophical Works of Descartes*, trans. E. S. Haldane and G. R. T. Ross (Cambridge, 1967). "The light that lighteth ... understanding" is from Aphorism 7 of Samuel Taylor Coleridge, *Aids to Reflection*, ed. Henry Nelson Coleridge (New York, 1863), p. 162.

[35] Sir Thomas Browne, *Religio Medici* (1642), ed. James Winny (Cambridge, 1963), p. 86.

The eye of reason may, it is true, reveal the traditional cosmology to be a mere fiction. But the ear of reason, hearing the light, reinstates the lost cosmic music as a metaphor – a metaphor for the divine truth inscribed in the order of nature. Haydn's music makes Addison's radiant orbs, the heirs to Milton's crystal spheres, touch our human senses as a primary image for Enlightenment itself.

This image even has its political side, which bears once more on the utopianism of *The Creation*. Though the *harmonia mundi* was a common, even a commonplace topic in traditional Creation narratives, its relationship to common life in the created world was marginal, esoteric both by definition and in practice. Outside of literature, the topic figured primarily in learned debates – did such music really exist? – and in the arcana of Renaissance magic, which took "the recovery of cosmic harmony ... [as its] persistent, supreme end."[36] Haydn's music, with its show-stopping C major cadence, brings the music of the spheres into public life, where its metaphorical sounding becomes the *introit* to a great communal occasion, a performance widely understood to be a quasi-religious festivity. In this role, the cosmic harmony becomes popular as well as public: democratic, if you will, or at least a vehicle for the Enlightenment ideal of universal sympathy. Anyone who wished to could hear the primal consonance and applaud it like one of the sons of God.

The first great event in *The Creation*, then, looks forward to the "Kuss der ganzen Welt" of Beethoven's Ninth Symphony. This gesture is reinforced by the choruses that close each part of the oratorio, all of which emphasize the oneness and humility of an awed humanity confronted with the works of God. Yet *The Creation* also forms a celebration of rigid social hierarchy. Underwritten by a consortium of aristocrats, composed by a man whose enormous success was inextricable from his unprotesting subordination, the music could hardly do otherwise. Haydn's libretto takes up this theme in terms that would have seemed both natural and emblematic to his audience: the subordination of Eve to Adam. The subject comes up both in Uriel's aria, "Mit Würd' und Hoheit angetan" (no. 24), and in the recitative, "Nun ist die erste Pflicht erfüllt" (no. 31), for Adam and Eve themselves. A full discussion of the way the music subscribes, indeed oversubscribes, to the hier-

[36] Thomas Greene, "Magic and Festivity at the Renaissance Court," *Renaissance Quarterly* 40 (1987), p. 645.

archical theme would lie outside the scope of this essay. Suffice it to mention that in the recitative Haydn's Adam repeats the imperative "folge mir" in his concluding phrase, "Komm, folge mir, ich leite dich." In response, Eve repeats "dir gehorchen" in her own concluding phrase, "Und dir gehorchen bringt / Mir Freude, Glück und Ruhm." Eve is also given an elaborate celebratory melisma on "Freude" – a gesture that resonates throughout the oratorio. By diverting emphasis from obedience to pleasure, Haydn smudges the contradiction between the communal ideal invoked by his cosmic harmony and the social conservatism fixed in his Garden of Eden.

For a final perspective on the ideological value(s) of *The Creation*, we can turn to a pair of comparisons. In his "Ode for St. Cecilia's Day," composed in 1692, Henry Purcell also depicts the creation. His representation both begins and ends with a deep organ point, which draws a link between the words "Soul of the world" and "one perfect harmony." Milton's image of "the bass of heav'n's deep organ" ("Nativity Ode," 130) may well hover behind this expressive choice. The music also depicts the binding of primeval atoms into "one perfect harmony" by a shift from imitative counterpoint to homophony. In the next number of the Ode, Purcell sets a couplet that praises God for tuning the music of the spheres. This music is simply a stately dance in the French style, with dotted rhythms. What is striking about the representational resources at work in these pieces is their easy accessibility. Purcell has no need to stretch his musical vocabulary as Haydn does; the material he needs comes ready to hand. Writing just five years after the publication of Newton's *Principia Mathematica*, Purcell still finds the figure of *harmonia mundi* both viable and obvious – impossible, really, to avoid. For Haydn, who lives in a fully Newtonian world, the same metaphor embodies an awesome mystery that arises at the crossroads of human reason and transcendental truth. By articulating a natural alliance between these terms, *The Creation* voices a principal Enlightenment ideal. Yet the extravagance of Haydn's expressive means, and perhaps of their reception, too, suggests a certain strain, a penumbral acknowledgment that the ideal is already breaking down.

If so, the finale of Beethoven's Ninth Symphony is built upon the ruins. With this music, Haydn's progression from naked tone to harmony is radicalized as a movement from cacophony to voice. In a typical Romantic reversal of traditional religious imagery, Beethoven's humanized Word does not descend from the heights but rises from the depths, as the recitative of the double basses is "incarnated" in the bass voice that calls out in appeal to a community of friends.[37] The music of the spheres has become the still, sad music of humanity. No other prelude is possible to Beethoven's "Ode to Joy," music that is compelled to seek the assurances that *The Creation* can still simply find.

In these compositions by Purcell, Haydn, and Beethoven, the music becomes a site on which cultural forces converge in considerable numbers. In terms that are important to recognize, the opening of *The Creation* takes this convergence as basic to its design. As we have seen, the movement from chaos to creation proceeds in cycles. By continually reinterpreting the cardinal features of its first four measures, the music achieves a progressively fuller clarification until the creation cadence refashions Haydn's *Urklang* as the root of a C major triad. From one standpoint this cyclical structure forms an extended representational metaphor; it suggests the circle as a traditional symbol of perfection, the circular shape of the heavenly spheres, the celestial sphere of astronomy, the swirl of planetary nebulae. More important than any of these associations, however, is the larger action that embeds them. With each new structural cycle, a greater density of allusion comes to bear upon the music. What is clarification or resolution at the level of musical structure is complication and interpretive provocation at the level of discourse. Haydn's chaos thus becomes cosmos by enveloping the *Urklang*, the epitome of what is meaningless, with gradual accretions of meaning. Logos in this music becomes a process: cultural, hermeneutic, open-ended.

I would claim that what Haydn does here is emblematic of musical representation as a whole, and implicitly of musical meaning as a whole. If the claim holds good, a summary view of musical representation would run about as follows. First, music becomes representational not in direct relation to social or physical reality but in relation to tropes. A musical likeness is the equivalent of a metaphor, and more particularly of a metaphor with a substantial intertextual history. Once incorporated into a composition, such a metaphor is capable of influencing musical processes, which are in turn capable of extending, complicating, or

---

[37] On Romantic reversals of traditional imagery, see Northrop Frye, "The Drunken Boat: The Revolutionary Element in Romanticism," in *Romanticism Reconsidered*, ed. Frye (New York, 1963), pp. 1–15.

revising the metaphor. Thanks to this reciprocal semiotic pressure, musical representation enables significant acts of interpretation that can respond to the formalist's rhetorical question, "What can one say?" with real answers.

9

Musical analysis as stage direction

David Lewin

I propose here two linked ideas about Classical music theater. First, I suggest that each analytical observation about the music-cum-text intends (*inter alia*) a point of dramatic direction. Second and conversely, I suggest that each intuition we have about the behavior of characters on stage naturally seeks its validation (*inter alia*) through musical–textual analysis. To oversimplify the matter in a brief maxim: no analysis without direction; no directing without analysis. The maxim makes my ideas sound more like imperatives than they need be taken as here; for present purposes I will propose only that it is often fruitful to proceed according to the maxim. Meaning to demonstrate that method, rather than to promulgate my particular readings as such, I shall study fairly closely a short passage from Mozart's *Le Nozze di Figaro*. The passage, comprising a solo by the Count, and a subsequent solo by Basilio, opens the First Act trio "Cosa sento!"

We shall consider the Count's solo first. In numerous analysis courses I have found most people ready to articulate a directorial intuition that the Count is confused, uncomfortable, not in good control of himself or his situation. Most people will also articulate an analytic observation that the Count has trouble making a firm cadence on the tonic, that the cadence on "sento" is somehow unconvincing, that the Count must work hard – too hard – to achieve the eventual cadence at the end of his solo. These people readily accept the implications of the maxim here, that their directorial intuitions and their analytic observations about the music are bound together in a reciprocal relation. That is: one feels the Count is not in control because one observes a musical problem about his early attempt to assert a tonic cadence; conversely, one's attention is drawn to the feebleness of the cadence on "sento" because one has a directorial impression of the Count as unsure of himself, as not in command.

163

(IL CONTE *si alza da dietro la poltrona.*)	LE COMTE *se lève.*
IL CONTE: Come! Che dicon tutti?	-- Comment, tout le monde en parle!
DON BASILIO (*a parte*): Oh bella!	SUZANNE. -- Ah ciel!
SUSANNA (*a parte*): O cielo!	BAZILE. -- Ha, ha!

[The recitative ends; the trio begins]

IL CONTE: Cosa sento! Tosto andate E scacciate il seduttor.	LE COMTE. -- Courez, Bazile, et qu'on le chasse.
DON BASILIO: In mal punto son qui giunto; / Perdonate, o mio signor.	BAZILE. -- Ah! que je suis fâché d'être entré!
SUSANNA: Che ruina! Me meschina! Son oppressa dal terror!	SUZANNE, *troubleé.* -- Mon Dieu! Mon Dieu!

Figure 9.1 Italian and French text for the opening of the First Act trio in Figaro

The idea of command will be a useful point of departure for the continuation and elaboration of our analysis-cum-direction. It will be helpful to inspect the text. Figure 9.1 gives in its left column Da Ponte's text for the end of the recitative and the beginning of the trio; in the right column, the figure aligns the corresponding French of Beaumarchais.[1]

The trio begins just where the Count, in the French, issues his first command of the play: "Courez, Bazile, et qu'on le chasse." The preceding scenes of the play, in which we have seen the Count behaving as a philanderer, not an overt authority figure, are set as recitative in the opera.[2] Da Ponte and Mozart thereby put emphasis on the Count as someone who is supposed to take charge of things; his command to Basilio is virtually the first thing he sings in the opera with full orchestral support.

But the qualification of "virtually" is critical. Da Ponte inserts into the text at the opening of the trio, before the Count's command, the exclamation "Cosa sento!" Da Ponte's Count begins the trio still in the grip of confusion and outrage, and only

[1] The Italian text is taken from Robert Pack and Marjorie Lelash, *Mozart's Librettos* (Cleveland, 1961), 114–16. The French is taken from Beaumarchais, *Le Mariage de Figaro*, vol. 1, ed. Pierre Richard in the series Classiques Larousse (Montrouge, 1934), p. 60.

[2] To be sure, Susanna has been made all too aware of the Count's political authority, while he has gone through the cruel pretence of approaching her as a simple lover. We share her awareness through her. Still, we have not seen his authority exercised on stage before this point.

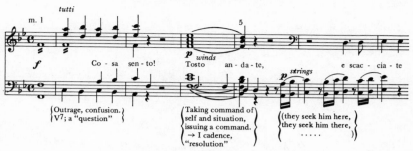

Example 9.1 Hypothetical setting for mm. 1–7

then pulls himself together to issue his command. In a play without music the exclamation would be redundantly ineffective. Its point has already been made more effectively on the stage by the Count's rising from concealment at the beginning of Figure 9.1, and by his text at that point. Da Ponte presumably inserted the text "Cosa sento!" so that Mozart could portray the Count's confusion and outrage by a big orchestral effect at the beginning of the trio. Da Ponte, specifically, might have anticipated something like Example 9.1.

Measures 1 through 3 of the example portray the confused outrage of "Cosa sento!" by a loud agitated tutti that elaborates a dominant-seventh harmony, demanding resolution. Measures 4 and 5 provide the resolution into a tonic cadence; here the hypothetical Count, with calm and quiet accompaniment takes command both of himself and of the situation; here he can appropriately issue the textual command "Tosto andate." The new motive of measures 6 and 7, which continues past the end of Example 9.1, is appropriate to the gesture of searching; it can easily take the text "e scacciate." The hypothetical setting of Example 9.1 is useful as a norm to keep in mind when analyzing Mozart's actual setting, shown in Example 9.2.

Mozart essentially sets the gestural profile of Da Ponte's text as per Example 9.1. But he consistently displaces the actual words forward in time; thus in Example 9.2 the text for measures 4–5, "Cosa sento," goes gesturally with the music of measures 1–3, and the text for measures 6–7, "Tosto andate," goes gesturally with the music for measures 4–5. The text "e scacciate," which goes gesturally with the music of measures 6–7, has not yet appeared on Example 9.2; like the preceding text, it will also appear a couple of measures "too late."

Example 9.2 Actual setting for mm. 1–7

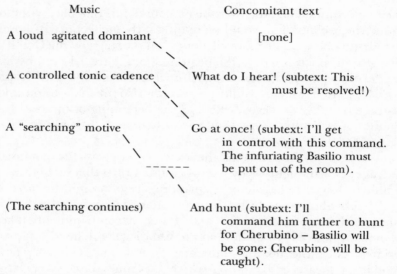

Music   Concomitant text

A loud agitated dominant   [none]

A controlled tonic cadence   What do I hear! (subtext: This
                                                  must be resolved!)

A "searching" motive   Go at once! (subtext: I'll get
                                                  in control with this command.
                                                  The infuriating Basilio must
                                                  be put out of the room).

(The searching continues)   And hunt (subtext: I'll
                                                  command him further to hunt
                                                  for Cherubino – Basilio will
                                                  be gone; Cherubino will be
                                                  caught).

Figure 9.2 The Count takes cues for his text from the immediately preceding music

    This analysis of Mozart's setting gives pointed theatrical direction to the actor singing the Count. Mozart's Count does not give impetus to the music by his verbal utterances, as an effective authority figure should – as the hypothetical Count of Example 9.1 does. Rather, he consistently takes his verbal cues from whatever music he has just heard, and then reacts to his impressions. As a stage director I am specifically suggesting, for example, that the actor should take the loud agitated music of measures 1–3, and not Basilio's earlier gossip, as a cue for the reaction "Cosa sento!" during measures 4–5. "What do I hear" in measures 1–3? Mozart thereby rehabilitates Da Ponte's theatrically redundant exclamation, providing a new, completely musical cue for the Count, a cue to which he can respond on the spot. The notion may seem farfetched to a scholar, but it will be very clear (and welcome) to an actor. Mozart's setting proceeds through Example 9.2 in a similar vein, as suggested by Figure 9.2.

Throughout the first big section of the trio, up to "Parta, parta ...," the Count continues to take his cues, both thematic and tonal, from preceding music. And throughout that section, Basilio and Susanna struggle to take control of those cues. They contend in initiating themes and harmonic moves to which the Count responds; each tries thereby to win the authority of the Count to use against the other.

It is primarily the observations we have been making, I believe, that make us feel the dominant-to-tonic cadence on "sento" is somehow weak and unconvincing. Specifically, there is a rhythmic dissonance in the syncopation between musical gesture and textual utterance, a rhythmic dissonance which makes us unable to accept the harmonic formula as authoritative and governing here. According to our maxim, we are thereby fleshing out our intuition that the Count is not authoritative and governing.

Once the maxim has turned our attention to the weakness of the cadence on "sento," we can make other interesting analytic observations. For instance, there is a particularly fine touch of orchestration in the bass under "sento!" The annotation on Example 9.2 points out that the Count's would-be cadence is not supported by a tonic note in the bass – the Count's third degree is the lowest note of the texture. To be sure the ear supplies a low B♭ for a number of psychoacoustical reasons; still the effect, subtly unhinging the authority of the would-be cadence, is remarkable. One would expect the accompaniment of Example 9.1 for this cadence, an accompaniment that does provide the low B♭.

Example 9.3 gives the complete vocal line for the Count's opening phrase. After his search over measures 6–12, the Count finally manages at measure 13 to enunciate an authoritative textual command, "Tosto andate," together with an effective tonic arrival in the music, on the high B♭. Characteristically, he does this only by recycling old text, text that did not work before. Characteristically, too, he does it only on the high B♭. Even at measure 15, where one strongly expects the low B♭, the Count is still unable to project the ground tone that should govern the number. He is still projecting the high B♭ on his later downbeat at "Parta, parta";

Example 9.3 Vocal line for the Count's opening phrase

Example 9.4 Vocal line of Basilio's solo

he will not project the low B♭ effectively until "Onestissima signora," after he discovers Cherubino. These analytic observations all arise, via our maxim, from a directorial intuition noted above, "that the Count must work hard – too hard – to achieve the eventual cadence at the end of his solo." At the beginning and the end of Example 9.3 are displayed the respective Roman numerals V and I. These symbolize the overall progression of the pertinent music, from dominant to tonic. Indeed, the convincing projection of a dominant-to-tonic cadence is as it were the essence of the Count's problem.

Example 9.4 displays the vocal line of Basilio's following solo, which reverses the Count's progression: it departs from the tonic and arrives at the dominant.

The reversal leaps to our analytic attention. The Count has labored mightily to construct a commanding move from dominant to tonic; Basilio's solo wipes out the Count's labors, abandoning the Count's hard-earned tonic command and leading back to the dominant whence the Count started out in rage and confusion. According to our maxim, we should look for directorial correlates to go with the musical analysis. I have sketched some of my own intuitions in Figure 9.3; the figure will be fleshed out by later commentary.

In these features, Mozart's Basilio goes far beyond Beaumarchais's and Da Ponte's. To see how much Mozart's music has contributed, it will be useful to consult the texts of Figure 9.1 again.

We know that Beaumarchais's Basilio is enjoying himself, but we know this only because of his earlier laughter at the end of what has

Analysis	Direction
1. Basilio does not confirm the Count's tonic cadence.	1. Basilio has no intention of leaving the scene, as commanded by the Count in that cadence.
2. Basilio moves back to the dominant harmony, whence the Count began the number.	2a. Basilio is specifically undoing the Count's previous labors; he is thwarting him, not just defying his command to leave.
	2b. Basilio is manipulating the Count.
	2c. Basilio expects to enjoy the Count's rage and confusion some more.
	2d. Not only is Basilio unwilling to leave, he attempts specifically to prolong the delightful situation at the beginning of the number.

Figure 9.3 Correlation of musical analysis and stage direction, as regards Basilio's harmonic plan

become Mozart's recitative. We know, therefore, that the Beaumarchais character enjoys witnessing the scandal at hand. But we do not find in his "je suis fâché" line any overt irony or taunting, let alone disobedience, defiance, or manipulation. In the French scene, a director could consistently have Basilio here on the verge of obeying the Count's command to leave, when Susanna distracts both men by her fainting spell, already "troublée" as she begins her text.

Da Ponte's Basilio goes farther: he speaks with irony, and he taunts his superior. The Count has been discovered by a notorious gossip-monger in a highly compromising situation, and Da Ponte's Basilio enjoys rubbing that in. The Italian text draws attention to the Count himself as a seducer; the irony is especially nice because the Count himself has introduced the word "seducer," which was not in the French. To point all this, Da Ponte introduces a strong parody relation between the sounds of Basilio's text and the Count's preceding text. The parody structure is sketched in Figure 9.4

Still, Da Ponte's Basilio does not go beyond ironic impertinence

C.   Cosa   Sento! Tos -to andate, e scacciate il seduttor.
B.   In mal   punto
         son qui giunto;
                              Per -do - n - ate,   o   mio si–gnor.

Figure 9.4 Basilio's Italian text parodies the Count's

Example 9.5 Hypothetical music, if Basilio did confirm the Count's tonic cadence

Example 9.6 Hypothetical music, if the Count reacted to Basilio's cadential dominant as the Count had reacted to the orchestral dominant at the opening of the number

to outright disobedience, let alone manipulative defiance of the Count's authority. In Da Ponte's text, as in Beaumarchais's, we can still imagine Basilio preparing to leave, obeying the Count's direct command to do so. Example 9.5 shows how Da Ponte's text could be set in that manner. Here, Basilio's solo would not move to the dominant; rather it would append itself to the Count's solo as a confirming tonic coda. One hears how the musical initiative would pass at once to Susanna; we shall return to that observation very soon.

To Example 9.5 we can compare Example 9.6 which expresses in an imagined musical setting some of the directorial notions listed in Figure 9.3 above, notions implicit in Mozart's overall harmonic progression for Basilio. Example 9.6 gives the end of Basilio's actual music, and follows that with a hypothetical response from the Count which Basilio would be delighted to provoke.

The example emphasizes how Basilio's solo closes a musical loop involving himself and the Count: the Count can go on all day attempting to resolve Basilio's discombobulating dominant to an effective tonic cadence; Basilio can likewise go on all day returning the Count's would-be tonic command back to another dominant. In this infinite tennis game Susanna has no place whatsoever. (One contrasts Example 9.5, where the initiative passes automatically to Susanna.) The game is a struggle for power and control between the two males, a struggle which Basilio is delighted to initiate, feeling himself the stronger, for the befuddled Count – obsessed by thoughts of Cherubino and the Countess – scarcely apprehends what is going on.[3]

Like Iago, Mozart's Basilio is playing a dangerous game, trying to manipulate and defy a superior who wields absolute authority, a superior who is not in good control of himself. Because of that, Basilio's unctuous hypocrisy, only a flat character trait in the texts, becomes a dynamic and purposeful tool for the Mozartean actor. Mozart's Basilio *uses* his unctuousness to keep the Count duped and mollified; the unction becomes purposeful and tension-laden, rather than merely incidental and amusing. The Count, if not sufficiently distracted, could at any moment focus his indignant rage upon the insubordinate Basilio, who remains about as a potential target for that rage.[4]

[3] Susanna however quite understands Basilio's game, and she is quite aware that she must break up the game before it continues any farther; she must win the Count's attention herself, to secure his authority for her interests against Basilio's. That is why she proceeds immediately, in the music which follows, to attack Basilio's dominant in the most forceful way possible: she moves from Basilio's F major harmony towards a cadence in F minor, destroying the dominant function of F major by denying the leading tone A natural. Her F minor key will not press towards a tonic cadence in the key of Bb major. Unfortunately, just as she faints (or "faints") away in F minor, Basilio hastens with feigned solicitude to "console" her in F major, thus restoring the harmony he wants, the harmony she was trying to escape. There is not space in this study to analyze adequately the fantastic tonal duel that ensues between Susanna and Basilio, as they compete with each other for control of the Count during the farcical stage events which follow; I shall content myself with sporadic observations in later text and notes.

[4] I think that Susanna is fully aware of Basilio's danger. I believe she attempts precisely to focus the Count's rage against Basilio during her rape accusation later in the scene. Specifically, I believe she means not so much to cry rape against both men, as to cry rape to the Count against Basilio. Useful in this connection is the split in the two men's texts after the rape cry: the Count says "Do not be upset, darling," while Basilio at the same moment assures Susanna "Your honor is secure." I would therefore stage a pertinent part of her earlier faint (or "faint") as follows: the two men together sing "O God how her heart is beating"; the Count feels her left breast with genuine concern, – or so he persuades himself – or at least so he pretends; Basilio, taking advantage of the situation (and quite possibly realizing or believing that Susanna is fully conscious) symmetrically feels her right breast.

This interpretation of Susanna's rape cry makes sense of her seizing the dominant

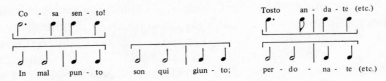

Example 9.7 Basilio smooths out the Count's rhythmic motive

We hear Basilio's hypocritical fawning in Mozart's music as well as in Da Ponte's text. Very audible, for instance, is the false solicitude with which Basilio's repetitive four-note rhythmic motive smooths out the jagged contours of the Count's four-note rhythms. The motivic transformation is displayed in Example 9.7.

Ostensibly calming the Count down, Basilio is actually duping him. Mozart uses to good effect here the ironic parody in Da Ponte's text, discussed earlier (Figure 9.4). The ostensible calming makes the musical impetus relax: the tonic has already been reached and now the rhythmic motives lose their drive as well. In order to maintain a suitable level of dramatic tension, it is useful for the actor playing Basilio to sense and project the danger underlying his Iago-like behavior, and his own Iago-like delight at his mastery over that danger. Among other things, as he leads the wandering harmonies of the solo along he must savor at all times his intention to arrive at the dominant when he closes.

The wandering harmonies themselves constitute another aspect of Basilio's hypocrisy. Figure 9.5 shows how the first three of Basilio's local tonics, Bb, G minor, and Eb, replicate and expand the harmonies of the Count's final cadence, just heard during measures 13–15. Basilio's solo thereby seems, up to its very end, to be confirming and extending the Count's final tonic cadence – as if Basilio were about to obey the Count's command.

Only at the end of Basilio's solo, as indicated by the parenthe-

harmony herself thereafter, when she urges the Count not to believe the "impostor" Basilio. One understands: "Take and resolve my dominant, not his, with your authority. Look how impertinent he is being."

The way in which the men treat Susanna during the trio, both musically and theatrically, would be intolerable to an audience of any sensibility, were that treatment not disguised by the heavily farcical mode that supervenes from time to time within the comedy for just that purpose. Mozart and Da Ponte are expert at moving along the edge of this line. (They do so throughout *Don Giovanni*.) In the French text, Basilio leaves Susanna completely alone and is completely silent during her fainting spell. There is no mention of Susanna's heartbeat; it is the Count's idea to put her in the chair; it is furthermore the Count, not Basilio, who reassures her after her indignant outcry that "il n'y a plus le moindre danger!"

m.13   m.15

Tosto andate, e   scacciate il   sedut-----------tor.

Bb   g   Eb   (F   Bb)

m.16

In mal punto son qui giunto;   Perdonate, o mio signor.

Bb   g   Eb   (c   F)

Figure 9.5 Basilio's harmonic progression compared to the harmonies of the Count's final cadence

F   D   (scalewise ascent. . . to)   Bb   G   Eb   (F   Bb)

Cosa sento! Tosto andate. . . , tosto andate e scacciate   il seduttor.

F   D   Bb   G   Eb   C

In mal punto   son qui giunto; Perdonate,

                                                 o mio signor.

Figure 9.6 Chains of falling thirds in the melodic structure of the two men's solos

sized harmonies in Figure 9.5, does Basilio reveal his true intention: instead of confirming the Count's final harmonies, F-to-Bb, Basilio substitutes C minor-to-F. He thereby sneaks in his insubordinate cadence on the dominant only after lulling the Count into supposing that he is about to confirm the Count's tonic cadence. The tactic is designed to keep the Count off-balance so that Basilio can get away with his game.

In Figure 9.5, Bb, G minor, and Eb build a segment from a chain of falling thirds, heard in the harmonic structure of both the Count's solo and Basilio's solo. Figure 9.6 shows how chains of falling thirds are also manifest in the melodic structure of both men's vocal lines.

As in the harmonic structure of Figure 9.5, so in the melodic structure of Figure 9.6 we hear how Basilio apes his master's model right up to the final cadence, as if he were about to confirm the Count's tonic closure. Instead, just where the Count breaks off his chain of thirds to form the melodic cadence F-to-Bb, Basilio extends his chain of thirds one link farther, arriving at a melodic cadence on the note C, the second degree of the scale, utterly incompatible with any possibility of tonic closure. One notes here the sudden vivification of Basilio's hitherto "unctuous" four-note rhythmic motive.

The manipulative mastery we have observed so far in Basilio's solo remains much in evidence during the remainder of the number. In particular, Basilio consistently manages to outwit and foil Susanna during their tonal duelling for the Count's authority. As a director, one wonders if our Iago-like Basilio would not be paying close attention to Susanna, as well as to the Count, during the solo we have been examining. Applying our maxim, we are thereby led to analyse the music of the solo even farther, to find some relation between Basilio and Susanna therein. The desired relation is indeed forthcoming. For Basilio's music does not refer alone to the Count's solo that immediately precedes it. It refers as well to Cherubino's famous aria, *Non so più*, the preceding number in the opera. Example 9.8 shows the relationship, which binds because it fits so clearly the repetitive motivic doggerel of each tune. In the example, Cherubino's tune has been transposed to the same key as Basilio's solo; this facilitates the comparison.

Now, applying our maxim again, let us see what we can infer in the way of stage direction from the musical analysis of Example 9.8. We can begin by inferring that Basilio has heard Cherubino's tune. (Basilio, we must remember, is a music master.)[5] Since Basilio has heard the tune, he must have heard its only performance. That is, Basilio must have been lurking about outside Susanna's door, listening to Cherubino, just before the Count went into the room.

Basilio, therefore, knowing or strongly suspecting that Cherubino is presently hiding somewhere in the room, is now making sure that Susanna knows his suspicion and suspects his certain

---

[5] I cannot entertain the possibility that Basilio's quotation is only Mozartean irony, like Wagner's irony when he makes Siegmund sing the Renunciation of Love motive in *Die Walküre*. That sort of irony seems to me not only pointless here but utterly foreign to the dramatic mode of *Figaro*. In any case, why reject a resource for deepening Basilio's character and his interactions with the others on stage?

For some time I believed that Basilio might not have heard the performance of *Non so più*; I thought that he might instead be looking at the score, which Cherubino or Susanna could have dropped in the scramble to conceal the boy. But this reading does not hold water: the score which Cherubino has brought to Susanna is *Voi che sapete*. Just before Cherubino will sing that song later on, Susanna will refer to it as "the song you gave me this morning." I am grateful to Edward T. Cone for the clarification.

Cherubino, *Non so più* (transposed)

Basilio, *In mal punie*

Example 9.8 Basilio's solo compared to Cherubino's Non so più

knowledge. Thus, while Basilio's solo is manipulating the Count in all sorts of ways, it is also keeping a tight grip on Susanna. This aspect of Basilio's solo will be very useful to the actress singing Susanna, as she responds with the punning text "Che ruina!" [= "Cherubino!"].

Since Basilio knows or suspects that Cherubino is in the room, a further delicious irony emerges: in defying the Count's first command – to leave the room – Basilio is deliberately and infuriatingly obeying the Count's second command – to hunt out Cherubino.

I assure those who are not musicians that I could go on exploring the two men's solos considerably farther in this vein, and I could go on for several times as long on Susanna's subsequent solo. But I think I have made the points I wanted to make; to continue would make little sense unless I were to analyze the entire number through in equal detail and also in its global musical structure – a worthy project but one so extensive as to be out of place in the context of the present volume. I should rather like now to stand back and comment upon what I think I have been doing.

First, I hope to have indicated the depth and thickness with which it is possible to explore Mozart's dramaturgy using my maxim. In one sense, I am only very belatedly attempting to show that one can perform as well for Mozart the traditional sort of close character analysis that A.C. Bradley and Harley Granville-Barker performed for Shakespeare some sixty to ninety years ago. I hope thereby to render less ephemeral the intuitions of critics who have ranked Mozart and Shakespeare together on the summit of theatrical art.[6]

Beyond that, I hope to have shown the utility of the maxim as

---

[6] For example: "Up to this winter I owed my most enjoyable evenings in the theater to Shakespeare and Mozart," Eric Bentley, "God's Plenty in Paris," (1949), *In Search of Theater* (New York, 1954), p. 55.

such. I think it is useful for opera at least from Mozart through Verdi, given some adjustments for a variety of musical styles and theatrical conventions over the period. I believe furthermore that the maxim is also useful for other vocal genres so far as the notion of "drama" pertains to them in some extended sense. I would put many Lieder into this category.[7]

Going farther still, I think the maxim might be useful for investigating the technical basis underlying the aesthetics of program music and programmatic criticism in nineteenth-century Europe. The urge to supply a program for an instrumental piece, either to help compose it or to help criticize it, might fruitfully be viewed as an urge to supply a theatrical dimension for the music at hand, enabling the composer or critic to move freely back and forth between musical analysis and dramatic direction, as I have been moving here. That sort of motion might well have been felt especially natural and constructive in the years following Mozart's theatrical achievements. Scott Burnham has recently approached one of A. B. Marx's programmatic analyses in this spirit, yielding results which seem to me very promising.[8] Thomas Grey's critique of another Marxian analysis, in the present volume, is suggestive in the same way. I sense that there are crucial distinctions to be made between drama and "narrative" in these contexts, but I do not have the expertise to formulate my impressions in a literary mode.

[7] The reader will find the notion developed at some length in my essay "*Auf dem Flusse*: Image and Background in a Schubert Song," in *Schubert: Critical and Analytic Studies*, ed. Walter Frisch (Lincoln, Nebraska and London, 1986), 126–52.

[8] "A. B. Marx and Beethoven's *Eroica*: Drama, Analysis and the *Idee*," lecture delivered to the meeting of the New England Conference of Music Theorists, Brown University, Providence, April 4, 1987. Mr. Burham's lecture is largely incorporated within his Ph.D. dissertation, *Aesthetics, Theory and History in the Works of Adolph Berhard Marx*, Brandeis University, 1988.

10

Poet's love or composer's love?

~

Edward T. Cone

I

Some fifteen years ago a short book of mine[1] put forward the idea of the *vocal persona*, a concept equally applicable to the characters in an opera and to the protagonists of art song (to use a barbaric but convenient locution). Such personas obviously differ from the purely verbal personas of the poetic text inasmuch as "they express themselves at least as much by melody as by speech, and as much by tone-color as by phonetic sound." That is to say, "the vocal persona adopts the original simulation of the poetic persona and adds another of his own: he 'composes', not the words alone, but the vocal line as well. We admittedly connive at this pretense when we watch an opera, but we should realize that a similar situation must obtain if we really attend to a performance of a Schubert Lied. For if we try to follow words as well as music, we must accept the song, no less than the opera, as a dramatic presentation."[2]

On the other hand, as I pointed out, very often – perhaps most of the time – such a persona "[f]rom the point of view of the implied or enacted drama ... is not 'really' singing at all." To be sure the *singer* sings, but the character portrayed is usually speaking. "From the realistic point of view, such a character is unaware of singing, and of being accompanied. Yet on the musical levels he must in some sense be aware of both." I then proposed that the paradox might be resolved, or at least mitigated, by a recognition of the verbal component as stemming from the conscious levels of the protagonist's psyche, and the musical components, vocal and instrumental, from the subconscious levels. "Consciously, he neither knows that he is singing nor hears the accompaniment; but his subconscious both knows and hears."[3]

[1] Edward T. Cone, *The Composer's Voice* (Berkeley, Los Angeles, and London, 1974).
[2] *Ibid.*, pp. 9–10 and p. 23.
[3] *Ibid.*, pp. 30, 33 and 36.

177

Today I am unwilling to be so categorical. Recently, when I had occasion to reconsider a number of familiar operas, I realized that it is often unwise or even impossible to try, as I formerly did, to "contrast the normal state of an operatic character with his behavior in situations where the libretto requires him to *enact* the singing of a song."[4] Indeed, I found the distinction so often blurred that I was forced to conclude that operatic characters are most fruitfully construed as inhabiting a strange but wonderful world in which singing is the normal mode of communication, and in which composing is a well-nigh universal activity.[5]

If that is the case, then the distinction between conscious and subconscious is equally blurred. If operatic characters are aware of singing, and of composing their own parts, that must be because their subconscious lies so close to the surface as to be available for scrutiny – by themselves, by one another, and by the audience. Such personalities must wear their hearts on their sleeves – and that is exactly what we feel that they do. That is what it means to be an operatic character.

I cannot review here the evidence and the arguments by which I arrived at my conclusions concerning opera, but they parallel those by which I shall now try to support a similar claim with respect to accompanied song in general ("art song"). For I now believe that the world of song is likewise inhabited by composer-poets who communicate by singing, and who are for the most part fully aware of their media of expression.

In the first place, as my book pointed out, there are many protagonists who must perforce be construed as "actually" singing. Some of their songs, such as stylized ballads, simulate traditional types of public performance. Others are imitations of what I described as "a persuasive or rhetorical song, possibly improvised for the occasion, in which, for example, the singer propitiates the Deity, or woos a beloved, or puts a baby to sleep." Still others refer to my hypothetical category of "pure natural song expressing simple emotions – singing for joy, singing for sorrow ... An interpretation of this kind, applied to a number of the songs in [*Die schöne Müllerin*, for example], would explain their emphasis on simple melodies and strophic forms: these songs represent not

[4] *Ibid.*, pp. 30–31.
[5] See Edward T. Cone, "The World of Opera and Its Inhabitants," in Edward T. Cone, *Music: a View from Delft* (Chicago, 1989), 125–38.

merely the thoughts of the protagonist, but songs composed (improvised) by him."[6]

What I wish to propose now is that we accept the foregoing model as more the rule than the exception. By acknowledging the protagonist as the conscious composer of words and music alike (often including, as I shall argue, the accompaniment), we can frequently – if not regularly – arrive at a more just appreciation of the dramatic portrayal inherent in a song.

I believe that we normally accept a parallel claim with respect to poetry – that is, whenever we stop to think about it. For what is the first thing we know about any poetic persona? Certainly it ought to be this: whether, as in a lyric, the persona is a representative of the poet's own ego, or whether, as in a monologue or dialogue, it is a dramatic character – in every case, it expresses itself in poetry. The persona is, in a word, a poet. Not the poet who actually wrote the poem, but the poet who is dramatically portrayed as reciting a poem that he or she is probably improvising. That is why it is quite natural for poems to call attention to themselves as poems, as they so often do. One immediately thinks of Shakespeare's Sonnet LV ("Not marble nor the gilded monuments/Of princes shall outlive this pow'rful rhyme"), but that is merely the most obvious of many such references in the cycle. Shakespeare speaks through a protagonist who not only is a poet but constantly thinks and speaks of himself as a poet.

Let me ask now, correspondingly, what is the first thing we ought to know about the protagonist of a song? Again, that he or she is a poet – but this time a singing poet, or, to give an old phrase something of its original meaning, a lyric poet, in the sense of one who composes words and music together. Many lyrical poems embody protagonists who, following that tradition, make it clear that they regard themselves as musicians; and it should not surprise us that composers in search of texts should be attracted to those. Thus, on the one hand, songs like the "Ständchen" from Schubert's *Schwanengesang* contain obvious proclamations of musicianship; on the other, an entire cycle like *Die schöne Müllerin* may be colored by subtle references that encourage such an interpretation.

I have already suggested that a number of the songs in that set might represent a kind of natural, spontaneous music-making;

[6] *The Composer's Voice*, pp. 52 and 55.

ironically, the one that provides us with the most concrete evidence
of the protagonist's musicianship is the one in which he pretends to
forgo musical expression: "Pause." When he hangs his lute on the
wall, singing "Ich kann nicht mehr singen, mein Herz is so voll,"
he confirms his own status as a musician, just as his rhyming
insistence that he can no longer rhyme ("Weiss nicht wie ich's in
Reime zwingen soll") implies that he is equally a poet. And finally,
the remaining numbers of the cycle are presaged in his reference to
"das Vorspiel neuer Lieder."

The hero of *Die Winterreise* is no doubt a more complex character, both verbally and musically. He, if anyone, might be
expected to exemplify my former "typical protagonist [who] is
assumed to be actually unconscious of singing".[7] But is he
unconscious of singing? His last words, addressed to the organ-
grinder, are: "Willst zu meinen Liedern/Deine Leier drehn?"
What we have been hearing, then, are real songs – not just poems
but compositions which, the hero feels, have some kinship with the
melancholy music of the hurdy-gurdy.

When I discussed the role of that instrument in *The Composer's
Voice* I insisted that one must distinguish between what the protagonist may be presumed to hear and what we, the audience,
hear. "The protagonist of 'Der Leiermann' hears a hurdy-gurdy,
but he does not hear what the actual singer and the audience hear:
a pianist playing a stylized version of what a hurdy-gurdy might
sound like ... [T]he sound as heard or imagined by the protagonist
is only raw material; what the singer and his audience hear is the
composer's transformation of the sound into an element of the
accompaniment." And I defined this transformation of the actual
sounds as "their resonance in the subconscious of the protagonist as
interpreted by the consciousness of the instrumental persona."
That complication was necessitated by my hypothesis of the
unconscious protagonist – unconscious, that is, of singing and thus,
a fortiori, of being accompanied. I therefore assigned to the accompaniment a quasi-persona of its own that I dubbed a "virtual
persona," since, as I admitted, "the instrumental persona may
seem a creature of analogy, an imaginary construct."[8]

Now, I do not wish to dispense with the concept of the instrumental persona, for I find it invaluable in explaining such diverse
phenomena as the accompaniment that binds together the voices of

[7] *Ibid.*, p. 38.   [8] *Ibid.*, pp. 30, 36, and 18.

a Mozart operatic ensemble, the web of leitmotifs by which the Wagnerian orchestra comments on the action, and the interplay of voice and orchestra in Mahler's vocal–symphonic hybrids. But the acceptance of the typical protagonist of song as a conscious composer often permits a radical simplification. Composers, after all, have been defined as people whose heads are always full of music. Ever since the advent of harmony, the music in the heads of Western composers has seldom been purely melodic. Thus their songs generally imply their own harmony, and a full-fledged accompaniment is often an integral part of the original conception. It is therefore easy to think of the accompaniment we actually hear as a representation of what is going on in the inner ear of the composer-protagonist.[9]

That is possible, I now suggest, whether that accompaniment imitates actual music heard by the protagonist, as in "Der Leiermann," or transmutes natural or other sounds into music, as in "Erlkönig," or comments upon the situation in abstract or symbolic terms. Thus, where I formerly wrote, "[T]he instrumental persona conveys certain aspects of the subconscious of the vocal protagonist, but indirectly,"[10] I should now say, "the instrumental accompaniment directly conveys certain aspects of the musical consciousness of the vocal protagonist." Specifically, with respect to "Der Leiermann," I should now recast my former statement thus: "The sound as heard by the musician-protagonist is his raw material; what we hear is his utilization of that sound as an element of his accompaniment." (True, one has to accept the convention by which the pianoforte may represent, now a hurdy-gurdy, now a serenader's guitar – or may present generalized, instrumentally unspecified sounds ringing in the protagonist's musical imagination.)

In many cases, at least, it thus becomes unnecessary to posit, as I formerly did, "a triad of personas, or persona-like figures, involved in the accompanied song: the vocal, the instrumental, and the (complete) musical." According to that analysis, "The complete musical persona is to be inferred from the interaction of the other two"; I called it an *implicit persona*, or, "as the vehicle of the composer's complete message ... *the composer's persona*."[11] No: we may now appropriately reserve those complications for more

[9] Cone, "The World of Opera," discusses this point in relation to operatic characters, pp. 135–38.
[10] Cone, *The Composer's Voice*, p. 35.   [11] *Ibid.*, p. 18.

complex situations such as those mentioned above. But when the accompaniment proceeds directly from the imagination of the protagonist, a separate instrumental persona becomes superfluous, and therefore no complete persona is to be "inferred from the interaction of the other two." Instead, my three original figures have collapsed into one: a unitary vocal–instrumental protagonist that is coextensive with the persona of the actual composer of the song.

The model for such accompanied song has now come close to what I earlier called "simple song", one that "projects a single persona – a protagonist who in fact or in theory produces his own accompaniment." But whereas I limited simple song to "song with no accompaniment at all or with 'simple' accompaniment – that is, accompaniment that has no individuality,"[12] I am now applying that model to songs with full-fledged instrumental parts.

My hope is that an interpretation based on the foregoing principles might result in a closer and more sensitive relationship between voice and accompaniment than would otherwise be possible. Singer and accompanist, instead of taking for granted that each of them represents a unitary agent (to adopt the jargon of my book), would try to hear the song-texture as composite; and they would determine to what extent their parts could be made to coalesce in order to project a single persona.

A detail from Schubert's "An die Musik" will serve to illustrate. The perfection of this lovely song is often marred in performance by a failure of communion between voice and accompaniment at the end of the second phrase (mm. 9–10). If the singer assumes that she is ending the phrase at m. 9, she makes of the second cadence a rhythmically and harmonically weak echo of the first (see Example 10.1a). Moreover, the cadence arrives too early, skewing the graceful balance of phrases: 4–3–(1)–4–5 measures, in which the single measure is an instrumental orphan between the vocal phrases. What both singer and accompanist must realize is that the goal of the second phrase is the piano's downbeat in m. 10. That is made clear by the piano's off-beat doubling of the melodic line in mm. 8–9, followed by its downbeat resolution in m. 10. The cadence is no longer a tentative V^6–I but a much stronger I–V; and the proportion of measures reveals a double-period with an emphatic lengthening of the final phrase – 4–4–4–5 measures. The previously

---

[12] *Ibid.*, pp. 59 and 58.

Example 10.1a Schubert, "An die Musik," mm. 5–9

Example 10.1b Schubert, "An die Musik," mm. 9–11

orphaned measure has become firmly integrated into the texture; for its first chord is a resolution for voice and piano alike, followed by a lengthy anacrusis in which inner voices and bass prepare the inception of the following phrase (see Example 10.1b). It takes a careful adjustment on the part of both performers to project the required sense of identity – which must of course inform the interpretation of the entire song.

II

A complete subsumption of the vocal and instrumental personas under the all-embracing persona of the composer has an important effect on what I have called "the inevitable transformation of poetic and dramatic content" involved in setting to music a pre-existing poem. In every such setting "the poetic persona is transformed into . . . the vocal persona: a character in a kind of monodramatic opera, who sings the original poem as his part."[13] What I

[13] *Ibid.*, p. 21.

now suggest is the possibility of a more profound transformation. The poetic persona, originally a surrogate for the actual poet, now becomes, through its participation in the vocal–instrumental persona, a surrogate for the actual composer. The composer not only writes his own music but desires, as it were, to write his own words. Sometimes, indeed, he can do just that; but often he finds that another poet has already written them for him.

The transformation is facilitated when the poet, like Müller, has already adopted as his persona the figure of the poet-musician. On the other side, the task is eagerly undertaken by composers who like to think of themselves as poets. Certainly Schumann was such a one. As Sams puts it, "Schumann, we know, approved of the term 'Dichtungen' ... as applied to musical composition; and thought of himself as a 'Dichter', or imaginative writer, as in the piece entitled "Der Dichter spricht" in Op. 15."[14] Thus *Dichterliebe* – the title eventually chosen or accepted by Schumann for his own choice of Heine's texts[15] – involves a double meaning. Schumann, the composer-poet, found in the poems evidence that their protagonist, like those of Schubert's Müller-cycles, is a poet-composer: one who is inspired by bird-song (No. 1), whose sighs become nightingales (No. 2), who inspires the lily to sing for him (No. 5), who dreams of magical fairy-music (No. 15), and who finally buries all his songs at sea (No. 16). That persona, originally Heine's surrogate, was an easy one for Schumann to embrace and transform into his own.

When I speak of Heine's or Schumann's surrogate, I do not mean to imply that those figures are necessarily autobiographical. True, Heine's poems are considered to be full of personal references; and there is good evidence that Schumann, too, identified himself to a certain extent with the poet-lover.[16] But my position would remain unchanged even if it were established that the lover's experiences were purely imaginary in both instances. *For the purposes of the poems*, Heine spoke through the role of the unhappy *Dichter*. *For the purposes of the songs*, Schumann transformed that figure into a *Dichter* of his own.

Let me further stress the phrase "a *Dichter* of his own." Schumann has sometimes been castigated for his apparent failure to

---

14 Eric Sams, *The Songs of Robert Schumann*, 2nd edn. (London, 1975), p. 108.
15 See Arthur Komar, "From Heine's Poems into Schumann's Songs," in his edition of *Dichterliebe* (New York, 1971), p. 4.
16 See Sams, *The Songs*, p. 107.

recognize, or at least to respond musically to, Heine's often bitter irony.[17] But the protagonist of the songs is no longer Heine's: it is now Schumann's. Schumann's *Dichter* inhabits a different world from that of his poetic original: a world in which words give way to music as the primary vehicle of expression, in which to speak is to sing, and in which to sing is to imagine the full implications of one's melody by auralizing an elaborate accompaniment. We should therefore not expect the personality of Schumann's *Dichter* to be the same as that of his purely poetic original.

That melody and accompaniment must be construed as inseparable components of a single invention is attested by many details of the type already noted in "An die Musik". The best-known example is the piano's persistent completion of the voice's unfinished cadences in No. 2 – subtly orchestrated by the piano's retention of each B, which, relinquished by the voice, is allowed to resound briefly before its resolution on A. What is not so often noted is that the B–A really initiates a motif only completed by the D of the next song. Komar points out the recurrence of the same motif at the end of No. 3: "The last three notes of the vocal part – B–A–D – reiterate the connection in the voice part between Songs 2 and 3, with B delaying A in each case."[18] But the connection between the two songs is not confined to the voice. From the outset it is intertwined between voice and piano until the piano postlude finally lingers on the three notes presented simultaneously (see Example 10.2).

Similar interdependence is a characteristic feature throughout No. 14. Here neither voice nor piano ever presents a definitive version of the theme, which must rather be inferred from the collaboration of the two. In each stanza, depending on the text, the voice omits one or more upbeats and afterbeats, which must be supplied by the piano; and in each the piano alone states the E♮ of the fourth measure – a note that is both harmonically and rhythmically essential. On the other hand, the appoggiatura B of the eighth measure is reserved each time for the voice (see Example 10.3).

No. 7 exhibits another type of collaboration. Voice and piano essentially double each other throughout; but Schumann was willing to entrust the melodic outburst of the climax to the piano,

[17] E.g., Jack M. Stein, *Poem and Music in the German Lied from Gluck to Hugo Wolf* (Cambridge, Mass., 1971), pp. 98–110.

[18] Arthur Komar, "The Music of *Dichterliebe:* the Whole and Its Parts," in his edition of *Dichterliebe*, p. 75.

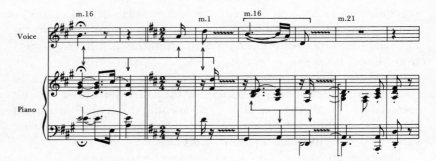

Example 10.2 Schumann, "Aus meinen Tränen spriessen," mm. 16–17; Schumann, "Die Rose, die Lilie, die Taube," mm. 1, 16–17, 21–22

Example 10.3 Schumann, "Allnächtlich im Traume," mm. 1–8, 14–21, 27–34

assigning to the voice a more singable inner part (see Example 10.4). The alternative version, in which the doubling continues, was apparently an afterthought.[19] It is as if the composer were saying, "Choose what line you will; voice and piano are one." The same message is conveyed, perhaps more explicitly, by the persistently converging vocal and piano lines of No. 5. No. 12 offers a variant of the same technique (see Example 10.5).

No. 6 exhibits a shifting method of doubling. The opening vocal phrase coincides with the cantus-like bass; but while the voice

---

[19] *Ibid.*, p. 83.

Example 10.4 Schumann "Ich grolle nicht," mm. 27–30

Example 10.5 Schumann, "Ich will meine Seele tauchen," mm. 1–4

repeats the cantus the bass continues independently. The voice next joins the upper line of the piano for two phrases. It concludes by moving freely from the piano's inner to its upper line and back again, coming to rest on a leading tone that must be resolved by the accompaniment alone. (Is this a facetious repayment for the opening upbeat tonic in the voice, which gave the accompaniment its pitch? Be that as it may, the original reversal of the expected roles prefigures the unification of voice and piano that characterizes the entire song.)

Doubling alternates with imitation in No. 4. The imitation, a contrapuntal device that might well have been used to emphasize the independence of the two parts, is used chiastically to underline their essential identity (see Example 10.6). In somewhat similar fashion the antiphonal fragments of No. 13 stress the unity of the two parts rather than their opposition, since the piano is a free echo of the voice. The final stanza brings them together for the first time. When, on the way to the climax, they diverge, it is impossible to grant the primacy either to the stationary vocal part or to the rising chromatic line of the piano. Their essential identity is established by their convergence on the high point, and by the voice's delegation of the descent to the piano (see Example 10.7).

Most subtle of all in the interpenetration of voice and accompaniment is the very first song of the cycle, which thus sets the tone for all that follows. The doubling is delicately heterophonic – as

Example 10.6 Schumann, "Wenn ich in deine Augen seh," mm. 1–6

Example 10.7 Schumann, "Ich hab' im Traum geweinet," mm. 28–33

Example 10.8 Schumann, "Im wunderschönen Monat Mai," mm. 6–10

when the voice, but not the piano, anticipates the resolution of a suspension; or when the piano, but not the voice, remains suspended; or when the voice, after inserting an appoggiatura, resolves such a suspension. The effect is the kind of blurring that might result if the piano could pedal the vocal line, so to speak, treating the voice as a strand of the piano texture (see Example 10.8). But that is exactly what the strategy of the whole song suggests. Its melody first unfolds in piano alone (mm. 1–4), adds fairly strict doubling by the voice (mm. 4–8), moves into the voice with selective piano doubling (mm. 8–12), and is continued by the piano alone (mm. 12–15) – at which point the entire process recommences.

The total ambiguity of the song is well known; what has not so often been discussed is the equally ambiguous periodic structure. Do mm. 1–8 form a period establishing A as tonic, or do mm. 1–4 constitute an introductory phrase to a period (mm. 5–12) modulating from A to its subdominant? Fortunately the strophic repetition allows both versions to be heard in a reading that insists on the essential oneness of voice and piano by their mutual periodic complementations.

X	Y	Z	X	Y	Z	X
(1–4)	(5–8)	(9–12)	(12–15)	(16–19)	(20–23)	(23–26)

(elision)

Piano—Voice   Voice——Piano   Voice——Voice   Piano–

The final piano phrase is of course incomplete both periodically and tonally. Periodically, it is answered by the next song, which once more turns the V^7 of F♯ minor toward A major. No. 2 thus functions as a consequent, not only for the final phrase but, as it were, for the entire No. 1. But the tonal completion – an F♯ minor chord that effectively resolves the V^7 and its acutely hanging leading tone – must wait for the concluding member of the cycle. No. 16 is in C♯ minor, but mm. 20–27 exhibit a powerful modulation to IV, in which voice and piano collaborate in making clear the origin of this key in the opening gesture of No. 1 (see Example 10.9). The resolution occurs in m. 27, which hammers out a reiterated V–I cadence in F♯ minor.

No. 9 may seem to be a counter-example to the argument I have been developing. It is difficult to hear the autonomous, dance-like accompaniment as proceeding from the same source as the relatively bare vocal line. Sams flatly refers to that accompaniment as "piano music, on which the vocal melody has somehow to be grafted."[20] And as Hallmark makes clear in response, the sketches demonstrate that Schumann wrote the song in just that way: "Here, in contrast to his methods for all the preceding songs, Schumann launched directly into a thorough sketch of the piano

[20] Sams, *The Songs*, p. 116.

Example 10.9 Schumann, "Die alten bösen Lieder," mm. 20–33
"Im wunderschönen Monat Mai," mm. 1–4

part, and indeed grafted on the vocal line."[21] But, dramatically considered, voice and accompaniment do not proceed from the same source, and the voice part is indeed applied to a preexisting instrumental composition. The accompaniment might reflect music the protagonist is hearing; more probably, it recalls recently heard music that, because of his agitation, keeps ringing in his ears, much as remembered music sometimes torments one in a feverish state. This explains the monotonous persistence of its melody and rhythm; and if, as Komar puts it, "the voice merely provides a rather square counterpoint,"[22] that is because the poet-composer's creative power is temporarily numbed by the memory.

In contrast stands No. 15, in which the accompaniment again imitates remembered music – this time one of the "uralte Melodei'n". But this tune the hero recalls with pleasure; and he makes it his own by appropriating it, at first literally, then in an augmented version that reflects his nostalgic regret.

Melodies resound in his ears also in Nos. 10 and 12. They are fainter and less insistent, for each is subjected to a delicate rhythmic shift that fixes it to a series of syncopated afterbeats. The displacements turn the beloved's song into a sad echo, and etherealize the imaginary voices of the flowers. In each song the device continues throughout the piano postlude, accompanying the hero's now wordless reflections. (It is interesting to find the same tech-

[21] Rufus Hallmark, "The Sketches for *Dichterliebe*," *19th-Century Music* 1 (1977), p. 123.
[22] Komar, *Dichterliebe*, p. 84.

Example 10.10 Schumann, "Die alten bösen Lieder," mm. 44–47
Beethoven, Symphony No. 3, second movement, mm. 171–72

nique used in one of the songs Schumann omitted from the definitive version of the cycle. "Mein Wagen rollet langsam" was originally one of two standing between the present Nos. 12 and 13.
Although the poem makes no specific mention of a remembered
tune, its mood is one of imaginative day-dreaming, for which the
syncopated melody – again persisting throughout the coda – is
appropriate.)

One other example of remembered music must be mentioned –
this time a well-known passage by a famous composer. In the
concluding number, as the poet-composer describes the sea-burial
of the coffin containing his songs, he rhetorically inquires, "Wisst
ihr warum der Sarg wohl/So gross und schwer mag sein?" At that
point the music refers to another burial by quoting, in both voice
and piano, two measures (mm. 171–72) from the "Eroica" Funeral
March (see Example 10.10). It is a detail to be pondered by those
who think Schumann incapable of irony. Beethoven's thematic
material is embedded in yet another return of the opening
harmony of the cycle, V^7 of F♯ minor. That juxtaposition under-
lines the protagonist's mock-heroic identification, but at the same
time it leads to a revelation of his stance as just a pose. He claims,
"Ich senkt' auch meine Liebe/Und meinen Schmerz hinein!"; but,
as he does so, a deceptive cadence initiates a transition confirming
the F♯ as a subdominant, and leading to the C♯–D♭ of the
coda. The concluding reminiscence of the flower-song of No. 12
confirms that it was pure bravado to pretend that his love and
sorrow were buried. Schumann's irony is not Heine's, to be sure,
any more than his hero is Heine's, but in its own terms it is both
dramatically effective and musically convincing.

The identification with Beethoven, whether taken seriously or ironically, is the final bit of evidence I offer for my theory of the protagonist as composer. Only a composer would be likely to think of such a comparison. As we know, Schumann acknowledged his own sense of kinship when he quoted from *An die ferne Geliebte* in his *Fantasie* and elsewhere. What could be more natural than for him to express his protagonist's similar intuition in similar fashion?

I once wrote, "Probably the singer's first task is to determine the nature of the protagonist – to ask, 'Who am I?' The answer is never simple."[23] Now I wish to suggest a simple answer: "I am a composer."

23 Cone, *The Composer's Voice*, p. 23.

11

The semiotic elements of a multiplanar discourse: John Harbison's musical setting of Michael Fried's "Depths"

Claudia Stanger

In one of the very few reviews ever published of John Harbison's song cycle *The Flower-Fed Buffaloes*, one critic observed that not only was Harbison's choice of poems too disparate for the work to be unified, the music was equally disconnected. The result was a farrago of ideas, a hodgepodge, a jumble that lacked any unifying elements, either musical or poetic.[1] Indeed, the work initially appears to be quite chaotic. Harbison was commissioned by the New York State Bar Association to set to music a speech titled "The Spirit of Liberty" by Judge Learned Hand. Judge Hand was for many years the highly regarded and extremely popular Chief Judge of the New York Court of Appeals, and he wrote "The Spirit of Liberty" in 1944 to deliver in a ceremony granting citizenship to immigrants. However, rather than composing music to this particular text, Harbison created a parallel text from various poems which offered a broader range of themes about the American experience. These poems range from the rhythmic lines of Vachel Lindsay to the blank verse of Gary Snyder. Harbison's settings, too, explore a broad range of musical possibilities, from the use of a chorus accompanied by an unusual combination of instruments to a solo dramatic reading with percussion and piano. In the liner notes accompanying the recording of *The Flower-Fed Buffaloes*, Harbison explains that his "musical language draws on American vernacular throughout" and that his objective is to make audible the "rhythmic and harmonic connections below the verbal surface."[2]

A summary of the genesis of Harbison's work highlights some of the most intriguing topics that concern not only those critics interested in musico-literary relations, but also interdisciplinarians

---

[1] Anon., *Down Beat Magazine* 47 (1980), 46.
[2] John Harbison, *The Flower-Fed Buffaloes*, Nonesuch Recording H–71366 (1979), liner notes.

from many different fields of study. The first issue, and perhaps the thorniest one, is to clarify what is meant by the word "language" and to differentiate, insofar as it is possible, between various kinds and uses of language. A peculiar history is at work between the two disciplines of music and the verbal arts; composers and musicians on one hand as well as writers and poets on the other have frequently adopted each other's vocabulary. Harbison's appraisal of his musical "language" as an "American vernacular" is typical of this tradition. Just as literary critics have claimed that certain writers musicalize language, so have music theorists frequently described music in terms of its linguistic qualities. The expression "the language of music" is as pervasive in music criticism as the expressions "the music of poetry" or "the musicalization of prose" are in literary studies. The historical ease of this exchange raises the basic question of whether or not these various applications of the word "language" in any way relate to each other across disciplinary boundaries.

This investigation will assess how models of communication developed in structuralist and semiotic theory are able to bring various applications of the word "language" into sharper focus. The major stumbling block in the comparative assessment of the languages at work in music and literature has been the problem of dealing with the concept of meaning in the two arts. However, the critical methodologies based on the structural linguistics of Saussure and Jakobson make it possible to shift the analytic focus away from what language actually says or means in order to concentrate on the relational structures that constitute the arena of language usage. Furthermore, semiotic models proposed by Louis Hjelmslev and A. J. Greimas that explicate relationships between the different signification systems at work in poetry and prose make it possible to compare the different signification systems at work in the arts of language and music. According to the basic principles of structuralist and semiotic theory, language consists of a highly complex range of discourses. However, natural language can be understood not merely as a semiotic system but as a model according to which other semiotic systems can be conceived.[3] This study will explore applications of semiotic theory across the broad range

---

[3] The question of using language as the model for examining the signification systems at work in either literature or the other arts is at the center of a complicated debate in post-structuralist and semiotic theory. This investigation will not attempt to resolve this issue but rather will suggest that the use of linguistic models helps us to perceive music in new ways.

of discourse fashioned out of prose, poetry, and music that comprise *The Flower-Fed Buffaloes*. Rephrased in semiotic terms, then, the compositional process at work in John Harbison's musical settings can be understood as a continuous one across different systems of signification. The two goals of this investigation will be, first, to demonstrate that similar devices are at work across all of the texts, and second, to suggest how these shared devices constitute a multiplanar, musico-literary discourse that yields a methodological basis from which to explore other structural relations between music and many different kinds of literary texts.

Legal texts and public addresses such as Judge Hand's speech are often cited as examples of practical language, what A. J. Greimas calls monoisotopic texts.[4] While these texts do contain certain ambiguities, the monoisotopic text provides both the discourse and the context for these ambiguities to be resolved. Everyday language, official language, informative language, committed as they are to communication, are also committed to unequivocal discourse and explicit context. It is significant that, although Harbison found Hand's text both rich and suggestive, he also found it inappropriate for a musical setting.[5] Harbison's construction of a parallel text out of various poems reveals a shift or transposition of language that raises a number of intriguing questions not only about semiotic relations between prose and poetry but also about the semiotic relations between language and music.

The first is whether there is something particularly unmusical about unambiguous texts. If so, does ambiguity (Greimas's term is pluri-isotopy) constitute a bridge or connection between languages both musical and literary? Furthermore, has this unsuitability of a particular linguistic discourse for musical settings been determined by culture and tradition alone, or are there other processes at work that determine what sorts of discourse are suitable for or even realizable in a musical setting? A rather absurd reformulation of this question might be to ask why musicians haven't set articles from *Scientific American* to music. Historically, composers have not

---

[4] A. J. Greimas and J. Courtes, *Semiotics and Language: An Analytical Dictionary* (Bloomington, 1982), pp. 163–65. For a complete discussion of isotopic spaces in narration see A. J. Greimas, "Elements of a Narrative Grammar," *On Meaning: Selected Writings in Semiotic Theory* (Minneapolis, 1987), pp. 63–83.

[5] In a March 1988 interview with this author, John Harbison further clarified his decision to set poetry rather than Hand's text to music. Harbison cited the compression of meaning in poetic language as well as the long rhythms in the poems as elements that lent themselves more readily to musical expression. Interestingly, Harbison also commented on the lack of images in Hand's text as a barrier to composition.

chosen to set monoisotopic texts to music. Especially in the twentieth century, composers have gravitated towards more radical
experiments with pluri-isotopic texts, for example by reorganizing
literary texts or by dismantling language itself in musical settings.
Because musico-literary criticism has not yet developed the
methods, models, or vocabulary to deal effectively with radical
musical experiments with language, Harbison's piece offers a rare
instance in which the process of transforming informative language
into poetic language is an overt and integral part of the musical
composition.

Two distinct but related transformations are at work in the
construction of *Buffaloes*. The first is the process by which the
relative unambiguity of Hand's prose has been translated into the
pluri-isotopy of poetic language, a subject clearly within the
boundaries of linguistic or literary analysis. The second is the
relationship between this process and the composition of the music
for *Buffaloes*, a more difficult but distinctly interdisciplinary topic.
Nevertheless, both of these processes lend themselves to semiotic
analysis, and approaching both processes from this analytical
point-of-view emphasizes the central question of this investigation:
does Harbison's transposition through two different levels of
linguistic discourse reveal processes that are integral to the composition of music?

Before examining this question in detail, it is helpful to describe
briefly the construction of the entire song cycle. *The Flower-Fed
Buffaloes* is composed of five songs, alternating between choral
settings in the first, third, and last song and baritone solos in the
second and fourth. After a short preamble of varying tempo, with a
rather threadbare clarinet and tenor saxophone duet, a choral
setting of Vachel Lindsay's "The Flower-Fed Buffaloes" opens the
work. A slow, rhythmic piano line is supplemented with very
traditional programmatic elements such as the sounds of cowbells
and a vocal line that mimics the drone of a locomotive. In the
second song, a solo baritone sings Hart Crane's "Enrich My
Resignation." The clarinet and tenor saxophone of the preamble
return, and clear thematic connections are established between the
poems: the extinction of buffalo from the windows of trains in the
nineteenth century finds a contemporary parallel in the hunting of
deer from airplanes. The third song, a choral setting of Michael
Fried's "Depths," functions in many ways as the linchpin of the
entire work, and it will be discussed later in detail. Suffice it here to

point out that the hounded shark in "Depths" perpetuates the theme of the hunt, albeit in a slightly different context, so that the hunter and hunted have been collapsed into one persona. Clearly, Harbison has chosen to emphasize certain tropes that connect the poems, particularly in the flower as a symbol of salvation and redemption, and the contrast of the Western frontiersman with the American Indian. In the fourth song, a scored dramatic reading for solo baritone of Gary Snyder's "Above Pate Valley," these thematic connections between the poems are again emphasized. The fifth and final song is a return to the rhythmic lines of Vachel Lindsay as well as to the rocking major chords that opened the piece, here expanded by strings and a vibraphone. The full chorus of the last song contrasts with the baritone solo in the fourth, but the poetic and musical themes are closely related.

Musically, Harbison's piece is not without a tonal center, but diverse and unexpected harmonies swirl around it. Similarly, a diversity of rhythms develops out of the regular meter that begins the piece. Just as his choice of poems radiates from the center of Hand's text, Harbison has constructed a musical analogy that explores, like a new frontier, the New World beyond the limitations of Classical tonality. However, these kinds of observations, so typical of much interdisciplinary criticism, represent a particular approach that is oriented towards finding (or conjuring up) parallels and analogies, in this case thematic ones, between the arts. Sometimes these parallels exist and sometimes they are important, but what warrant further investigation are the structures or the foundation that even allow us to perceive parallels or analogies between the arts in the first place. One way of working beyond analogy is to propose that the interface between music and language is the scene of a confrontation of different signification systems. The concessions or compromises that are made between these systems in the process of joining them together in an interdisciplinary work reveals characteristics about both systems.

Judge Hand's text is hardly an ideal monoisotopic text, one constrained by unequivocal statements and a clear context. It is, in fact, an interesting weave of rhetorical devices, constituted primarily out of opposition and negation.

We have gathered here to affirm a faith, a faith in a common purpose, a common conviction, a common devotion. Some of us have chosen America as the land of our adoption; the rest have come from those who did the same. For this reason we have some right to consider ourselves a picked group, a group of those who had the courage to break with the past and brave the dangers and the loneliness of a strange land. What was the object that nerved us, or those who went before us, to this choice? We sought liberty; freedom from oppression, freedom from want, freedom to be ourselves. This we then sought: this we now believe that we are by way of winning. What do we mean when we say that first of all we seek liberty? I often wonder whether we do not rest our hopes too much upon constitutions, upon laws, and upon courts. These are false hopes; believe me, these are false hopes. Liberty lies in the hearts of men and women; when it dies there, no constitution, no law, no court can save it; no constitution, no law, no court can even do much to help it. While it lies there it needs no constitution, no law, no court to save it. And what is this liberty which must lie in the hearts of men and women? It is not the ruthless, unbridled will; it is not the freedom to do as one likes. That is the denial of liberty, and leads straight to its overthrow. A society in which men recognize no check upon their freedom soon becomes a society where freedom is the possession of only a savage few; as we have learned to our sorrow.

What then is the spirit of liberty? I cannot define it; I can only tell you my own faith. The spirit of liberty is the spirit which is not too sure that it is right; the spirit of liberty is the spirit which seeks to understand the minds of other men and women; the spirit of liberty is the spirit which weighs their interests alongside its own without bias; the spirit of liberty remembers that not even a sparrow falls to earth unheeded; the spirit of liberty is the spirit of Him who, near two thousand years ago, taught mankind a lesson it has never learned, but has never quite forgotten; that there may be a kingdom where the least shall be heard and considered side by side with the greatest. And now in that spirit, that spirit of an America which has never been, and which may never be; nay, which never will be except as the conscience and courage of Americans create it; yet in the spirit of that America which lies hidden in some form in the aspirations of us all; in the spirit of that America for which our young men are at this moment fighting and dying; in that spirit of liberty and of America I ask you to rise and with me pledge our faith in the glorious destiny of our beloved country.[6]

Those who seek liberty, according to Learned Hand, are part of a courageous and elite group which has two characteristics: their willingness to break with the past and their fearlessness in confronting a strange land. It is this singularity of purpose and solitary frame of mind that characterize this American ideal. However, the spirit of liberty has three qualities that are far more nebulous, qualities that are repeatedly described in terms of what they are not. Liberty's spirit cannot be written down in laws or constitutions for it "lies in the hearts of men and women"; liberty's spirit cannot be clearly defined except that it "is not too sure that it is right"; and finally, liberty's spirit can never be tangibly realized for it "lies hidden in some form in the aspirations of us all." While the spirit of

6 Learned Hand, *The Spirit of Liberty: Papers and Addresses of Learned Hand*, 2nd edn. (New York, 1953), pp. 189–91. Harbison instructed that copies of this text be distributed to the audience before each performance of *Buffaloes*.

liberty is simultaneously deep within us yet beyond our grasp, the wisdom of this paradox can only be appreciated by those who seek liberty, knowing it is unattainable.

Hand's rhetoric resonates with the tangled logic of Romantic poetry: not much of a deconstructive push is required to reveal how easily meaning in monoisotopic texts can fail to coincide with itself. At this point, one might question whether monoisotopic texts can exist at all, the premise at the heart of the radical semiotics of Derrida and de Man. However, this study will not focus on this question but rather propose that this undoing of prose discourse reveals patterns that can be found first in the poetry and then in the musical settings of the poems. Harbison gives instructions in the score that Hand's text should be distributed to the audience before each performance of *Buffaloes*, so it is clear that the song cycle was conceived as an intertextual experience of prose, poetry and music. A complete analysis of the piece would consider the entire parallel text formed by all of the poems and their relationships with Hand's prose. For reasons of space, this analysis will focus on Michael Fried's "Depths" and the specific devices shared between it and the prose.

What Fried's poem says, in a strict sense, is quite different from what Hand's text says:

> Suddenly there is nothing that is not revealed by faces alone.
> America, like a hounded shark, not knowing where to turn,
> Makes for the depths
> Taking us down.[7]

As in Hand's address, the density of the poetic language is fashioned out of a weave of negation and opposition. The tension in the first line arises from the ambiguity of the modifier "alone," a word that can function doubly as an adverb meaning "simply" as well as an adjective "lonely" or "solitary" modifying "faces." The multiple readings forced by the ambiguity of the modifier are then compounded by the various readings offered by the double

---

[7] Michael Fried, *Powers* (London, 1973), p. 40. The text is given here as it appears in Fried's collection, but because of considerations of space, Harbison slightly alters the lines on both his score and the liner notes. The text of the poem appears in this form:

> Suddenly there is nothing that is not revealed
>   by faces alone.
> America, like a hounded shark, not knowing where
>   to turn,
> Makes for the depths
> Taking us down.

negative, the "nothing ... not revealed." Solitary faces will never, perhaps can never, reveal the great nothingness which they conceal, a "nothing" that lies hidden within them in the same way that the spirit of liberty hides itself within the hearts of those who seek her. The rhetoric of the second line, like America, the hounded shark or the spirit of liberty herself, turns on this process of not knowing, of not being too sure. It is precisely this undecidability that drags us down to the depths beneath the verbal surface of the poem.

Fried's terrifying assessment of the American consciousness might seem to be at odds with Hand's guarded optimism, and a thematic comparison of the two texts fails to clarify the connections between them. However, the differences between what is actually said, that is the truth claim of the statements, are easily undermined by the processes at work in both texts, particularly in the patterns of negation and opposition.[8] In this regard, a structural analysis of the relationship between prose and poem reveals a matrix, a set of differential relationships between modifiers and negation at work in both texts. Furthermore, the fact that these similarities are masked by the apparent contradictions on the verbal surface offers an interesting perspective on the compositional devices at work in Harbison's music. After the sense or meaning, that is the monoisotopic reading, of texts has been problematized, the similar deconstructive strategies implicit in both are revealed and provide a framework for the musical composition.

For example, new relationships between music and language are clearly at work in the musical setting of "Depths," and perhaps the best way to illustrate these new relationships is by a negative example. Prosody, or the alternation between stressed and unstressed syllables, has traditionally been viewed as one of the most fundamental characteristics shared by music and language, from Aristotle through Augustine to T. S. Eliot. Although Harbison's setting is concerned with rhythm, the setting actually masks the words, making them at times unintelligible. The elementary shift away from vocal clarity and diction reveals a fundamental change of focus in the relations between music and the verbal arts because prosody is, above all, a characteristic of language as it is

[8] In the March 1988 interview, Harbison acknowledged that he found virtually no similarities between Hand's address and the critical view of America given in Fried's poem. It is noteworthy that some members of the New York State Bar Association that commissioned *Buffaloes* left the New York premiere during the performance of "Depths." One of the main points I am trying to make in this analysis is that the deceptive qualities of Hand's text were not immediately obvious either to the composer or his patrons.

made audible through speech. Within "Depths," Harbison does investigate these traditional devices, but then he refuses to continue using just those patterns that most easily connect music to language across the mediating structures of voice.

A more revealing approach to Harbison's setting of "Depths" is to consider it as an exploration of the many qualities of voice that function beyond the coherence of clear enunciation, and a brief synopsis of the setting will clarify some of these. The piece opens with an uncanny reverberation of instruments behind five vocal parts that begin singing different melodies in a staggered entry (Example 11.1). Directions on the score specify that singers should use a jazz or a popular singing style that utilizes glides and slurred words, and what results is a vocal line in which the words are virtually unintelligible. There is a certain degree of playful humor at work in Harbison's selection of popular songs for this passage, and the five tunes resonate thematically with some of the basic themes established in the five poems: the chorus sings the blues songs "I Have Had my Fun if I Don't Get Well No More," "I Only Have Eyes for You," "They Didn't Believe Me," "Always," and "Indian Love Call." Like Hand's address, these songs embrace a particularly uncritical view of American life. An important musical element is also at work in each of the pop songs: each begins with a C–D–F motive that will constitute an important musical sign in the rest of the setting.

The vocal and melodic confusion of the first few bars is suddenly interrupted in measure 20 by the first line of the poem sung in unison by the entire chorus (Example 11.2). The sharp entry of the voices on the word "suddenly" utilizes a mimetic device frequently employed in song settings, but the short, powerful staccato on the words "suddenly," "nothing," and "faces" contrasts with the note held on "revealed" and the sustained notes and chord change on "alone." In fact, the strongest application of rhythmic as well as melodic pressure is on the word "alone" in measure 25 (Example 11.3). The unison setting of the first line is then interrupted by the reappearance of the staggered voices and instruments beginning in measure 28. Again, traditional compositional considerations are at work in the setting of the second line with the obvious variation on the melody of "America" and the programmatic use of the canon to mimic the hounded shark. In the final bars, an uneven rhythmic line returns, and for the first time, a purely instrumental section dominates the piece and brings it to a close.

Harbison has incorporated many traditional compositional

Example 11.1 Harbison/Fried, "Depths," mm. 1–10

Example 11.2 Harbison/Fried, "Depths," mm. 16–22

Example 11.3 Harbison/Fried, "Depths," mm. 23–30

devices into this setting, but two characteristics which initially might not appear to be very important seem particularly note-worthy when compared with Fried's poem and Hand's text. If Harbison's music is heard through these texts, it can be understood as an acoustic trace of his transposition between different levels of linguistic discourse. This shifting between different kinds of lan-guage is simultaneously interpretive and constitutive. The reader-composer at once dissolves and invents new languages, and it is precisely this simultaneous undoing and reconstituting of language that reveals elements of Harbison's music not easily heard in traditional auditory terms. At this point the music has become written in a deconstructive sense: beneath the privilege accorded to the pure self-presence of what is heard at the verbal or acoustic surface lurks a graphic or inscriptional interplay of differential traces.

The first of these traces occurs on the sustained "alone" shown in Example 11.3. Not only has Harbison emphasized the ambiguous function of this word by holding it longer in unison voices than any other word in the setting, but he also uses this word to repeat the three-note motive of the popular songs as well as to introduce the melody of "America." The compositional connection between the words "alone" and "America" is direct and clear. On the word "alone" in measure 26 the piano and contrabass are in B♭ major. This key continues through the following measures, including in measure 28, where the bass and alto voices restate the three-note motive C–D–F in the retrograde F–D–C on "America." In addi-tion, the glisssando and slurred style of the C–D–F motive from the beginning returns. What Harbison has done is not only to exploit musically the function of "alone" as a shifting modifier but to expand its function so that "alone" now functions through its musical setting as a modifier of "America."

The second characteristic of Harbison's setting is that he uses various attributes of sound to create a network of acoustic oppo-sitions. There is a contrast in the vocal settings between slurred and clearly enunciated lines as well as a contrast between phrases sung in unison and those treated with a staggered entry. In the music, the unclear or subtle musical references to the popular songs that open the piece are contrasted with the clear musical reference to the melody of "America the Beautiful" and, as in the vocal lines, unison entries of instruments are set in opposition to staggered entries. The political critique of Fried's poem contrasts with the optimistic sentiment of the popular song lyrics, a tension Harbison captures by overlapping the word "always" from the famous Irving Berlin song with the initial "suddenly" of Fried's poem. Finally, the entire setting explores the limitations of voice, beginning with the distortion of slurred lyrics, moving through clearly enunciated words of the poem, and ending with a conspicuous absence of voice at the end of the setting. What Harbison has constructed is a network of contrast and opposition that works on multiple levels, and what we are to listen for are not merely what the setting "says" but more importantly the processes that are employed in the "saying."

Like many contemporary composers, Harbison is not so much interested in the poem as a finished product, as an object to be set. Rather, he is interested in the poet's method, the rules of the poet's game and the systematic patterns of meaning constructed within the poem. In semiotic terms, Harbison's musical setting of "Depths" clearly repeats two significant patterns that have been established in the discourses of both Hand's address and Fried's poem. How these intertextual devices relate to each other is not easily explained in either musical or literary terms. At this point discourse theory becomes a useful analytical tool. It should be clear that the term discourse as it has been used in this analysis does not mean a series of utterances that are connected to each other through grammatical rules to form sentences. This definition of discourse establishes levels of meaning, understanding, and competency, but this definition impedes rather than facilitates an examination of discourse in music. Hjelmslev has proposed a broader theory of discourse, one that interprets the structural linguistics of Saussure as a particular case of a more general semiotics. According to Hjelmslev, the term "discourse" includes the totality of operations at work within any system of communication, including how units of signification are defined, as well as the relations and operations of these units. Hjelmslev's model, taken directly from Saussure's *Course of General Linguistics*, delineates the fundamentally different operations of a combinatorial or syntagmatic axis and a substitutional or paradigmatic one. When applied to semiotics, Hjelmslev utilizes these terms to designate two universal distinctions used by a perceiver to understand any conceptual object of study. Perceived at the syntagmatic level, the object is understood as a process; at the paradigmatic level, as a system.[9]

---

[9] Louis Hjelmslev, *Prolegomena to a Theory of Language* (Bloomington, 1953), p. 24.

At the syntagmatic or process level, relations between signs are established by knowing how any sign connects with or relates to another sign in a linear chain. According to Hjelmslev, describing what an individual unit or sign might be and prescribing its functions are not a prerequisite of understanding how signs might function along a syntagmatic axis. Furthermore, the syntagmatic relations between signs are not fixed, and establishing a particular linear relationship between components does not exclude other linear relations.

Fried's text provides an excellent example of this dynamic in the way the modifier "alone" functions in the first line. The mobility of this word within the linear sequence, in fact the inability to fix it permanently, forces multiple readings because proper placement is always undecidable. The word "alone" is truly a loner, but it is important to recognize that it is the system of Fried's poem which generates this displacement. When Fried's text is read in conjunction with Hand's speech, the disintegration of the poetic line into its multiple texts actually demonstrates the American ideal, the spirit of liberty, that Hand found so difficult to capture in his address. In fact, it is precisely the organized confusion of the poem that manifests at a lexical level the ineffable qualities of liberty that Hand attempts to circumscribe in his speech.

This is, of course, a mediated reading made possible only by Harbison's musical setting, and it is the handling of the music that validates these observations. The three-note motive aligned with the word "alone" not only emphasizes the variant readings offered by the poem but, more importantly, adds to them. "Alone" is melodically joined to the noun "America," and both are in turn associated with the popular songs, with the melody from "America the Beautiful" as well as with the frantic sounding of the shark. On a syntagmatic level, Harbison's setting reformulates and expands the function of the problematic quantifier in the poem. By reordering this melodic sequence, Harbison creates a musical sign that, like the word with which it is most closely identified, both generates new syntagmatic chains as well as connects these new readings with each other.

In Hjelmslev's second mode, in which the conceptual object is perceived paradigmatically or as a system, relations between signs are established through disjunction.[10] Rather than being linked

---

[10] *Ibid.*, p. 22–25. Hjelmslev's discussion is concerned with "language (in the ordinary sense of the word)," and in the conclusion to this section he states that the process can be

It is now possible to give a definitive representation of what we call the semiotic square:

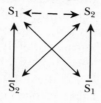

$S_1 \longleftarrow - - \longrightarrow S_2$

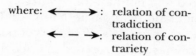

$\bar{S}_2 \qquad \bar{S}_1$

where: $\longleftrightarrow$: relation of contradiction

$\longleftarrow - \rightarrow$: relation of contrariety

Figure 11.1 Greimas's semiotic square

through a linear set of syntagmatic relations, signs along the paradigmatic axis are able to act as substitutes for each other. While the syntagmatic axis can be envisioned as a horizontal one, the paradigmatic axis is usually understood as a vertical one along which selections are made from a class of elements that can occupy the same position in the syntagmatic chain. The process of selecting from this hierarchy is the systematic elimination of like to similar terms. One simple example of this linguistic concept is that Fried chose to use the word "America" in his poem instead of its synonym "United States."

Both Saussure and Jakobson characterized the paradigmatic axis as one of binary opposition and, as Jakobson has demonstrated, an example of paradigmatic selection that frequently occurs in poetry is the use of metaphor.[11] In Fried's poem, the paradigmatic axis of selection is clearly at work on a linguistic level in the simile of the hounded shark which is substituted for America in the second half of the poem. However, it is important to remember that metaphors, unlike synonyms, require that a differentiation of terms is maintained. The hounded shark can work as a metaphor for America only if the difference between the terms America and shark be maintained. The richness, the literariness, of

thought of as a text and language itself as a system. Hjelmslev also stipulates that no process can exist without a system. It is Hjelmslev's broader discussion of relationships between process and system rather than his specific focus on language that are most useful in interart analysis.

[11] Roman Jakobson and Morris Halle, *Fundamentals of Language* (The Hague, 1956), p. 76 *passim.*

metaphors stems from the delicate web established through simultaneous recognition and rejection: America is indeed most horrifically a shark only when it is recognized as not a shark at all in the ordinary sense. However, even in unequivocal discourse, selecting from a hierarchy of synonyms is a complicated process. In Hand's address, various terms for the concept of liberty are considered and then rejected, and finally the spirit of liberty is defined not by suggesting similar terms but rather by creating a matrix of unacceptable synonyms. Liberty becomes that which is not written, not defined and not tangibly realized.

Because paradigmatic relations in many kinds of discourse are more complicated than models of binary opposition are able to convey, A. J. Greimas has proposed a model that more fully elaborates this complexity. In his semiotic square, Greimas suggests that paradigmatic selections should be arranged in terms of both their contradiction and contrariety (Figure 11.1). With this model, Greimas attempts to describe the entire system at work behind narration and the deep structures from which all individual narratives are derived. However, the most significant aspect of Greimas's semiotic square is that initial relations of opposition generate highly complex and contradictory trajectories, and it is the multiplicity and variety of oppositions that distinguish one discourse from another.[12]

The music in Harbison's setting of "Depths" is not easily understood in terms of harmonic, melodic, and rhythmic structures. Rather, as pointed out earlier, masses of sound are juxtaposed in various combinations. Greimas's semiotic square offers another perspective on Harbison's composition. Greimas's definition of contrariety describes the relations that are established between vocal and instrumental sections in the musical piece because both vocal and instrumental sections are present together and separately in the setting. In addition, both vocal and instrumental sections have what Greimas terms contradictions. Instrumental sections characterized primarily by staccato notes and sharp attacks are set against, that is contradicted or opposed by, instrumental sections of primarily slurred notes and pedaled instruments. This same pattern is repeated in the vocal sections. Clearly articulated vocal lines are set against, that is contradicted by, inarticu-

---

[12] A. J. Greimas, "Interaction of Semiotic Constraints," *On Meaning: Selected Writings in Semiotic Theory* (Minneapolis, 1987), pp. 48–62. The source of this diagram is Greimas and Courtes, *An Analytical Dictionary*, p. 309.

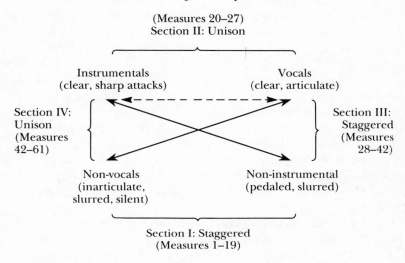

Figure 11.2 Harbison's setting of "Depths" according to the parameters of the semiotic square

late or slurred vocal sections. It is precisely the system of these musical contrarieties and contradictions that constitutes the discourse of Harbison's musical setting of "Depths," and Harbison's composition can be mapped out in terms of Greimas's notion of variable opposition (Figure 11.2).

In Section I, a section distinguished by the staggered entry of voices and instruments, inarticulated vocal lines sound against a pedaled vibraphone and piano while the rest of the instruments play predominately slurred notes. In Section II, another combination is explored: clearly articulated voices enter in unison over the sharp attack of various instruments. In Section III, the various oppositions are juxtaposed in a different way. A clear vocal line returns in a staggered entry over slurred notes and pedaled instruments. In the final Section IV, clear instrumental attacks are punctuated by staccato percussion. Although voices return primarily in unison, the last section of the setting of "Depths" is characterized by a total absence of voice, particularly in the canon on the three-note motive that dominates the final eleven bars.

On the basis of an examination of these structural features, it is possible to discern the common elements of discourse in the texts by Hand, Fried, and Harbison. In all of the texts, a matrix has been created wherein something is understood not by knowing what it is, but rather by apprehending and exploring its various relationships with what it is not. In his recent work on the semiotics of literary texts, Michael Riffaterre identifies what he terms hypersigns, or textual conundrums that simultaneously arrest the process of understanding and provide multiple solutions through reference to other texts.[13] According to Riffaterre, the reader apprehends the hypersign or compound sign which, in turn, determines an interpretation in an open-ended process of discovery and decoding. The relationship between music and language in a musical setting might be understood in similar terms, except that, rather than expanding outward infinitely, the musical setting realigns poetic language to music so that the hypersigns in each refer to solutions proffered by the system of the other.

The intertext created by Harbison's setting is, in semiotic terms, the expansion and connection of three different bi-planar systems. Just as the functions of ambiguity in the syntagmatic axis are connected across the texts by the setting, so are the relations of opposition and contradiction connected across paradigmatic axes. Furthermore, this makes possible a mediated reading of all three texts. A mediated reading neither obscures nor privileges one art or the other but rather seeks to connect the semiotic elements of each text. An interpretation of Harbison's composition made possible by a mediated reading is that his setting of "Depths" investigates the problematic nature of voiced language. The intertext created by the amalgam of prose, poem, and music concerns the nature of voices which, like faces and like the spirit of liberty, are more revealing when they are hidden, masked, unclear, or silent.

In current interdisciplinary inquiry, it is no longer sufficient or satisfactory simply to offer analogies between the literary and musical arts. The reason that expressions such as "the music of poetry" or "the language of music" offer so little insight about either literature or music is that these expressions demarcate oppositions between the arts without elaborating the middle ground between the two poles. The trajectory of a traditional interdisciplinary vocabulary based on analogy is simply to reduce or collapse one art into the other. Fundamental adjustments of interdisciplinary focus are necessary in order to recognize that the intertext created by the multiple inscriptions of different arts generates a

---

[13] Michael Riffaterre, "Hypersigns," *The American Journal of Semiotics* 5:1 (1987), pp. 1–12.

discourse of its own, a discourse that is substantially different from those of each individual text.

One such adjustment is provided by what I will call mediated readings. The mediated reading is acutally a more sharply defined application of the combinatory principles at work in Lévi-Strauss's *bricolage*[14] or Greimas's application of multiple cross-reference in the *Analytical Dictionary*.[15] Mediated readings function between different kinds of discourse and attempt to make each text transparent so that the semiotic elements of all the discourses are allowed to refer to each other. In addition, mediated readings are always multiple because the objective is not to fix a single interpretation on the interdisciplinary work of art but rather to allow the work to generate its own structure, as Lévi-Strauss suggests, somewhere between aesthetic perception and the exercise of logical thought.[16] Furthermore, as soon as the interdisciplinary work has been revealed as an interface of different communication systems, the many new discourses generated by the work can be examined. For example, Harbison has constructed a new narrative out of the five poems he selected for *Buffaloes* – a technique long employed by composers in song cycles, but one that has yet to receive rigorous examination in interdisciplinary scholarship. While the challenges posed by musico-literary texts have yet to be fully answered, one conclusion is clear. Interdisciplinary discourse is a collective discourse, and the interdisciplinary work of art is the creation of strata of discourses, each of which successively alters and reshapes the others. What is currently required by interart inquiry is an archeology of analysis with theories and methods as resilient as the works under investigation.[17]

---

[14] Claude Lévi-Strauss, *The Savage Mind* (Chicago, 1966), pp. 17–20. For a discussion of the combinatory and music see the preface to Lévi-Strauss *The Raw and the Cooked* (London, 1970).

[15] A complete discussion of multiple cross-referencing can be found in the preface to the *Analytical Dictionary*.

[16] Lévi-Strauss, *The Raw and the Cooked*, p. 14.

[17] I would like to thank William P. Dougherty for his thoughtful remarks on the early drafts of this study.

Part IV

Gender and convention

12

Whose life? The gendered self in Schumann's *Frauenliebe* songs

Ruth A. Solie

Women have served all these centuries as looking-glasses possessing the magic and delicious power of reflecting the figure of man at twice its natural size.   Virginia Woolf[1]

[An ordinary woman] is the unutterable which man must forever continue to try to utter . . .   D. H. Lawrence[2]

Feminist scholarship in all disciplines has insisted on the study of cultural context, whatever the project at hand. This is because gender relations, while seldom brought to the surface for scrutiny in mainstream scholarship, are constructed by culture and are always among the most fundamental ideological structures operating in any society. It is part of the project of feminist work to keep pointing out, as a character in one of J. M. Coetzee's novels puts it, "how scandalously, how outrageously a meaning can take up residence in a system without becoming a term in it."[3] This is as good a description as any of my purpose here, to investigate how gender as a "meaning" resides in the *Frauenliebe und -leben* songs by Adelbert von Chamisso and Robert Schumann.

We have in these songs a particularly focused, not to say fraught, ideological situation. For one thing, because nineteenth-century listeners expected music to carry messages, the songs would have been understood in their own time to be doing "cultural work," and indeed would have been used by their culture in ways that made that work explicit and gave social sanction to their message. For another, as Christine de Pisan insisted five hundred years ago, "nothing gives one so much authority as one's own experience,"[4]

---

[1] Virginia Woolf, *A Room of One's Own* (New York, 1929), p. 35.

[2] D. H. Lawrence, "Study of Thomas Hardy," in *Phoenix: The Posthumous Papers of D. H. Lawrence*, ed. Edward D. McDonald (New York, 1936), p. 496.

[3] J. M. Coetzee, *Life & Times of Michael K*, quoted by Denis Donoghue in *The New York Times Book Review*, 22 February 1987, p. 1.

[4] Joseph L. Baird and John R. Kane, *"La Querelle de la Rose": Letters and Documents* (Chapel Hill, 1978), p. 143.

and it is entirely to the point that these songs were not made by a woman – in which case they might conceivably (though not necessarily) convey the authority of experience – and they are not even a man's portrait of a woman – in which case they would make no pretensions to that authority: rather, they are the *impersonation* of a woman by the voices of male culture, a spurious autobiographical act.[5]

1. She has seen him for the first time, and now he is the only thing she can see.
2. She describes his many perfections, and her own lowliness.
3. He has chosen her, and she cannot believe it.
4. She sings to his ring, which she now wears, and promises to belong to him totally.
5. She asks her sisters to help her prepare for the wedding; at the end she takes leave of them.
6. She confides to him the reason for her happy tears, and shows him where she will put the cradle.
7. She rocks and plays with the baby.
8. His death, she says, is the first wrong he has ever done her, and she can no longer live.

Figure 12.1 Summary of the events of the story

Today it is awkward to hear this song cycle. All its recent commentators seem to recognize that it creates what Judith Fetterley would call "resisting readers,"[6] and with good reason, considering the very different view of gender relations we have from the one represented here by Chamisso and Schumann. It seems that we have developed a number of defensive strategies that enable us to listen in relative ease: one is to seek refuge in autonomism, to focus on "the music itself" and to insist that it, on its own, carries no "meaning." Another is to take comfort in a kind of naive historical relativism, to assume that "things were like that" then,

---

[5] The term is from Elizabeth W. Bruss, *Autobiographical Acts: The Changing Situation of a Literary Genre* (Baltimore, 1976). On authoritative tellings of women's lives in the period, see for example Ruth-Ellen Boetcher Joeres, "Self-Conscious Histories: Biographies of German Women in the Nineteenth Century," in *German Women in the Nineteenth Century: A Social History*, ed. John C. Fout (New York and London, 1984), pp. 172–96.

[6] See Judith Fetterley, *The Resisting Reader: A Feminist Approach to American Fiction* (Bloomington and London, 1978). Perhaps the cycle is also difficult to perform: Will Crutchfield has recently commented that "women today face a considerable acting challenge to perform it without putting the whole thing in quotation marks or a picture frame." We sense, that is, its inauthenticity. See Will Crutchfield, "Christa Ludwig Sings Schubert's 'Winterreise'," *New York Times*, 17 July 1988, p. H 27.

and that it is simply inappropriate to hold 1840s society to 1990s social standards. For a third, there is a thin but helpful veil of distance for us in the kinds of performance situations in which we encounter such songs, formal and professional, so unlike the intimate domestic *Liederabend* of their own period.

A few comments from the literature will reveal these strategies at work. Astra Desmond cautions that "we must ... bear in mind the position of women at that time ...,"[7] and Hans Tischler that the songs portray "truly all that, in the nineteenth century, the title implied."[8] Jack Stein believes that the poems show an "amazing empathy" with a woman's sensibility[9] although he would also agree with Martin Cooper's observation that "certainly the humble adoration of the chosen male that breathes from [these poems] ... wakes very little echo in a modern listener."[10] Eric Sams evidences a truly breathtaking failure of perspicacity, insisting that while "some complain that [the cycle] makes women seem inferior," that complaint is unwarranted because "the girl sings of herself as a lowly maid because she was one, if that helps. In any event, the objection that a modern woman takes a quite different view of her love-life seems hopelessly irrelevant ... "[11]

But such defensive arguments are merely sloppy intellectual habits, and historically inaccurate as well. That is, the peculiarity of these commentaries results from their insistence upon a view of history according to which women "must have" viewed themselves differently in the nineteenth century than modern women do, and in which Lieder texts transparently report these quaint views. (Among the commentators I have read, only one has an inkling of the social facts: Stephen Walsh describes the message of the poems as "an elegant view of how the more authoritarian paterfamilias hoped to be regarded by his wife, and particularly how he assumed she would greet his death."[12]) More to the point is an interpretive strategy which views these songs, like all intellectual products, as bearers of culture, objects that, as Jane Tompkins says, "offer powerful examples of the way a culture thinks about itself, articulating and proposing solutions for the problems that shape a

[7] Astra Desmond, *Schumann Songs [BBC Music Guides]* (London, 1972), p. 32.
[8] Hans Tischler, *The Perceptive Music Listener* (Englewood Cliffs, N.J., 1955), p. 157.
[9] Jack Stein, *Poem and Music in the German Lied from Gluck to Hugo Wolf* (Cambridge, Mass., 1971), p. 119.
[10] Martin Cooper, "The Songs," in *Schumann: A Symposium*, ed. Karl Abraham (Westport, Conn., 1977), p. 104.
[11] Eric Sams, *The Songs of Robert Schumann* (London, 1969), p. 129.
[12] Stephen Walsh, *The Lieder of Schumann* (New York, 1971), p. 52.

particular historical moment."[13] Peter Gay has recently elaborated upon this point:

> Any group that has a solid grip, and can therefore make a strong claim, on its
> members – a religious sect, a social class – attempts to perpetuate itself by
> imposing styles of feeling and expression. It forces appetites into what it considers
> proper channels and organizes communities of fantasies that will appear in the
> attitudes they foster, actions they deprecate, conflicts they exhibit or provoke.[14]

Works of art, that is, provide what Kenneth Burke calls "equip-
ments for living."[15] What we have here, I will suggest, *is* in fact an
accurate portrayal, but of fantasy rather than of reality, of male
ideology rather than of female acquiescence.[16]

My argument comes in two parts. First, I want to demonstrate
the ways in which the *Frauenliebe* songs might have done "cultural
work" in their own time with reference to the actual historical
situation that is their context. I will argue, that is, that these songs
invoke powerful mythic images of women, of marriage, and of
domesticity that had rather recently entered that culture from
surprising sources and for remarkably pragmatic reasons. Second,
I want to suggest that, perhaps because these songs are a sort of
costume role, an examination of the music reveals – despite the title
– a *Herrenleben*. (Whether or not there is also *Herrenliebe* involved is a
moot point.) This masquerade, the "he" behind the "she," is,
moreover, not a symptom of aesthetic failure but a necessary part
of the social message it was the cycle's job to transmit.[17]

---

[13] Jane Tompkins, *Sensational Designs: The Cultural Work of American Fiction, 1790–1860* (New York and Oxford, 1985), p. xi. I have borrowed the useful term "cultural work" from Tompkins.

[14] Peter Gay, *The Tender Passion* (New York and Oxford, 1986), vol. 2 of *The Bourgeois Experience: Victoria to Freud*; p. 140.

[15] Kenneth Burke, *The Philosophy of Literary Form: Studies in Symbolic Action*, 2nd edn. (Baton Rouge, 1967), p. 262. Wendell Stacy Johnson has studied the role of literary work in the transmission of similar aspects of bourgeois sexual ideology in Victorian England in his *Sex and Marriage in Victorian Poetry* (Ithaca and London, 1975).

[16] For an analysis of a like situation in literature, see Mary Kelley, "The Sentimentalists: Promise and Betrayal in the Home," *Signs* 4 (1979), 434–46.

[17] Although it is not my purpose in this paper to explore the biographical aspects of this cycle's genesis in Schumann's own experience, preferring to deal here with larger cultural forces, nonetheless the timing of its composition is suggestive. *Frauenliebe* was written on two afternoons, 11 and 12 July of 1840, according to Schumann's diary. Five days earlier a positive but provisional court decision had been handed down in Clara Wieck's suit to marry Schumann without her father's permission; they had ten days to wait, however, to see whether Friedrich Wieck would file an appeal. Since Clara's father had conducted his side of the case by disseminating scurrilous and slanderous reports of Schumann's character throughout Leipzig – his court depositions are described in detail in Nancy B. Reich, *Clara Schumann: The Artist and the Woman* (Ithaca and London, 1985), p. 97 ff. – and since, surely, only worse could follow if an appeal were filed, these texts with their reassuringly noble and complacent portrait of a young husband must have fairly leapt off the page at Schumann during this tense week.

I

Man's love is of man's life a thing apart,
'Tis woman's whole existence ...   Byron[18]

Present-day critical commentary on the Lied repertory seldom takes the *Frauenliebe* songs very seriously. As it becomes more sophisticated, and more sensitive both to the connection of such songs to underlying tenets of literary Romanticism and to the complex intertextual subtleties created by the musical setting of poetic texts, such criticism proceeds as if the Romantic subjectivity characteristic of other major song cycles is universal, a defining trait of the genre. Against that backdrop, of course, these songs are anomalous at the least; elements that are important in other canonical cycles – the *Wanderjahr*,[19] the struggle of subjectivity against the external world, romantic self-consciousness and irony – are simply not available subject matter, within nineteenth-century ideological parameters, for a story with a middle-class female protagonist.

Not available, that is, for cultural reasons. The normative confinement of women within the domestic sphere – whether real or hortatory – hardly provides the opportunity for "adventures" even of the mild internal sort experienced by the heroes of song cycles. The difficulty is not merely empirical, though, but conceptual as well, arising from a set of essentialist dichotomies dear to the Romantic mind. A male–female polarity, to cite one instance, was so widely equated with one between culture and nature – the female thus identified with natural forces – that the relation of "human" subjectivity to nature, so common a theme in early nineteenth-century poetry and song, is only conceivable if that subjectivity is taken to be male.

---

[18] Byron, *Don Juan*, Canto I, cxciv.
[19] Barbara Turchin has discussed the *Wanderlied* convention and its implications, including the symbolic goal of union with a "female other," in "The Nineteenth-century *Wanderlieder* Cycle," *The Journal of Musicology* 5 (1987), 498–526. Roland Barthes has characterized the special genius of the Romantic lied as its "forgetting" of the gender markings of vocal ranges, its use of a voice *"unisexual*, one might say, precisely insofar as it is *amorous.*" ["The Romantic Song," in *The Responsibility of Forms: Critical Essays on Music, Art, and Representation*, trans. Richard Howard (New York, 1985), p. 287.] This observation seems convincing, viewed from the standpoint of the performance tradition as we know it. From that same standpoint, it is a mark of the anomalousness of the *Frauenliebe* songs that, as Edward Cone has quite correctly noted, we do not accept their performance by a man. [*The Composer's Voice* (Berkeley and Los Angeles, 1974), p. 23.] Will Crutchfield has recently written astutely about the performance by female singers of the

There is by now a considerable literature on the invention, in late eighteenth-century Germany, of *Geschlechtscharakter*, a kind of mythic definition of the sexes which gave rise to such familiar poetic tropes as *das Ewig-Weibliche*. What is perhaps surprising from our standpoint is that such a notion would not have been available to an earlier period; many researchers have documented the transition, in encyclopedias and dictionaries, from functionalist definitions of "man" and "woman" according to social roles and household tasks, to essentialist ones purporting to show that behavioral differences were nature-based – as indeed so much else was taken to be during the nineteenth century.[20] This development has been attributed by some scholars to governmental efforts to stem the tide of certain socially disruptive behaviors, from divorce to infanticide – women could perhaps be most efficiently controlled by persuading them to control themselves, through fear of appearing "unnatural."[21] Others connect it to the development of capitalism, with its attendant need for men to encourage and justify in themselves certain traits of character that might in other circumstances appear undesirable – in Bram Dijkstra's words, for instance, the need of the male "predator" in the business world to keep a female "conscience" at home[22] – and such references to economic arrangements may serve to remind us that the social phenomena in question here belong exclusively to the bourgeois world; that is, no one would expect – or tolerate – such decorative

male-persona cycles and the striking asymmetry of the gender system which makes a male performance of *Frauenliebe* seem a "repulsive" possibility. See note 6 above.

20 See in particular Karin Hausen, "Family and Role-Division: The Polarisation of Sexual Stereotypes in the Nineteenth Century – An Aspect of the Dissociation of Work and Family Life," in *The German Family: Essays on the Social History of the Family in Nineteenth- and Twentieth-Century Germany*, ed. Richard J. Evans and W. R. Lee (London, 1981), pp. 51–83, and Marilyn Chapin Massey, *Feminine Soul: The Fate of an Ideal* (Boston, 1985). For evidence that even female anatomy and physiology were similarly reconceptualized in this period, see Thomas Laqueur, "Orgasm, Generation, and the Politics of Reproductive Biology," in *The Making of the Modern Body*, ed. Catherine Gallagher and Thomas Laqueur (Berkeley, 1987), pp. 1–41.

21 Massey comments: "In order to force mothers to conduct themselves for the benefit of the state, the reformers turned not only to law but also to ... ideological power ... The second [of these strategies] was to prize and praise 'the salutary influence of the mother' and of natural femininity" (*Feminine Soul*, p. 37). In a vignette named for the opening line of this poetic cycle – "Seit ich ihn gesehen" – Theodor Adorno has dourly commented on this phenomenon: "The feminine character, and the ideal of femininity on which it is modelled, are products of masculine society ... Whatever is in the context of bourgeois delusion called nature, is merely the scar of social mutilation." *Minima moralia: Reflections from a Damaged Life* (1951), trans. E. F. N. Jephcott (London, 1974), p. 95.

22 Bram Dijkstra, *Idols of Perversity: Fantasies of Feminine Evil in Fin-de-Siècle Culture* (New York and Oxford, 1986), p. 9.

vacuity from a working-class woman. The historical context of this long-term shift of focus is explained by Herbert Marcuse:

Running *parallel* to the liberation of man as a "citizen" whose whole existence and energies are devoted to "society" and its daily economic, political, and social struggles, is the commitment of woman and her whole being to her house and family, and the utilization of the family as "refuge" from daily struggles.[23]

Medicine, anthropology, psychology, and many other academic disciplines were gradually able to contribute to the effort, as they were later, notoriously, to do in helping socially dominant groups "recognize" differences among the races. And popular culture at mid-century "recognized" a nervous disorder common among young women, familiarly referred to as "green-sickness," whose onset was caused by the contemplation of an impending marriage and its attendant intimacies. Eventually, of course, the sickness was not only expected but *required* in a young woman of good breeding, as evidence of her purity.[24] Thus, when our heroine tells us, in the very first song, that she has been *blinded* by her first vision of this glorious man, we can anticipate with confidence that she will, in a few decades, find her way to the consulting rooms of Sigmund Freud.

Such profound changes in cultural definition often do not rest on very stable social consensus, however; by the *Vormärz* period there was a thriving women's movement in Germany challenging the basis of this new social contract – there was, as well, a first generation of professional women writers – and debates about marriage in particular were widespread and vigorous. In a study of the contemporary situation in England and America, for instance, Carl Degler reports that "in fact there is some reason to believe ... that the so-called Victorian conception of women's sexuality was more that of an ideology seeking to be established than the prevalent view or practice of even middle-class women ... "[25] The cultural work of the arts becomes particularly crucial in this

---

[23] Herbert Marcuse, "Autorität und Familie in der deutschen Soziologie bis 1933," quoted and translated in Renate Möhrmann, "The Reading Habits of Women in the *Vormärz*," in Fout, *German Women in the Nineteenth Century*, p. 108.

[24] See Helena Michie, *The Flesh Made Word: Female Figures and Women's Bodies* (New York and Oxford, 1987), pp. 16 ff. This notion is distinct from, though not unrelated to, "greensickness" as a nickname for chlorosis, or iron-deficiency anemia, common among adolescent girls at this time. I am grateful to Miriam Whaples for reminding me to make this distinction clear.

[25] Carl Degler, "What Ought to Be and What Was: Women's Sexuality in the Nineteenth Century," *American Historical Review* 79 (1974), 1471.

endeavor – the attempt to establish an ideology;[26] Schumann's
songs are entirely consonant, for instance, with Coventry Patmore's slightly later long poem, *The Angel in the House*, published in
England in 1854, which also charts the courtship and marriage of
an exemplary middle-class couple and which prescribes for the
young wife – tellingly named "Honor" – similarly self-effacing
sentiments.[27] But *Frauenliebe* would also have found itself in cultural dialogue with such works as Luise Mühlbach's 1839 tetralogy
of novels, collectively entitled *Frauenschicksal*, whose first volume,
Das Mädchen, portrays a woman's life in seven stages. According to
one critic, " ... Mühlbach describes the destruction of a female
existence from the perspective of the person concerned. Christine
[her protagonist] goes under because ... she does not take to heart
the rules of resignation which applied to her class ... "[28]

Songs such as the *Frauenliebe* cycle have in their presentational
character a stronger and more immediate power to convey such
cultural messages than any literature could. They have, that is,
considerable performative meaning. Though actually conveying
the sentiments of men, they are of course to be performed by a
woman, in a small and intimate room in someone's home, before
people who are known to her and some of whom might well be
potential suitors;[29] she is unlikely to be a professional singer but,
rather, someone's daughter or niece or cousin – an ordinary
woman, significantly enough – and she sings, in the native tongue
and contemporary idiom of herself and her hearers, texts which
seem already to have been popular favorites, no doubt to an
audience of approvingly nodding heads. We are irresistibly
reminded of the familiar cultural trope in which woman is posi-

26 A similar situation in the history of French painting is studied by Carol Duncan in
   "Happy Mothers and Other New Ideas in Eighteenth-Century French Art," in *Feminism
   and Art History: Questioning the Litany*, ed. Norma Broude and Mary D. Garrard (New
   York, 1982), pp. 201–19. Duncan says of this phenomenon, "What these images of happy
   families and contented mothers reflect is not the social reality of the eighteenth century,
   nor even commonly accepted ideals. Rather they give expression to a new concept of the
   family that challenged long-established attitudes and customs" (p. 204).
27 "Man must be pleased; but him to please / Is woman's pleasure: down the gulf / Of his
   condoled necessities / She casts her best, she flings herself ... She loves with love that
   cannot tire; / And if, ah woe, she loves alone, / Through passionate duty love flames
   higher, / As grass grows taller round a stone." Coventry Patmore, *The Angel in the House*
   (Boston, 1856), Canto IX (I:135–6).
28 Renate Möhrmann, "Women's Work as Portrayed in Women's Literature," in *German
   Women in the Eighteenth and Nineteenth Centuries: A Social and Literary History*, ed. Ruth-Ellen
   B. Joeres and Mary Jo Maynes (Bloomington, 1986), p. 67.
29 See Gay, *The Tender Passion*, pp. 7 ff. and William Weber, *Music and the Middle Class: The
   Social Structure of Concert Life in London, Paris, and Vienna* (New York, 1975), p. 31.

tioned, docile and immobile, under the male gaze; and we are reminded, moreover, that it is a crucial part of the effectiveness of this fantasy that she appear to present *herself* so, to speak for herself. The classic formulation of this situation is from John Berger:

... *men act* and *women appear.* Men look at women. Women watch themselves being looked at. This determines not only most relations between men and women but also the relation of women to themselves. The surveyor of woman in herself is male: the surveyed female. Thus she turns herself into an object – and most particularly an object of vision: a sight.[30]

Given the situation, it is particularly striking that the first song introduces "her" as having (already) looked at "him," a transgression swiftly punished by blinding and by her consequent obsessive inability to see anything else – "wo ich hin nur blicke, seh' ich ihn allein." At the close of the song, moreover, the combination of Chamisso's rounded text with Schumann's strophic setting requires her to reiterate her blindness to the same music which originally announced the increasing brilliance of his image – "heller, heller nur empor." The prescriptive forcefulness of this experience helps us to understand what Virginia Woolf meant about women serving as mirrors, and the more so when, in the seventh song of the cycle, our protagonist has learned to rejoice in the observation that her child – male in the songs, as we shall see, though less clearly so in the poems – looks at her ("du schauest mich an ... ").

The postlude to *Frauenliebe*, a recapitulation of the music of the first song, is no mere epilogue in Schumann's customary manner, nor a simple homage to Beethoven's *An die ferne Geliebte*, as many have suggested. It is rather a representation, perhaps one might say a symptom, of cyclicity itself and of the *Ewigkeit* that mythically stands for the feminine, and its presence is heavily overdetermined from the beginning. The opening figure (Example 12.1) is already cyclic, its ending elided to its beginning both rhythmically and

---

[30] John Berger, *Ways of Seeing* (London and Harmondsworth, 1972), p. 47. Later in his text, Berger explains the implications of this cultural behavior for the forms of art: "Women are depicted in quite a different way from men – not because the feminine is different from the masculine – but because the 'ideal' spectator is always assumed to be male and the image of the woman is designed to flatter him" (p. 64). On this point see also Myra Jehlen, "Archimedes and the Paradox of Feminist Criticism," in *Feminist Theory: A Critique of Ideology*, ed. Nannerl O. Keohane, Michele Z. Rosaldo, and Barbara C. Gelpi (Chicago, 1982), pp. 189–216. On the more sinister ramifications of this particular cultural trope, see Suzanne Kappeler, *The Pornography of Representation* (Minneapolis, 1986), especially "Subjects, Objects, and Equal Opportunities" (problem 5) and "Why Look at Women?" (problem 6).

Example 12.1 Song 1, opening figure

harmonically. It frames – both begins and ends – the music of the
first song, which in its turn frames – both begins and ends – the
song cycle as a whole. It is well enough known that Schumann's
epilogue replaces a ninth poem in the Chamisso cycle, in which the
protagonist looks back on her life from some later point and passes
on her accumulated wisdom to her granddaughter. Both poet's and
composer's versions of the story stress the endless repeatability of
the woman's experience, the "all-encompassing and infinite" time
that, as Julia Kristeva has told us, represents the feminine in many
cultures throughout history.[31] There is no question, though, that
Schumann's reading is the more extreme. Torn from all connection
to women's culture – her relation to her daughter and granddaughter, and in other ways, as we shall see, mother and female
companions – as well as from the specificity of her own historical
experience, Schumann's heroine retains only a ritualized, mythic
existence (a modern commentator might, less poetically, call her
"generic") which she, or perhaps another of her kind, is doomed to
repeat each time it comes to an end: though Lawrence is
undoubtedly right to deem woman "unutterable," she clearly is
iterable.[32]

Not only has the female often been associated with cyclic temporality, but shifting gender relations in uneasy cultures have as often
been seen as attempts by the female to break into historical, linear
time – an effort, in Leslie W. Rabine's words, to "enter the historic
process and to become an active agent of history."[33] While Chamisso's heroine has attempted to rupture the surface of her cyclic

[31] Julia Kristeva, "Women's Time," trans. Alice Jardine and Harry Blake, in Keohane, et
al., *Feminist Theory*, p. 35.
[32] In her study of heroines of Victorian fiction, Helena Michie has suggested that the
rampant occurrence of cliché in descriptions of these heroines itself plays an ideological
role as it "defines and perpetuates an unceasingly iterable notion of 'woman' ... " *The
Flesh Made Word*, p. 89.
[33] Leslie W. Rabine, *Reading the Romantic Heroine: Text, History, Ideology* (Ann Arbor, 1985),
p. 5.

time, to live on beyond the death of the hero who (as she has apparently forgotten!) is the only historical ground of her being, Schumann has caught her out in this attempt and returned her securely to her orbit.[34]

II

> ... man dreams of an Other not only to possess her but also to be ratified
> by her.   Simone de Beauvoir[35]

The first poem of Chamisso's cycle presents to us a protagonist in the dark, in a trance, blind. It is across this featureless background that "he" – the genuine hero of the story – will streak with cometlike brilliance. The peculiarly circular motive with which Schumann begins his setting, *ma fin est mon commencement*, heightens this trancelike impression as it continues, obsessively, to interject itself each time she stops singing. One notes, for instance, its precipitate entry in measure 4, on the wrong "foot" in its haste to reassert its seamless presence (Example 12.2). Appropriately, the singer's stanzas do not conclude, each first subverted by a deceptive cadence and then, as closure approaches, subsumed again into the ending-beginning of the cyclic motive. Indeed, there is no complete closure here: even at the last measure the piano's tonic chord is voiced with the suggestive third topmost; its inconclusiveness is, *a fortiori*, replicated in the epilogue at the "close" of the cycle.

But our heroine herself tells us that she is merely background to his foreground – "wherever I look, I see only him" – and his ubiquity, at once constant and protean, is the subject of the second song. Represented by a characteristic dotted arpeggiated *Heldenmusik* figure, he modulates freely and energetically during the course of the song (on this point, more below), and thus more or less literally turns up wherever one looks. In this song the composer's interpretive contribution is particularly evident. The text

---

[34] It seems to me both curious and misguided that musicians always refer to recurring musical material as "reminiscences." Such a notion gives undue interpretive privilege to the first occurrence of any "recalled" music, whereas the recurrence itself may be much more to the point, as so often in life – many of the songs in this cycle suggest instead the appropriateness of the psychoanalytic notion of "repetition compulsion." In the present situation, the common assumption is that Schumann's postlude represents more or less happy memories for the solace of the new widow. But she does not speak of memories – indeed, in several texts including the first and fourth poems she has explicitly repudiated memory; rather, she speaks, dissociatively, of turning within herself, where he now is.

[35] Simone de Beauvoir, *The Second Sex*, trans. H. M. Parshley (New York, 1970), p. 170.

Example 12.2 Song 1, measures 4–5

Example 12.3 Song 2, measures 32–34

consists of six strophes, to which Schumann has added (as often in this cycle)[36] a rounding restatement of the first. For Chamisso, the initial burst of heroic rhetoric lasts only two strophes before the speaker lapses into self-abasement; it is strophe 4 in which the self-styled "lowly maid" advises him, in effect, to pay her no mind. But Schumann's rondo-like arrangement of musical stanzas (AABA′CC′A) oddly reintroduces the heroic figure at just this point (Example 12.3), preempting the "nied're Magd" with its militaristic rhythm and rendering her just short of ridiculous if, indeed, present at all.[37]

But, of course, it is precisely Virginia Woolf's point that she is *not* present: a mirror must show only what looks into it, not itself. Throughout the cycle, our presumptive heroine's disavowals of,

[36] Schumann adds recapitulatory roundings to four of the texts; in poem 1 Chamisso has already done so. This text treatment, in combination with the unusual predominance of rondo-like musical settings, creates a strong and consistent impression of cyclicity in this piece.

[37] This motive is strongly marked by its plagal harmony. Gretchen Wheelock has pointed out to me how the extraordinary prominence of the subdominant throughout this cycle reinforces its generally worshipful aura.

Example 12.4 Song 3, conclusion

and distancings from, her own affective states are extraordinary, and in every case underlined by the musical setting. Song 3 ("Ich kann's nicht fassen") is about misperception, about her having been "tricked" ("berückt") and unable to understand her own experience. The word itself is first set with an appropriate diminished seventh chord, and its implications more fully played out in the song's postlude which proceeds from deceptive (and altered) to plagal cadential patterns (strongly defining dominant harmony occurs before the deceptive cadence; only passing vii follows it), and is further marked by a devious Picardy-esque shift to the major mode (Example 12.4). What the mode change evokes, in retrospect, is the most strikingly alienated stanza in the song, in which Schumann has subverted her melodramatic wish for death by a major-mode setting (mm. 37–40), and her hopes for "unendliche Lust" with a sudden turn to minor (mm. 49–51). Whereas the poetic text moves, albeit limply, toward affirmation – although she does not much trust her perception, she is willing to settle for the illusion of "endless joy" – the composer, cycling yet again, returns her not once but twice to her original state of tricked bewilderment.

Ultimately – in the last song, at his death – the protagonist refers to herself in the third person, "die Verlass'ne." Her dissociative usage initiates an equally dissociative harmonic process, which veers dangerously close to the nonfunctional and thus forms quite an exceptional passage in this cycle. She sings over a V/iv pedal whose meaning, placed as it is under a series of chromatically shifting chords, is not fully interpretable. After a passage in which the bass line drops out completely (while she tells us, twice, that the world has become "empty") the resolution of the pedal occurs, like a thought that has been lost and later recovered. The text echoes this process, as "die Verlass'ne" now tells us that *"ich* bin nicht lebend mehr."

There is no better emblem for the absence of woman in these songs than the narrative gaps apparent in the whole.[38] Such gaps occur on a number of levels and are the artifacts of both poet and composer. In the poetic cycle alone they are evident enough, given a sentimental imagination that could conceive only love and motherhood as discriminable "events" in a female life. But Schumann has created others – eliminating the ninth poem and excising, as well, a strophe from the sixth ("Süsser Freund") in which our heroine confides her suspicion of pregnancy to her mother and receives apparently welcome comfort and advice. The result is her even more total confinement within the space of patriarchy, as the feminist critical metaphor has it, and, perhaps more to the point, the opportunity for Robert Schumann to appropriate those gaps and, thus, control their meaning. Indeed, it is musical structuring that interprets the meaning of all the events of this life, as the tonal layout of the whole makes abundantly clear.

Song:	1	2	3	4	5	6	7	8	Postlude
Key:	B♭	E♭	c	E♭	B♭	G	D	d	B♭
	I	IV	ii	IV	I	VI	III	iii	I

Figure 12.2 Tonal plan of the cycle

Except for songs 6 and 7, all large-scale tonal relations in the cycle are diatonic; it is surely no accident that those two exceptions

---

[38] Elaine Showalter explains that feminist criticism "has allowed us to see meaning in what has previously been empty space. The orthodox plot recedes, and another plot, hitherto submerged in the anonymity of the background, stands out in bold relief like a thumbprint." See her "Review Essay: Literary Criticism" in *Signs* 1 (1975), 435. See also Millicent Bell, "Narrative Gaps / Narrative Meaning," *Raritan* 6 (1986), 84–102.

represent the appearance of a new and intrusive element, the child – or, in proper Biedermeier terms, the "little stranger." (Perhaps it is not excessively Freudian to point out the Oedipal drama here, to observe that the son's birth in D major is immediately followed by the father's death in D minor.) With the addition of the postlude as a ninth piece, the fifth song falls precisely in the middle of the cycle. It is in the course of this song ("Helft mir, ihr Schwestern") that the protagonist is taken from her former life and transposed by wedding march into a new order, an act of musical appropriation which will be detailed below. On the other hand, ironically, all the songs of the first half – until the moment when her bridesmaids are dressing her – are actually about him: his image, his character, his choice of her, his ring. It is only after her enclosure within established patriarchal rules that she is entitled to the events unquestionably her own, pregnancy and childbirth. Her unseemly rupture of the diatonic surface, which might be seen as an attempt to fill a gap of her own making, is repaired by his death and her subsequent recuperation into an infinitely iterable recurrence.

Song 6, in which, as Astra Desmond aptly puts it, "it takes our heroine twenty-three bars of slow tempo to tell her husband that she is going to have a baby and even then it is the piano that has to tell him,"[39] contains the most striking composer-created and composer-filled gap. Notorious, largely because of the coyness with which its vocal line simpers its way among treacly harmonies, the song nonetheless paints a somewhat darker picture than might at first appear. It is entirely in keeping with contemporary social ideology that the virtuous wife should be unable to impart this information, not merely from modesty but, indeed, from ignorance.[40] As the female and the male are associated with emotion and reason, respectively, the song makes clear that, for all her emotional investment, she is not the possessor of the required information. Coventry Patmore again:

> mere love alone,
> Her special crown, as truth is his,
>   Gives title to the worthier throne;
> For love is substance, truth the form;

---

[39] Desmond, *Schumann Songs*, p. 33.
[40] On the censorship and "pruning" of women's literature to preserve this ignorance, see Renate Möhrmann, "Reading Habits," cited in note 23 above.

Truth without love were less than nought;
But blindest love is sweet and warm,
And full of truth not shaped by thought ...[41]

Blind we already know that she is. But we also recall that this gap, this unshaping of her thought, is Schumann's invention; in the poem we learn that knowledge was available to her in female-defined form – "Hat die gute Mutter alles mir gesagt."[42] In the song, by contrast, it is patriarchal knowledge and another form of mirroring that fill the gap, as the composer inserts the heroic dotted rhythms, heretofore associated with the lover/husband, into the space presumably intended for whispering her happy news. The happy news, it turns out, is himself. It appropriates the musical "wedge" figure that enters the marriage in the opening measure of the song, much as the non-diatonic key has intruded itself into the cycle at this point (Example 12.5). Thus, although in the omitted ninth poem the protagonist speaks to "her daughter's daughter," the music seems to insist that the child is a son, the mirroring image of his father. This reading is markedly reinforced by other events in the song, most notably Schumann's singling out for repetition, after the completion of the text and of what would otherwise be a piano postlude, the words "dein Bildniss!" Like the musical icon for the husband/lover, this little image also has pervasive tendencies. The second song closes with this figure – before we have learned its verbal association – as does the seventh song, twice, immediately following the strophe in which she gloats that the child looks at her (Example 12.6).

The acts of mirroring are also acts of male appropriation. Particularly striking is the handling of the fifth song, the central point of the story and the narrative of the woman's transformation from maid to wife. As the song begins, she addresses her companions, enlisting their help in her bridal preparations, accompanied by typical female-identified *Spinnrad* music. Toward the end, her expression of ambivalence at separating from them is momentarily represented with darkened harmony and slowed tempo (mm. 41–42), but then is briskly recuperated within two measures, her flat-VI efficiently reinterpreted – resolved, presumably along with

[41] Patmore, *The Angel in the House*, Canto V (I:81). This passage is discussed in Carol Christ, "Victorian Masculinity and the Angel in the House," in *A Widening Sphere: Changing Roles of Victorian Women*, ed. Martha Vicinus (Bloomington, 1977), p. 148.
[42] *Adelbert von Chamissos Werke*, 4th edn. (Berlin, 1856), vol. 3, p. 14.

Example 12.5 Song 6: (a) opening
(b) gap, measures 22–24

her anxieties – as the Neapolitan of V.[43] She makes up her mind, apparently, that she leaves them "freudig", and the text phrase in which she does so is repeated by Schumann as entree into the transformative appropriation of her melody in the postlude passage which commentators universally interpret as a wedding march. March indeed it is, a veritable patriarchal display: we recognize the rhythmic signature of the husband, "heroizing" the character- istic pattern of her opening invocation to her sisters; thus trans- formed, and fenced in by a double pedal in the bass, she is initiated into a literal process of canonic imitation (Example 12.7).

The events of this story are, of course, not unusual in their cultural context; nor are they unexpected from the heroine's point of view. From the first, she has bravely announced that she is ready to give up her life among her female companions – "nach der Schwestern Spiele nicht begehr' ich mehr" – and we should recognize, furthermore, her culturally-approved payoff in the seventh song as, with the tempo speeding more and more nearly

---

[43] I am grateful to Raphael Atlas for the observation that her disruptive beginning here, on the "wrong" rhythmic half of the phrase, requires the compensatory, recuperative addition of two extra measures.

Example 12.6 "dein Bildniss!"
(a) Song 2, postlude
(b) Song 6, postlude
(c) Song 7, postlude

out of control, she accepts her infant son instead as companion and playmate. A couplet from this text appears on a popular pattern for decorative needlework (Figure 12.3): no doubt, brightly embroidered and hung upon the nursery wall, it reminded young mothers of the sanctity of their calling during 2 a.m. feedings.[44]

As in the society at large, so within the *Frauenliebe* cycle such tidy role assignments may rest upon an uneasy truce or, indeed, turbulence may lurk beneath the gratifying domestic surface. The second song here illustrates such a threatened disruption and its containment with particular vividness. From the beginning,

[44] The illustration is from Ingeborg Weber-Kellermann, *Frauenleben im 19. Jahrhundert: Empire und Romantik, Biedermeier, Gründerzeit* (Munich, 1983), p. 160.

Example 12.7 Song 5: (a) original melody (here, measures 37–40)
(b) transformation (postlude)

Figure 12.3 Needlework pattern with text from Song 7.

melodic material comes in two forms, the striding arpeggiated
figure of "er, der Herrlichste von Allen" and a clearly contrasted
descending second – at first, to be sure, no more than a resolving
appoggiatura, buried unobtrusively in the inner voices of the
accompaniment. As the stanzas go by, the second asserts itself more
and more prominently. After four strophes (set AABA' by Schumann) the music reaches its first real closure (m. 38), which,
however, is immediately subverted by this heretofore subsidiary

motive, now come into its own both rhythmically and melodically, and even able to leap out of its confinement in the accompaniment and prompt the singer into action (Example 12.8). It is to this motive that she describes "die Würdigste von Allen" – dare she imagine it to be herself? – who will be worthy of his choice.[45] With mounting hysteria the accompaniment goads her on through two stanzas of such speculation. More, her distraught energy gradually takes control of the harmonic structure of the piece, as its motion copies the pattern of that appoggiatura figure, from Db major to C major in strophe 5, from Bb major to A major in strophe 6. At this point, in a nihilistic frenzy worthy of a *fin-de-siècle* heroine – "brich, o Herz, was liegt daran?" – she has brought herself and the music to the absolute of alienation, the key of the tritone. Here patriarchal rule reasserts itself; her crazy tonality is tamed and recaptured by the original, triadic motive, which pulls it into an inexorable, rule-governed circle-of-fifths progression (A–D–G–C–F–Bb) that reintroduces the "Herrlichste von Allen" in place of the neurotic, presumptuous "Würdigste." It is almost needless to say that this is one of the songs Schumann has rounded by recapitulating the opening strophe of the text.

This is not the only instance in which such ruptures threaten. Indeed, within the eight songs of the cycle Schumann has provided us with a consistent iconography for their control. In each case melodic–harmonic sequences are involved (representing, generally speaking, mounting emotion), in each the piano accompaniment resorts to obsessive repeated chords in regular eighth-note pulsations,[46] and in each the song's melodic high point is reached, invariably associated with text of a particularly lurid self-abasement. In the fourth song, the otherwise cheerful and calm

---

[45] Eric Sams's elaborate system of ciphers would identify the opening Eb major arpeggio as spelling ROBERT, and another phrase – at "wandle deine Bahnen," m. 21 – as CLARA. Quite apart from the convoluted argument in which Sams has "reconstructed" Schumann's ciphering process, these melodic figures are of course perfectly in keeping with a by then long familiar rhetoric for contrasting the masculine and the feminine. It is inconceivable that if this couple had had different names – Carl and Roberta, say – Schumann would have "cross-dressed" them with the wrong melodic shapes; rather, the putative "cipher-table" would have had to be constructed differently. See Eric Sams, "Did Schumann Use Ciphers?" *Musical Times* 106 (1965), 584–91; "The Schumann Ciphers" and "The Schumann Ciphers – A Coda," *Musical Times* 107 (1966), 392–400 and 1050–51.

[46] In a powerful analysis of Charlotte Perkins Gilman's story "The Yellow Wallpaper," Mary Jacobus has observed of the wallpaper's reiterative design that "the function of figuration is to manage anxiety; any figuration is better than none." See her *Reading Woman: Essays in Feminist Criticism* (New York, 1986), p. 246.

Example 12.8 Song 2: (a) original material, measures 2–5
(b) measures 38–41

"Du Ring an meinem Finger," the fourth stanza is such a passage, its melodic climax coinciding with her expressed intention to belong to him "ganz" and subsiding with her reiteration (at the composer's behest, not the poet's) that his radiance will transform her – another recuperation, one surmises. Song 5, which we have already looked at and which hardly needs further pointing of its motive, also contains one of these distraught strophes (mm. 27–35), in which the relentless patterning of the accompaniment pushes the vocal line gradually upward to its high point on "lass mich verneigen dem Herren mein." Here, as in Song 2, she is immediately recaptured – reminded, by the reappearance of the song's two introductory measures, of what she is supposed to be saying and made, as it were, to begin again.

These analytic vignettes do not, of course, exhaust the revisionary possibilities of a feminist critical reading of this song cycle. They do, I hope, serve to illustrate the usefulness of feminist method as one among several available responses to the formalism which still somehow lingers in musicology beyond its effective demise in other academic quarters. It is formalism, of course – or what, in music, we might more pointedly call autonomism – that has operated most strenuously to obliterate all presence of a cultural Other,[47] and it does so at a great price: the loss of cultural context from critical discourse.[48]

[47] See Michel Certeau, *Heterologies: Discourse on the Other*, trans. Brian Massumi (Minneapolis, 1986), p. 181. See also Craig Owens, "The Discourse of Others: Feminists and Postmodernism," in *The Anti-Aesthetic: Essays on Postmodern Culture*, ed. Hal Foster (Port Townsend, Wash., 1983), pp. 57–82.

[48] My thanks for careful reading and insightful suggestions to Raphael Atlas, Peter Bloom, Jeffrey Kallberg, Marilyn Schuster, Elizabeth V. Spelman, Susan Van Dyne, and especially to Gretchen Wheelock. At the Dartmouth conference for which this paper was written, the comments of Joseph Kerman and Hayden White were particularly helpful and welcome.

13

Operatic madness: a challenge to convention

~~~

Ellen Rosand

Madness might be regarded as a particularly operatic condition. Irrational characters, featured in operas from the seventeenth century to the present, claim, by definition, the right to abnormal behavior; their instability legitimizes their singing. In spoken drama, the mere fact of singing was almost sufficient for a diagnosis of insanity. Ophelia's songs (*Hamlet*, IV, v) offer incontrovertible evidence of her dementia.[1]

Ophelia's appearance in IV, v is prefaced by an account of her mode of speech:

> She speaks much of her father, says she hears
> There's tricks i' the world, and hems and beats her heart,
> Spurns enviously at straws; speaks things in doubt,
> That carry but half sense: her speech is nothing,
> Yet the unshaped use of it doth move
> The hearers to collection; they aim at it,
> And botch the words up fit to their own thoughts;
> Which, as her winks and nods and gestures yield them,
> Indeed would make one think there might be thought,
> Though nothing sure, yet much unhappily.

And Ophelia herself then proceeds to confirm the report, speaking almost entirely in songs until the end of the scene. And she kept singing until she died, according to the Queen's report to Laertes (IV, vii):

> When down her weedy trophies and herself
> Fell in the weeping brook. Her clothes spread wide,
> And mermaid-like a while they bore her up:
> Which time she chanted snatches of old tunes,
> As one incapable of her own distress,

---

[1] Singing was a symptom of madness in the Italian comic tradition as well; cf. below, note 11; also Vanna Gentili, *La recita della follia: Funzioni dell'insania nel teatro dell'età di Shakespeare* (Turin, 1978), p. 46, n. 3 and J. T. McCullen, "The Functions of Songs Aroused by Madness in Elizabethan Drama," in A. Williams, ed., *A Tribute to G. C. Taylor* (Chapel Hill, 1952), pp. 185–96.

> Or like a creature native and indued
> Unto that element: but long it could not be
> Till that her garments, heavy with their drink,
> Pull'd the poor wretch from her melodious lay
> To muddy death.

Ophelia shows other symptoms of her disease, of course, than an exaggerated propensity for song. She also speaks, but in unshaped prose rather than the "normal" language of poetry.[2] And the content of her expression, not just its form, testifies to her damaged condition. Released from the conventional inhibitions of a girl of her social class, her songs are bawdy and her speech ostentatious in its compulsive invocation of folk customs and rituals, of natural lore, to which her madness grants her special access. Uncensored, she readily sees and tells the truth, a truth that is bare, unvarnished by decorum.[3] According to Claudius, she is "Divided from herself and her fair judgment,/Without the which we are pictures, or mere beasts" (IV, v).

Paradoxically, Ophelia's singing represents a loss of control, something akin to her overt expression of libidinous thoughts and desires, a regression to a kind of primitive behavior (to the state of the "mere beast"). She gains credibility by flaunting not only the conventions of behavior (singing instead of speaking, prose instead of poetry), but those of language as well: by breaking rules of logic with abstruse allusions, incongruous juxtapositions, disconnected exclamations. Succeeding one another apparently at random, her ideas are triggered by unfathomable associations as she swings wildly between funereal and sexual imagery and between literal and figurative truth. She is at once strangely cognizant of the impression she is making on her audience – real and imagined – and firmly controlled by her own inner rhythms.

The mere act of repeated singing might have been sufficient evidence of Ophelia's deranged state, but in opera everyone sings; in opera singing is the normal mode of discourse. Clearly the portrayal of operatic madness needs more. It requires that *its* language be shaped in an extraordinary, abnormal way; and its language is really two: music and text.

---

[2] Prose or blank rather than rhymed verse was commonly used for mad characters as well as for fools during the Renaissance; cf. Gentili, *La recita della follia*, p. 46, who cites, in addition to Ophelia, Hieronomo in the *Spanish Tragedy*, Lady Macbeth, and King Lear.

[3] On the invocation of folk customs and the absence of inhibition as symptoms of madness, see Paolo Valesio, "The Language of Madness in the Renaissance," *Yearbook of Italian Studies* 1 (1971), 199–234.

Music and text: two distinct modes of discourse, each with its own potential for expression, rational or irrational, its own rules and conventions, to be followed or broken. The portrayal of madness in opera enlists the power of both – and the conventions of both – as two separate but simultaneous languages, working independently, in conflict, or else conjoined, reinforcing and complementing one another.

Operatic madness can rely primarily on text. In such cases, abuses of the conventions of verbal logic and syntax, of rhetorical order, determine musical expression. By subordinating its own logic to the illogic of the text, music can sustain textual madness. But music can be independently, actively mad; that is, it can ignore or subvert its own laws of structure and syntax with discontinuities or unconventional juxtapositions. Such music serves to intensify or compound – or even substitute – the irrationality of the text with its own. Finally, it may be the combination itself that is mad rather than either of the two components, each element retaining its own syntactic and expressive logic but failing to synchronize or mesh with the other. In this way operatic language can literally imitate the divided self of madness.

Undoubtedly one's most immediate association with operatic madness is the benighted Lucia, who stands for a whole host of demented nineteenth-century heroines. But Lucia comes late in a generic lineage, separated from her progenitors by some two centuries: and it is with those progenitors that I will be concerned here.

The first composer to attempt a portrayal of operatic madness was also the most obviously self-conscious about it – and the most articulate. Claudio Monteverdi recorded his ideas on the subject in a famous series of letters of 1627 concerning an opera on which he was working with the librettist Giulio Strozzi, *La finta pazza Licori* (*The Feigned Madwoman Licoris*).[4] As always, Monteverdi was most interested in exploring the mimetic powers of music. He had recently developed the *stile concitato* for the portrayal of violent, war-like emotions, and he had been turning increasingly to poetry with concrete visual imagery that suggested translation into

---

[4] The letters, to Alessandro Striggio in Mantua, are published in Domenico de' Paoli, *Claudio Monteverdi, Lettere, dediche, e prefazione* (Rome, 1973), Nos. 91–104. For English translations, see Denis Stevens, *The Letters of Claudio Monteverdi* (Cambridge, 1980), Nos. 92–104, and 106.

specific musical figures. In advising Strozzi about the kind of text he wanted, Monteverdi was particularly concerned with the character of Licori, the "finta pazza" herself. He emphasized the need for her continually to express new ideas, actions, and moods that would lend themselves to frequent and strong musical contrasts. He wished the singer of the role to be able to effect rapid transformations, to play "first a man, then a woman with lively gestures and distinct emotions", "to become a brave soldier, timid and bold by turns," because he was "constantly aiming to have lively [and varied] imitations" in the music.[5]

The composer's most revealing formulation deals directly with the musical setting of Licori's mad texts. He says:

> since the imitation of such … madness must take into account only the present and not the past or future, therefore it must be based on the single word and not on the sense of the phrase; when, therefore, war is mentioned, it will be necessary to imitate war, when peace, peace, when death, death, and so on. And because the transformations and their imitation happen in the shortest space of time, the person who takes the principal part, which should arouse both laughter and compassion, must be a woman who can lay aside every sort of imitation except that which is dictated by the word that she is saying.[6]

Once the poetry was composed properly, with the requisite amount of contrast, then it was up to the composer to "imitate" or mime (or create) the madness. Clearly what Monteverdi had in mind here was a special – atypical – treatment of the text that would render individual words as disembodied, disconnected entities rather than parts of sentences, in effect making nonsense out of them. A potential for madness implicit in the highly contrasting, unusually vivid text would be brought out by this particular, unconventional kind of musical setting.[7]

---

[5] Letter of 7 May 1627 (de' Paoli, No. 92): "E vero che la parte di Licori per essere molto varia, non dovera cadere in mano di Donna che hor non si facci homo et hor Donna con vivi gesti, et separate passioni."

[6] *Ibid.* "perchè la immitatione di tal finta pazzia dovendo haver la consideratione solo che nel presente et non nel passato et nel futuro[,] per conseguenza la imitatione dovendo haver il suo appoggiamento sopra alla parola et non sopra al senso de la clausula[,] quando dunque parlerà di guerra bisognerà inmitar di guerra, quando di pace pace[,] quando di morte di morte, et va seguitando, et perchè le transformationi si faranno in brevissimo spatio, et le immitationi; chi dunque haverà da dire tal principalissima parte che move al riso et alla compassione, sarà necessario che tal Donna lassi da parte ogni altra Immitatione che la presentanea che gli somministrerà la parola che haverà da dire."

[7] The setting is unconventional because it removes individual words from their context for the purpose of imitating them. For a somewhat different view of the significance of this kind of localized imitation for Monteverdi's art in general, see Gary Tomlinson, *Monteverdi and the End of the Renaissance* (Berkeley and Los Angeles, 1987), pp. 204–5, esp. note 21.

For unknown reasons, *La finta pazza Licori* was never performed. Indeed, it was probably never even completed.[8] But Monteverdi's ideas left strong marks on a second *Finta pazza* (of 1641) by the same Giulio Strozzi, this one with music by Francesco Sacrati. The text of the mad scene in act II, scene 10 of this second *Finta pazza* – Deidamia feigns madness in order to convince Achilles to marry her – follows Monteverdi's prescriptions for the first *Finta pazza* quite closely, in fact almost programmatically (Figure 13.1).[9]

Like her missing predecessor Licori, Deidamia pretends to be a soldier; she speaks repeatedly of war (letter A) and also of death (at the end of the scene); she effects quick transformations, switching sex and character several times, becoming now man, now woman; first a soldier, then Helen of Troy, finally returning to herself, the abandoned lover; and her moods shift rapidly and wildly from anger through irony to despair.

Beyond Monteverdi's prescriptions, though, Deidamia's text reveals other, even more compelling evidence of her disoriented state, or rather, the fiction of her disoriented state. Deidamia is the author of her own madness; her task as artist is to portray that fiction persuasively, and she presumably knows what will be effective. The symptoms she manufactures to create her mad self recall those of Ophelia: an absence of sexual inhibitions (letter B), the recitation of esoteric imagery – mythological as well as ornithological (at letters C and D); sudden exclamations; imagined

---

[8] An early version of Strozzi's text, in dialogue form, may have been performed at the Palazzo Mocenigo some time before 1627. This is suggested by Monteverdi's letter to Striggio of 5 June 1627 (de' Paoli, No. 95, Stevens, No. 96): "Giulio Strozzi ... having been urged by me very insistently to do me the honour of adapting *La finta pazza Licori* to my way of thinking ... willingly offered his services, confessing that in writing this play he did not achieve the degree of perfection he had in mind, but wrote it in dialogue to provide entertainment at a musical evening which a certain Most Illustrious Signor Mocenigo, my lord, had arranged to give. I, visualizing its presentation with some by no means straightforward rearrangement, did not want to set it to music." This information seems to conflict with that in an earlier letter, of 7 May 1627, in which Monteverdi claimed that *La finta pazza* had been "so far neither set to music, nor printed, nor even acted on the stage." Perhaps, then, the performance at the Palazzo Mocenigo was a spoken one. In any case, Strozzi's three-act libretto, which he revised for Monteverdi, was never performed. The tortured history of this project is unraveled in Gary Tomlinson, "Twice Bitten, Thrice Shy; or Monteverdi's 'finta' *Finta pazza*," *Journal of the American Musicological Society* 36 (1983), 303–11.

[9] There are actually two mad-scenes in *La finta pazza*, this, more extended one, and another in Act III, scene 2. Deidamia is not alone in either scene; in this one, the brief contributions of the other characters, the Eunuch, Diomede, and a member of the chorus, have been omitted from the example (the omissions indicated by ellipses). The text is taken from Giulio Strozzi, *La finta pazza* (Venice: Surian, 1641).

Figure 13.1 Giulio Strozzi, La finta pazza *(1641), Act II, scene 10*

Guerrieri, all'armi, all'armi;	Warriors, to arms, to arms;
All'armi, dico, all'armi.	To arms, I say, to arms.
Ove, stolti fuggite?	Where are you fleeing, fools!
. . .	
La fiera d'Erimanto,	The wild beast of Erymanthus,
L'Erinne Acherontea,	the Acherontean fury,
Il Pitone di Tessaglia,	the python of Thessaly,
La vipera lernea,	the Lernean hydra
Ci sfidano à battaglia.	challenge us to a fight.
. . .	
Mugge il Toro di Pindo,	The bull of Pindus bellows,
Rugge il Nemeo Leone,	The Nemean lion howls;
Udite, udite Cerbero, che latra.	Listen, listen to Cerberus who barks.
. . .	
Volete, che v'insegni,	Should I teach you,
Ingegnosi discepoli di Marte,	resourceful disciples of Mars,
A brandir l'hasta, à maneggiar lo scudo?	to brandish your lances, to handle your shields?
A ferir, à vibrar, di punta, in giro,	To wound, to wield head on, in motion,
Di dritto, e di rovescio,	frontwards, backwards,
Questa fulminea spada?	this flashing sword?
A farsi piazza, e strada	To clear a place and path
Sovra i corpi nemici? ecco un fendente	over enemy bodies? Here's a downward stroke
Come in testa si dona.	to be given in the head.
. . .	
Sù stringete le file,	Come, tighten the lines,
Formate lo squadrone,	form a squadron,
Abbassate le picche;	lower the swords;
Soldato dormiglione,	Sleepy soldier,
Camerata d'Acchille,	Achilles' comrade,
Destati, che il nemico	wake up, for the enemy
Di quì poco è lontano.	is little distant from here.
Armi, armi, armi alla mano.	Arms, arms, arms in hand.
Fermate, o là, fermate,	Stop, hey, stop,
Oh, Dio silentio, oh Dio,	Oh god, silence, oh god,
Tacete, homai, tacete,	be still now, be still.
Chetatevi, chetatevi, che chiede	Hush, hush, for
Il traditor perdono,	the traitor asks pardon
Della schernita fede.	for his betrayal.
Elena bella io sono,	I am beautiful Helen,
Tù Paride Troiano,	You Trojan Paris,
Sù rapiscimi, sù, ladro melenso,	Come, carry me off, come stupid crook,
Stendi, stendi la mano.	Extend, extend your hand.
Ti picchi? ti rannicchi? t'incrocicchi?	You hit yourself? you crouch? you crisscross?
Giacer io volea teco,	I wanted to lie with you
E lasciar il mio Giove,	and leave my Jove
Ch'ogni notte stà meco:	who stays with me every night
Mà stanco dal lunghissimo camino,	but tired out from the long journey
Ch'ei fà dal Cielo in terra,	that he makes from heaven to earth,
Mi riesce sovente il gran tonante	the great thunderer often turns out to be
Un sonnacchioso Amante.	a sluggish lover.
Deh, dimmi, dimmi il vero,	Alas, tell me, tell me the truth,
Se lo dicesti mai,	if ever you told it,
Che fissa pecoraggine ti assale?	what fixed stupidity assails you?
Di che ti meravigli?	Why are you surprised?
Cutrettola, Fringuello, Ocha, Frusone,	Yellow wagtail, chaffinch, goose, hawfinch,
Barbaggianni, Babusso;	Barn owl, idiot,

Non sò per quale influsso,	I don't know from what planetary influence
Ne' miei segreti amori,	in my secret loves
Urto ogn'hora in soggetti	I collide always with subjects
Più stolidi, e peggiori?	ever duller and worse?
Non si può più parlare,	One can't speak any more.
Ogn'un, à quel ch'io sento,	Everyone, from what I hear,
Hoggi mi vuol glosare,	wants to gloss me today,
Mi vuol far il comento,	to comment on me.
A stride quiete, dunque,	Let's be quiet, then
Ad intendersi à cenni,	and communicate with signals,
Alla muta, alla muta,	mutely, mutely,
Pronta man, occhio presto,	Ready hand, quick eye,
Quel che diria la lingua, esprima il gesto	what the tongue would say, let gesture explain ...
. . .	
Aita, aita, aita.	Help, help, help.
. . .	
Ohimè quest'onda, ohimè	Alas, this wave, alas,
E l'ultima per me;	is the end for me;
Dunque pietade in voi non hà più luogo?	Has pity no place in you then?
Non vedete ch'affogo?	Don't you see I'm drowning?
. . .	

E

Verga tiranna ignobile,	Tyrannic, ignoble rod
Recide alti papaveri;	cuts down tall poppies;
Per questo io resto immobile,	For this I remain stationary
Frà voi sozzi cadaveri.	among you loathsome corpses.
Il foco mesto, ardetemi:	The funeral fire, light for me;
Il sepolero apprestatemi:	Ready my sepulcre:
Donne care, piangetemi;	Dear women, weep for me.
Pace all'alma pregatemi.	Pray for the peace of my soul.
. . .	
Son forzate, ò vicini;	I am being violated, o neighbors,
Il mio honor è perduto,	My honor is lost.
Aiuto, amici, aiuto.	Help, friends, help.

fears – of drowning, imprisonment, kidnapping; confusion of identity; and response to imagined voices.[10]

Deidamia's madness is conveyed primarily through her text. Essentially a formless succession of *versi sciolti*, its vivid imagery and rhetorical disorder dominate and control her music, which unfolds a series of literal images in recitative style. Textual contrasts find direct translation in musical ones. Strident, obsessive arpeggios and martial rhythms suggesting the trumpet fanfares of Deidamia's imagined battle yield to extended passages of repeated notes or softer melodic lines to accompany more poignant phrases of text (Example 13.1a).

Particularly on the local level of the individual word, text maintains firm control: words suggesting height or depth, distance,

[10] The method in Deidamia's madness permits apposite allusions to her surroundings, to the theater, the production of the opera itself, and even the sexual orientation of one of the other characters, the Eunuch, naturally. Like Ophelia, she is an uncensored observer of reality.

Example 13.1a Francesco Sacrati, La finta pazza *(1641)*, Act II, scene 10
(from MS I- Isola bella, private collection, [69ʳ–73ʳ])

Example 13.1a (*cont.*)

Example 13.1a *(cont.)*

Example 13.1a (*cont.*)

fe - de. E - le-na bel - la io so - no. Tu Pa - ri - de la - sci - vo.

Sù, ra - pi - sci - mi. sù la - dro me - len - so. Sten-di. sten - di. sten-di. sten - di la

ma - no. Ti pic - chi? ti ran - nic - chi? t'in-cro-cic - chi? Gia - cer io

vo - lea te - co, E la-sciar il mio Gio - ve. Ch'o - gni

not - te stà me - co. Mà, stan - co del lun - ghis - si - mo ca - mi - no.

Ch'ei fa dal cie - - - lo in ter - ra Mi ri - e - sce so -

-ven - te il gran to - nan - te Un son - nac - chio - so a - man - te. [Diomede, then Uno del Coro]

[#]

Deh, dim-mi, dim-mi il ve - ro. Se lo di - ce -sti mai. Che fis - sa pe - co - rag - gi - ne ti as -

Example 13.1a (*cont.*)

Example 13.1a (*cont.*)

sounds or silence are mimed musically, the images essentially
unconnected to one another. And in a final imitation, Deidamia
literally screams as she is forcibly removed from the stage in chains
(Example 13.1b). Only once, near the end of this lengthy scene
does Deidamia's music abandon the role of faithful follower of text

Example 13.1b Sacrati, La finta pazza, *Act II, scene 10*

to display any special awareness of itself as music, an awareness
manifested by interruption of the prevailing prosaic duple meter
with an expanded lyrical section in triple meter (Example 13.1c).

And even here the inspiration comes from the text, from its single
formal gesture, at letter E: two parallel stanzas of *versi sdruccioli,* a
verse form traditionally associated with the powers of the Under-
world.[11] This mournful passage, set as an aria, exploits some of the
associations of affective intensity that are standard for music of this
period: string accompaniment, suspensions, and chromaticism; it
thus completes an emotional swing from the aggressive, confront-
ational opening mood to the soft, poignant mood of lament. Here
music, held in reserve, finally (though briefly) asserts itself.

[11] On the associations of *versi sdruccioli,* see Wolfgang Osthoff, "Händels 'Largo' als Musik
des goldenen Zeitalters," *Archiv für Musikwissenschaft* 30 (1973), 177–81; and "Musica e
versificazione: funzioni del verso poetico nell'opera italiana," in *La drammaturgia musicale,*
ed. Lorenzo Bianconi (Bologna, 1986), pp. 126–28; also Ellen Rosand, *Opera in Seventeenth-Century Venice: The Creation of a Genre* (Berkeley and Los Angeles, 1991), Chapter 11.

In its responsiveness to the contrasts and vivid images of the text, Deidamia's music realizes – though perhaps somewhat palely –

Example 13.1c Sacrati, La finta pazza, *Act II, scene 10*

Monteverdi's concept of localized imitation, whereby individual words are extracted from their context for mimetic purposes. In so doing it sacrifices much of the structural coherence it might otherwise have claimed as music. The niceties of rhythmic flow, prepared dissonance, melodic shape, yield to exaggerated patterning and abrupt juxtapositions – but all in the service of the words. Through its imitative response, the music confirms the discontinuities built into the text, thereby amplifying its madness.

Though itself modelled on the conventions of *commedia dell'arte*,[12] *La finta pazza* may in turn have inspired the development of madness as an operatic convention; certainly Deidamia was followed by a long line of operatic protagonists whose temporary madness, feigned or real, contributed to the resolution of their difficulties. The depiction of Deidamia's madness, dependent as it is on the special setting of a special text, certainly leaves the impression of representing Monteverdi's ideas in action; but, as I have suggested, chief responsibility for the portrait lies with Strozzi's text rather than Sacrati's music.

The power of music is more fully tapped and Monteverdi's ideas more fully realized, not surprisingly, in a work by the composer himself: his Homeric *Il ritorno d'Ulisse in patria* (1640). The opening scene of the third act is a monologue for the parasite, Iro, who laments his hunger, the death of the suitors having deprived him of his source of nourishment (figure 13.2).[13] Although this is not ostensibly a mad scene, Iro's fear of starvation becomes increasingly exaggerated and irrational until, in a radical reversal of mode, it leads him abruptly to take his own life. A strange comic character who achieves a kind of tragic status at the end, Iro evokes a disturbing mixture of laughter and compassion, precisely the combination of affects Monteverdi had sought from Licori. And, in

---

[12] On the convention of madness in *commedia dell'arte*, see Maria Paola Borsetta, "Teatro dell'arte e teatro d'opera nella prima metà del Seicento," tesi di laurea (University of Bologna, 1986), p. 143; also Cesare Molinari, *La commedia dell'arte* (Milan, 1985), p. 122. The topos, which seems to have originated with *Orlando furioso*, became a favorite tour de force for some of the most famous actors (mostly female) in the troupes of *comici dell'arte* who roamed the courts and cities of Italy during the sixteenth and seventeenth centuries. One of the earliest vehicles was *La pazzia d'Isabella*, named for Isabella Andreini, who performed it with the Gelosi troupe in Florence in 1569. In describing Isabella's mad behavior, a contemporary chronicler reported that she spoke in foreign languages, imitated the accents of her fellow players, and sang. The chronicle is quoted in Borsetta, p. 143.

[13] In Badoaro's libretto the scene occurs at the opening of the fifth act. The text is taken from I- Vmc, Ms Cicogna 564.

fact, Monteverdi seems to have used Iro's scene to test this combination, since it was he (and his librettist) who added its tragic conclusion; in Homer Iro ends up as Odysseus' victim, his mangled body propped against the courtyard wall, spear in hand, to scare away the dogs and stray pigs.[14]

Figure 13.2 Giacomo Badoaro, Il ritorno d'Ulisse *(1640), Act III, scene 1*

O dolor, o martir che l'alma attrista,	Oh pain, oh martyrdom that saddens the soul,
Onesta rimembranza	Honest memory
Di dolorosa vista,	of a painful sight.
Io vidi estinti i Proci,	I saw the suitors dead,
I Proci furo uccisi, ah, ch'io perdei	The suitors were killed, alas, and I lost
Le delizie del ventre, e della gola.	the delights of the stomach and the throat.
Chi soccorre il digiun, chi lo consola,	Who will save the starving one, who will console him,
O flebile parola,	O pitiful word,
I Proci Iro perdesti,	You have lost the suitors, Iro,
I Proci, i padri tuoi	The suitors, your fathers,
Sgorga pur quanto vuoi	Shed as much as you want
Lagrime amare e meste,	bitter, mournful tears,
Che padre è chi ti ciba, o chi ti veste,	For a father is the one who feeds you, or dresses you.
Chi più della tua fame	Who now will satiate
Satollerà le brame,	your hungry yearnings?
Non troverai chi goda	You won't find anyone to enjoy
Empir del vasto ventre	filling the voracious caverns
L'affamate caverne,	of your vast stomach.
Non troverai chi rida	You won't find anyone to laugh
Del ghiotto trionfar della tua gola,	at the gluttonous triumph of your gullet.
Chi soccorre il digiun, chi lo consola.	Who will save the starving one, who will console him?
Infausto giorno a mie ruine armato	Unlucky day armed for my ruin,
Poco dianzi mi vinse un vecchio ardito	A short time ago an insolent old man conquered me.
Or m'abbatte la fame	Now hunger prostrates me.
Dal cibo abbandonato	Abandoned by food,
L'hebbi già per nemica,	It was once my enemy,
L'ho distrutta, l'ho vinta hor troppo fora,	And I destroyed it, I conquered it. Now it would be too painful
Vederla vincitrice,	to see it victorious.
Voglio uccider me stesso e non vo' mai	I want to kill myself so that it never
Ch'ella porti di me trionfo e gloria,	shall triumph or glory over me.
Che si toglie al nemico è gran vittoria,	To be able to remove oneself from one's enemy is a great victory.
Coraggioso mio core,	My brave heart,
Vinci' l dolore e pria	vanquish your pain; and before
Ch'alla fame nemica egli soccomba,	it succumbs to inimical hunger,
Vada il mio corpo a disfamar la tomba.	let my body go feed my tomb.

[14] *Odyssey* XVIII, ll. 1–107. This character, and this opera, are discussed more fully in Ellen Rosand, "Iro and the Interpretation of *Il ritorno d'Ulisse*," *Journal of Musicology* 7 (1989), 141–64.

Iro's disorientation is already evident in the text of his monologue. (We may imagine that the composer had as much to say
about this text as about the role of Licori.)[15] Comprising thirty-five
lines of irregularly rhymed recitative verse, structured only by a
brief refrain placed asymmetrically near the beginning and in the
middle of the speech (italicized), it is marked by free-associated
flow from idea to idea that produces a succession of incongruous
images – on the local level they parallel the central incongruity of
suicide as Iro's solution to his deprivation; dissociation is manifested in repeated shifts between first and third person address; and a
disjuncture of tone and subject matter juxtaposes objective, heroic
rhetoric and locutions ("trionfo e gloria," "infausto giorno,"
"lagrime amare e meste") against the basest and most personal of
human needs, hunger. As it gradually gains control over him, Iro
begins to personify his need: hunger becomes his enemy, every bit
as powerful as the "vecchio ardito" Ulisse who has just finished
beating him. "Abbandonato dal cibo," the parasite describes his
suffering with an exaggerated intensity, using a plethora of vivid,
affective imagery that is highly suggestive for musical translation:
"dolor," "dolorosa," "lagrime amare e meste," "l'affamate
caverne."

It would be an understatement to observe that Monteverdi's
setting capitalizes on the verbal discontinuities and incongruities.
For the music so exaggerates these features as actually to dwarf
them in the text (Example 13.2). Monteverdi's approach is, of
course, mimetic, and his musical images include many that are also
found in Deidamia's mad scene: *stile concitato* trumpet imitations for
expressions of aggression, wide leaps and extremes of range to
portray words describing distance and direction, and lyrical dance
patterns.[16] What is especially striking about this scene, however,
and what distinguishes it from Deidamia's, is the musical action,
the impact of the music on the text. For rather than merely
mirroring the verbal discontinuities, the music compounds them

[15] Monteverdi's intervention in Badoaro's text, amply documented by a comparison
between the score and the various manuscript versions of the libretto, is specifically
acknowledged in a letter to the composer from the librettist, who claims not to recognize
his creation in Monteverdi's musical setting. The letter is transcribed in Wolfgang
Osthoff, "Zu den Quellen von Monteverdis Ritorno d'Ulisse in patria," *Studien zur
Musikwissenschaft* 23 (1956), 73–74.

[16] Mimetic treatment of text is hardly limited to the portrayal of madness; it is one of
Monteverdi's most powerful dramatic devices and is employed for a wide variety of
purposes. For a discussion of some of these, see Ellen Rosand, "Monteverdi's Mimetic
Art," *Cambridge Opera Journal* 1 (1989), 113–37.

Example 13.2 Claudio Monteverdi, Il ritorno d'Ulisse in patria *(1640, Act III, scene 1* (from MS A-Wn 18763)

Example 13.2 (*cont.*)

Example 13.2 (*cont.*)

Example 13.2 (*cont.*)

Example 13.2 (*cont.*)

by following its own devices, generating its own gestures. These musical gestures, or images, which attach themselves to individual words, further fracture the sense of the text by breaking it up and stretching it out, imposing upon it multiple, irrational repetitions.

The multiple repetitions, extending in one case to eleven, tend to isolate the word or phrase, causing it to shed its semantic meaning, to turn it into an object embodied in a musical shape. While the choice of words to repeat is usually justified rhetorically – "l'ho distrutta" (eleven times; mm. 101–6), "ah" (six times; mm. 22–25), "rida" and "m'abbatte" (four times each; mm. 61–66 and 88–93), "mai" (seven times; mm. 117–19) – the appropriateness of the particular musical association is not always immediately evident. The exuberant setting of the parallel phrases "non troverai chi goda ..." and "non troverai chi rida" (mm. 55–66), though literally interpreting the words "goda" and "rida," is so inappropriate to the pathetic context of those words as to contradict the sense of Iro's utterance.

But literalism is the key here. For though intensive repetition of a particular literal musical image may decontextualize the word to which it is attached, it increases its psychological resonance. Monteverdi repeats the end of Iro's desperate textual refrain "chi lo consola" ("who will console [the starving man]") as a whole and in part numerous times, setting it to an extended triple-meter arioso over a ciaccona bass (mm. 31–36, 73–83). The musical image, a protracted, patterned dance, may seem incongruous, but, in its reassuring regularity, it actually offers temporary consolation – on the most concrete level of meaning: it provides a calm, patterned oasis within the frenetic, sputtering context of the monologue as a whole. Iro asks for comfort and he literally gets it, however briefly, from the composer. Monteverdi's fragmented treatment may fracture the sense of Iro's verbal discourse, but it thereby heightens its instability – and poignancy.

Some of Monteverdi's literal images are more obviously mimetic and more immediately expressive. Iro's opening whine on a single pitch (mm. 1–8) gains intensity through exaggerated extension, its length measured out and emphasized by an eighth-note ostinato figure in the bass. The word "estinti," repeated three times to a disjunct sequence of descending thirds separated by several interruptive rests, finally extinguishes itself (mm. 16–19). "M'abbatte" pits two overlapping five-beat melodic figures in the voice and bass against a six-beat measure – the three patterns literally beat against one another, creating palpable conflict (mm. 88–93). And Iro's laugh image (mm. 62–66) is so extreme, so exaggerated and stylized that it turns itself from musical imitation to singer's trill to real laugh: Monteverdi here actually enacts the transformation of music into mimetic gesture.

The momentum, spontaneity, and exaggeration of these musical gestures actually succeed in creating some confusion as to who is responsible for them, composer or character; the two seem to merge into a single voice. Having wrested the initiative from Monteverdi, Iro seems to take charge; he becomes the musical image maker madly following some inner drive, a compulsion to repeat and to dissociate.[17]

In tuning itself so closely to its images – madly literal rather than rationally contextual – Monteverdi's setting completely transforms Iro's text into musical language, leaving behind the word – word as specific meaning. But by engulfing and finally displacing Iro's words, Monteverdi's music touches and releases the emotions within them, the vast expanse and depth of feeling below their iceberg tip – feelings too deep for a comic character. What Monteverdi's music supplies, finally, is the justification of Iro's incongruous gesture of suicide.

Music bears a much greater responsibility for the portrayal of Iro's madness than it does for Deidamia's. But it does not adhere any more closely to abstract musical laws. Iro's music is madder than Deidamia's because it is even less continuous, more fragmented and contrasting – and more self-indulgent. That is, in following its own impulses, music departs further from the control of the text. It is irrationally obtrusive and dominant. Though generated by the text, music ends by transcending it.[18]

Although their effects, in the end, are quite different, the musical depiction of Deidamia's and Iro's madness could only succeed within a context that was highly word-oriented, where text interpretation was fundamental to the style itself. In the 1640s, close attention to text was normal. The *seconda prattica* had challenged an older rhetorical system by asserting the dominant role of words in determining musical expression. But words were regarded as parts of phrases or sentences and understood in their context. The sense of a word normally affected an entire musical phrase rather than just the setting of itself. Isolating or objectifying the single word was thus abnormal: it upset the reason and structure of conventional discourse. But it had enormous expressive impact: musical fixation assumed psychological dimensions.

---

[17] The merging of the composer with the character and/or singer who enacts his music is a phenomenon considered at length in Edward T. Cone, *The Composer's Voice* (Berkeley and Los Angeles, 1974), esp. Chapter 2 "Persona, Protagonist, and Characters."

[18] This is an exaggeration of an effect inherent in all vocal music, according to Cone: "... when, as in song, a musical line is combined with a text, it is natural for us to accept the music as referring to a subconscious level underlying – and lying under – whatever thoughts and emotions are expressed by the words" (*The Composer's Voice*, p. 35).

The portrayal of madness, then, exploits and subverts the assumptions of stylistic decorum on which it builds. In so doing, it exposes those assumptions with glaring clarity. The mad-music of Deidamia and Iro worked because it acknowledged the extreme text-orientation of the *stile rappresentativo*. But as operatic language evolved, other features began to take priority. Intimate word-oriented rapport between text and music yielded gradually to a more general, formal relationship, one determined by more exclusively musical considerations. By the eighteenth century, operatic language had coalesced into two conventional procedures: recitative and aria. Recitative, the normal carrier of neutral speech, culminated at regular intervals (usually at ends of scenes) in arias (usually in da capo form) that expressed crystalized emotions (usually a single, specific one per aria). These emotions were generally conveyed by a conventional set of musical associations.

A new conception of normalcy naturally required a revised conception of the abnormal.[19] Thus, in this style, rather than by obsessive attention to individual words, the rapid emotional changes associated with mental instability are portrayed by the unexpected and the inappropriate on a larger scale – by formal or affective improprieties: by unpredictable juxtapositions of recitative and aria or of arias of wildly contrasting moods or irregular form; by the totally inappropriate setting of a particular text; or by the use of music and text unsuitable to the dramatic situation at hand. And, since its own rules were stricter and more prominent – and thus more breakable – music could assume a role independent from that of the text.

In Handel's *Orlando* (1733), one of the many musical incarnations of Ariosto's paradigmatic madman, the portrayal of madness depends on text and music operating as separate entities as well as together, on the subverting of both musical and textual conventions. In his mad scene at the end of Act II, Orlando's thoughts are irrational; the form of his text is irregular; and the musical setting, even apart from the text, is unconventional.

Handel's text, an anonymous adaptation of an earlier libretto by Sigismondo Capeci, presents Orlando's multi-stage vision of hell,

---

[19] This is one of the basic premises of Michel Foucault's classic *Histoire de la folie* (Paris, 1961), revised and translated into English as *Madness and Civilization* (New York, 1965). It is central as well to most of the recent studies of madness in literature and art, including, among others, Lillian Feder, *Madness in Literature* (Princeton, 1980), and Sander Gilman, *Seeing the Insane* (New York, 1982).

S C E N A XI.

O R L A N D O *solo.*

Ah *Stigie* Larve ! Ah fcelerati fpettrì,
Che la perfida donna ora afcondete,
Perchè al mio amor offefo
Al mio giufto furor non la rendete ?
5 Ah mifero e tradito !
L' Ingrata già m' ha uccifo ;
Sono lo fpirto mio da me divifo ;
8 Sono un ombra, e qual' ombra addeffo Io voglio
Varcar là giù nè Regni del Cordoglio.

Ecco la *Stigia* barca.   [*Come s' entraffe in barca.*
Di Caronte a difpetto
12 Già folco l' onde here : Ecco dì *Pluto*
Le affumicate Soglie, e l' arfo Tetto.
    I Già latra *Cerbero*
       E già dell' *Ereba*
       Ogni terribile
       Squallida furia
       Sen viene a me.   *Già, &c*

II Ma la Furia, che fol mi diè Martoro
Dov' è ? Quefta e *Medoro.*
A *Proferpina* in braccio
Vedo che fugge.   Or a ftrapparla Io corro.
23 Ah ! *Proferpina* piange !
Vien meno il mio furore,
Se fi piange all' Inferno anche d' amore.
    III ⎧ Vaghe pupille, non piangete no,
         ⎪ Che del pianto ancor nel Regno
       A ⎨ Può in ognun deftar pietà ;
         ⎪
    29 ⎩ Vaghe pupille non piangete no.
       ⎧ Ma sì pupille sì piangete sì
       ⎪ Che fordo al voftro incanto
       B ⎨ Ho un Core d' Adamanto,
         ⎪ Nè calma il mio furor.
    34 ⎩ Ma sì pupille sì piangete sì.

[*Si getta furiofa mente dentro alla Grotta, che
 fcoppia, vedendofi il Mago nel fuo Carro, che ti-
 eue fra le braccia Orlando, e fugge per aria.*

Fine dell' A T T O Secondo.

Figure 13.3 Anon., Orlando (1732), Act II, scene 11.

SCENE XI.
ORLANDO *solus.*

Ah Stygian *Monſters! Ah ye impious Spectres!*
Who hide that faithleſs Woman from my View!
Why render ye not up your guilty Charge
To my juſt Vengeance and offended Love!
Wretch that I am! abandon'd and betray'd!
The proud Ingrate has robb'd me of my Life!
I'm now a Shade divided from my Self,
A fleeting Shade, and I as ſuch determine
To ſink into the gloomy Realms of Woe!

This is the Stygian *Bark! In ſpite of* Charon
I navigate the dark and dreary Waves!
There the Throne riſes of tremendous Pluto,
Black with redounding Smoak!— *Behold the God!*
How dreadfully he nods his flaming Head!

    New Cerberus *begins to howl,*
    And hideous Furies *grimly ſcowl;*
    From each dark Quarter of the Dead,
    The haggard Forms around me ſpread.

But where's the Fury that alone torments me!
This is Medoro *in the guilty Arms*
Of Proſerpine, *who skims from my Revenge!*
I fly to rend him from her wanton Claſp!
But ah ſhe weeps! Ev'n Proſerpine *can weep!*
My Fury ſoftens, and I'm calm again,
Since, ev'n in Erebus, *Love calls out Tears.*

    O lovely Eyes, no longer flow!
    For; even in theſe Realms of Woe,
    A Sight ſo moving will engage
    Each Fury to renounce his Rage.
    O lovely Eyes, no longer flow!
    — Yes, rather weep for ever ſo!
    For I, to your inchanting Woes,
    A Heart of Adamant oppoſe.
    No Softneſs ſhall my Fury khow—
    —Yes, rather weep, for ever, ſo.

                    O lovely, &c.

Ruſhes furiouſly into the Grotto, which burſts
open, and diſcovers the Magician ſeated in
his Car, who claſps *Orlando* in his Arms, and
flies thro' the Air.

The End of the ſ   nd ACT.

with a piling up of infernal imagery and *versi sdruccioli* reminiscent of earlier mad scenes.[20] The requisite instability is provided here by three major textual articulations (and several minor ones), marked with Roman numerals I, II, and III in Figure 13.3. Conventionally irregular recitative poetry is interrupted twice by unusual metrical passages (indented); unusual because, although their meter signals aria style, neither passage exhibits the da capo form that characterizes virtually all of the other arias in the opera (and virtually all of the other operas of this period).

The unconventionality of these two formal interruptions becomes especially striking when compared with Capeci's original libretto of 1711. There, both passages (marked with Roman numerals I and III on Figure 13.4) were normal da capo arias. It is obvious, then, that in depriving both arias of their da capos and the first aria of its B section as well, Handel's poet deliberately rejected conventional form for this scene.

The musical setting capitalizes on and intensifies the formal unconventionality of the text (Example 13.3). The composer multiplies its discontinuities through musical means. Although he exploits the contrasts built into the libretto between recitative and formal poetry, setting both metrical sections in aria style, Handel imposes his own more frequent, more localized contrasts indiscriminately over the entire text, on recitative and aria alike. In his setting the three changes of mood become eleven. His Orlando is far less stable than the librettist's.

That instability infects the entire fabric of the scene. Within the opening accompanied recitative, for example, comprising thirteen lines of text, Orlando's musical mood shifts at least four times – at lines 5, 8, 12, and 13 (mm. 10, 16, 22, 25, and 28) – the shifts marked by abrupt changes of tempo, meter, harmony, texture, accompaniment, and vocal style in various combinations. The orchestra is especially mobile during this recitative, varying between active engagement with the voice and passive accompaniment, even participating gesturally in Orlando's hallucination

---

[20] The musical setting of Capeci's libretto, by Domencio Scarlatti, is unfortunately lost. On the origins of Handel's text and its relationship to Capeci's libretto, see Reinhard Strohm, "Handel and His Italian Opera Texts," in *Essays on Handel and Italian Opera* (Cambridge, 1985), pp. 65–66. The entire Capeci libretto, edited by Lorenzo Bianconi to show the derivation of Handel's text, is given in the program book published in conjunction with a performance of Handel's opera at the Teatro La Fenice, Venice, in 1985. The mad scene is discussed briefly in Winton Dean, *Handel and the Opera Seria* (Berkeley and Los Angeles, 1965), p. 96.

ATTO

La memoria fcolpita; e in me rinovo
Quel dolor, che levar mi dee la vita.
Non ti trovo, e tù forfe qui vicino
Col tuo Drudo novello vai fcherzando,
E del tradito Orlando
Alle lagrime ridi, & a i fofpiri;
Ma lagrime non fon quelle che miri;
Del mio vitale humore
Sono l'ultime ftille,
Che manda agl'occhi il moribondo core:
Non fon fofpiri, nò, quefti che il feno
Par che languendo efali;
Amor battendo l'ali
Intorno al fuoco fuo fa quefto vento,
Perche viva l'ardor nel fen già fpento,
Et io più non fon'io
Poiche l'ingrata di fua man m'hà uccifo;
Sono lo fpirto mio da me divifo,
Son l'ombra, che n'avanza,
Efempio a chi in amor pone fperanza.
Sì, l'ombra fono, e voglio   III
Ne' Regni del cordoglio,
Fra l'ombre tormentate,
Cercar fe alcuna v'è, che fi contenti
Di cambiar con i miei li fuoi tormenti.
Or sù la ftigia barca
Di Caronte a difpetto,
Già folco l'onde nere; ecco di Pluto
L'e affumicate foglie, e l'arfo tetto.
   Già latra Cerbero;
   E già dell'Erebo

SECONDO.

Ogni terribile
Squallida furia
Sen viene a me.
Ma tra quei moftri
Degl'empii chioftri
Dov'è il più horribile?
Che l'alta ingiuria
Soffrir mi fè!   Già &c.
Quello, quello cerch'io,
Che con volto giocondo, e chioma d'oro.
E' il più indegno, e più rio
Moftro, ch'habbia l'abiffo; & è Medoro.
A Proferpina in braccio
Vedo che vuol fuggir; ma farà invano;
Strappargielo dal feno,
Saprà ben quefta mano.
Ah Proferpina piange; e già vien meno
In me tutto il furore,
Nel veder che fin dentro al cieco Averno,
V'è chi pianga d'Amore.
   Vaghe pupille, non piangete- nò,
   Che ne i Regni del pianto
   Il voftro folo può,
   Deftar pietà:
   Ma sì, piangete sì,
   Che quefto dolce incanto
   Se un giorno mi tradì,
   Hoggi cötro il mio cor forza non hà.
      Vaghe &c.

Fine dell'Atto Secondo.

Figure 13.4 Sigismondo Capeci, Orlando (1711), Act II, scene 11.

by miming his entrance into Pluto's realm with a strangely disembodied, harmonically ambiguous sequence of ascending scale
passages in an extremely abnormal, irregular meter (5/8; line 12,
mm. 22–27).

The major textual articulation between the recitative and the
first metrical interruption of five *settenari sdruccioli* (the former A
section of Capeci's aria text), is marked by a full stop (m. 30), the
standard closing of a recitative that is to be followed by an aria; but
the conventionality of the relationship is minimized by the
repeated earlier contrasts and by the absence of an articulating
ritornello to prepare the potential aria. The aria (or arioso,
because it is so truncated) in turn moves straight into another

Example 13.3 George Frederic Handel, Orlando *(1732), Act II, scene 11*
(from *G. F. Händels Werke,* ed. F. W. Chrysander [Leipzig, 1858–94],
vol. 82)

Example 13.3 (*cont.*)

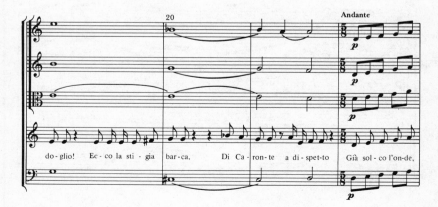

Example 13.3 (*cont.*)

Example 13.3 (*cont.*)

O - gni ter - ri - bi - le   Squal-li - da fu - ri - a   Sen vie-ne a me,   sen vie-ne a me,

40

sen vie -ne a me!   Già la - tra Cer - be-ro,

45

e già dell' E - re-bo   o - gni ter - ri - bi - le   squa - li - da fu - ri - a

Example 13.3 (*cont.*)

sen vie-ne a me,   sen vie-ne a me!   Mà la fu - ria, che sol mi die mar - to-ro, Do-v'è?

Que-sto è Me-do-ro!   A Pro - ser - pi - na in brac-cio   Ve - do che   fug-ge.   Or a strap-

par-la io cor-ro.   Ah!   Pro - ser - pi - na   pian-ge?   Vien

Example 13.3 (*cont.*)

Example 13.3 (*cont.*)

Example 13.3 (*cont.*)

Example 13.3 (*cont.*)

Example 13.3 (*cont.*)

Example 13.3 (*cont.*)

Example 13.3 (*cont.*)

Example 13.3 (*cont.*)

Example 13.3 (*cont.*)

Mà sì, pu - pil - le, sì, sì, pian-ge - te, sì, sì, sì, pu - pil - le, sì,

Tutti

sì, pian - ge - te, sì, pian - ge - te, sì.

Si getta furiosamente dentro alla grotto che scoppia, vedendosi il mago nel suo carro, che

tiene fra le braccia
Orlando, e fugge per aria.

Example 13.3 (*cont.*)

labile recitative passage (Roman II, m. 49), shorter than the first (only seven lines this time) and marked by only a single – and a more subtle – change of mood, at line 23. This passage, too, ends with a complete cadence in preparation for the following aria, creating a major articulation (m. 62). But this aria also begins without an opening ritornello; and its effect is even more jarring, since it brings with it a grotesque change of mood, from adagio, lamenting chromaticism cadencing in D minor, to a hallucinatory Gavotte in F major.

This final aria, rather than representing the conventional point of arrival, culmination, or stability of a typical *opera seria* scene, actually intensifies the instability that preceded it. In altering the original da capo form of this text, Handel's librettist constructed a bipartite aria whose form matches and maintains the rather schizoid dichotomy of its meaning: the opposition between "Non piangete, no" in the first line of the A section, and "Si piangete, si," in the first line of B, a dichotomy that the poet emphasized by repeating each of the opposing lines at the end of its own section (lines 29, 34). This repetition allowed for a direct juxtaposition between the two contrasting ideas at the juncture between A and B (lines 29–30), a juxtaposition that would not have occurred if the original da capo form had been retained.

Handel's setting fully confirms the contrast between A and B. But, not satisfied with his librettist's single juxtaposition of opposites, the composer introduces several of his own by further sectionalizing each of the aria's two parts, creating three additional contrasts to supplement the one in the libretto. He does this by startling changes in style for the setting of lines 2–3 of the A section and the final line of B, changes that heighten the impression of Orlando's irrationality. The opening Gavotte mood of the aria lasts only briefly, for a single line, yielding unexpectedly to a much longer, more fully developed lament (mm. 75–107), laden with all of its traditional attributes: minor key, descending chromatic tetrachord ostinato bass, suspensions, and extended, overlapping phrases. And this is succeeded, just as suddenly, by the return of the Gavotte. The juxtaposition of Gavotte and lament takes advantage of the contradiction built into the text, a translation of which might read: "Don't cry, because even in this kingdom tears evoke pity. But, go ahead, cry."

Handel sets the B section (mm. 120–78) in the style of a typical Baroque rage aria, with its emphatic scalar passagework in the strings and mixture of disjunct leaps and angry coloratura in the voice. The intensity of the rage portrayed here matches that of the lament in A, and the contrast between them certainly embodies Orlando's emotional instability. But Handel adds a final, dramatic touch. Instead of maintaining the momentum of rage to the end, he introduces one further, unexpected contrast, setting the final line of B ("yes") to the music of the opening line of A ("no") (mm. 170–78), which then lends its thematic material to the closing ritornello. The mad Orlando evidently cannot distinguish between yes and no. The result, in spite of the form and meaning of the text, is a kind of musical da capo (or rondo). Ignoring his text, this madman yields insanely to the da capo urge. Orlando's behavior throughout the scene, in fact, suggests that, like Iro, he has taken over the composer's role. He gives the impression of creating and then following his ever new images with a narrative momentum propelled by his torment. But then, some blind, subliminal impulse toward the da capo causes him to disregard even those irregularities given him by his librettist. Having lost contact with the words he is saying, he reverts to his old music.

Orlando's madness implicates both his text and his music. His text is irrational in its ideas, in its discontinuities of thought. His imagined vision of Hades is populated by live ghosts, and his emotions shift wildly back and forth between fury and despair, between self-pity and aggression. The irrationality of his music lies primarily in its form, in the violence of its own discontinuities, which, in addition to intensifying those of the text, make their own mark. The rate of change (in recitative and aria alike), the violence of the changes, and the very nature of the musical gestures themselves are abnormal for the style: truncated, incomplete, incoherent, irregular. Operating against a very strong set of conventions, the conventions of simple recitative and da capo aria, of gradual build-up and culmination of affect, the music speaks an irrational language all its own, suggesting the possibility that it might convey madness even without its accompanying text.

In expressing operatic madness, Deidamia, Iro, and Orlando each depends on a different kind of interaction between text and music, and a different hierarchy between the two languages. Whereas Deidamia's text bears the brunt of the responsibility, forcing her music to mirror it, Iro's music dominates, consuming his text in its voracious grasp. In Orlando's case, text and music operate both together and separately, reinforcing one another but also making independent effects.

If madness is a peculiarly operatic condition because it licenses the suspension of verisimilitude, so opera itself can be said to be generically mad, for its double language provides a perfect model for the splitting or fragmentation of character. The opposition between text and music naturally embodies the conflicting forces that disturb or undermine equilibrium.

The portrayal of madness is an exercise in operatic consciousness raising. For just as each individual mad-scene sheds light on the stylistic conventions of its own period, so all such portrayals, in exploiting the tension between text and music, raising it to a level of primacy, call attention to the precariousness of "normal" reciprocity, of the balance of operatic discourse in general. The portrayal of madness tests the power of the two languages not only to cohere, but to separate.

14

Form, reference, and ideology in musical discourse

Hayden White

The issues raised in this collection of essays touch upon almost all of
the aspects of contemporary discussions of language, discourse, and
textuality: referentiality and theme, voice and expression, cognitive
and ideological codes, audience reception and affect, poetics or
style, figurative and literalist meaning, narration and description.
Moreover, these issues are considered within the context of the continuing debate between Formalists and Historicists over the relevance of knowledge of social–cultural contexts to the understanding of the forms and contents of artistic, and specifically musical
artifacts. Thus, Thomas Grey and Lawrence Kramer deal with the
function of metaphor in the musical production of meaning.
Anthony Newcomb considers the question of plot in the production
of narrative effects in instrumental music. Edward T. Cone discusses the nature of voice in sung speech. John Neubauer, Peter
Rabinowitz, and Charles Hamm deal with the "audience's share"
in the production of musical meaning. The topic of musical thematics is addressed by David Lewin (with respect to power), Paul
Alpers (with respect to "strength to world"), and Ellen Rosand
(with respect to madness). And the problem of ideology in musical
representation is analyzed by Claudia Stanger and Ruth Solie.

Marshall Brown provides a cultural–historical context for our
consideration of these issues insofar as they relate to contemporary musicological research. First, he notes a specifically formal
problem confronting the attempt to answer the question posed by
Newcomb: namely, how *might* music mean? He points out that, in
the musical work, structure is explicit and meaning difficult to
discern, while in the literary work meaning is easily discernible but
structure is elusive. This insight alerts us to the danger of what we
might call "the structuralist fallacy": namely, the belief that when
we have identified a structure in an artistic work, we have also
found its meaning.

Next, Brown reminds us of an historical circumstance that should be borne in mind in any effort to explicate a relationship of similarity and difference between musical and literary expression: our own cultural moment is one in which literature has been "striving toward the condition of music," while music has been "striving toward the condition of language." There has been, Brown argues, a tendency in both music and literature "to substitute *embodiment* for *designation* in order to restore *expressivity* where *formal control* has been lost" (my emphases). There has been a drive toward an "atonal literature" corresponding to Schoenberg's attempt to "emancipate dissonance" in music. Consequently, Brown concludes, the "polarizations" which informed earlier discussions of music and literature *and* of the possible relations between them have broken down. This implies that the critical terminology used in the analysis of both music and literature cannot be taken for granted and must be used with full understanding of its problematic nature.

While the breakdown of the familiar polarizations with which an earlier critical discourse operated has been disturbing, it does provide an incentive for a fresh consideration of the musical aspect of verbal expression, on the one hand, and of the extent to which a semantic content, similar to that figured forth in literary expression, might be said to inhere in musical form, on the other. Efforts in these directions are undertaken in the essays of this volume. Therefore, in my commentary, I will concentrate on our authors' treatments of such topics as metaphor and figuration in music; plot, time, voice, mode, and theme in musical narration; and the relationship between the musical text and its historical context, which encompasses the problem of ideology in musical expression. I will then offer some general thoughts on the viability of looking at music in terms of literary theory and literature in terms of musical theory.

TEXT, IDEOLOGY, AND CONTEXT: FORMALISM AND HISTORICISM

The essays brought together in this volume permit us to see the ways in which the long-standing conflict between formalist and historicist approaches to the study of cultural artifacts has changed in recent years. Charles Hamm remarks on the general reaction in musicology to the older formalist and positivist methods, and Ellen

Rosand speaks of a turn towards a "new historicism" in musicological studies today. The effects of this turn can be seen in the
generally "contextualist" orientation of the essays by Neubauer,
Solie, Kramer, Rabinowitz, Hamm, and Rosand. All urge the
desirability, as much ethical and political as it is theoretical, of
studying the relation of music to the social context(s) in which it is
composed, performed, transmitted, and received. They point to
the desirability of a *hermeneutic* operation, intended to reveal the
ways in which the social context bears upon, determines, influences, or otherwise informs the production, form, content, and
reception of the musical artifact and, conversely, the ways in which
the artifact may affect its context(s). Even the essays by Stanger,
Grey, and Newcomb, which remain rather more formalist in
method, indicate the need to correlate what is happening within
the musical artifact to its generally cultural and specifically
musical "intertext." In this respect, they too are more hermeneutic
than formalist in their basic approach to the problems engaging us
in this volume.

Hermeneutics, however, is no more critically neutral than any
other method of analysis. It, too, presumes a number of different
ways of construing the relation between cultural artifacts and their
contexts. When it comes to the hermeneutic consideration of artworks, two principal orientations predominate: *aestheticizing*, which
presumes that the work of art transcends the social conditions of its
production and consequently yields insight into the nature of
human creativity in general; and *politicizing*, which presupposes
that works of art at least reflect or may even be determined by the
interests – political, cultural, economic, and other – of specific
social groups and classes at specific moments of historical con-
juncture.

These two fundamental orientations of hermeneutic criticism
extend to the consideration of the nature of both "history" and the
kind of knowledge that we can have of it. As in aesthetic hermeneutics, so too in historical hermeneutics: the effort to historicize
the relation between works of art and their social–cultural con-
text(s) can take the form of an essentially aestheticizing or a more
openly politicizing analysis. In the former case, the relation
between works of art and their contexts will be construed as a
matter of certain *similarities and differences of form*; in the latter, the
relation will be conceived as a matter of an *identity of semantic
contents*.

Consider, for example, Stanger's approach to the problem of explicating the relation between the musical and the verbal elements in John Harbison's "Flower-Fed Buffaloes." She concentrates on the *implicit* strategies of structuration – the "codes" which authorize the complex condensations and displacements effected on the paradigmatic and syntagmatic axes of both music and language, not on any superficial similarities of form or reference. According to Stanger, it was the implicit and latent content of the speech by Learned Hand, its structure of oppositions and contrasts and its ideology, that served as the inspiration of Harbison's piece. Instead of setting Hand's speech to music, Harbison apparently chose a number of poetic texts – by Vachel Lindsay, Hart Crane, Michael Fried, and Gary Snyder – which he took to represent the deep structural content of Hand's address as the matter to be represented in his song cycle.

Accordingly, the musical settings of these poems replicate and comment on *the structure of relationships among the poems*; this is what Stanger's mentor, Louis Hjelmslev, would have called the "Substance of Expression" of Harbison's work. The musical settings also reinforce the "Substance of the Content" (the ideology) of the poetic texts, by their supplementary revision of "the Form of the Content" of these poems' thematizations. While generally sharing in the dire vision of America that these poems present, Harbison's settings of them also represent a revision of the traditional musical ideology, the ideology which promoted the view that a musical setting of a verbal text could consist of a simple and direct "translation" of the "meaning" of the latter. The ideology of "New Music," then, what might be called its "politics," is shown to be nothing other than a discovery of the "multiplanar" dimensions of both music and the relations between the tonal and verbal elements in mixed forms such as song or program music in general.

In his essay on Haydn's *Creation*, Lawrence Kramer mentions "a general skepticism about music as a bearer of meaning." If such skepticism still exists, these essays, taken together, should help dispel it. All of them address the question posed by Anthony Newcomb: how *might* music mean? Can music mean or produce meaning-effects similar to those produced in lyric or narrative poetry? In fabulistic or novelistic prose? In didactic and conceptual(izing) discourse? Can music mean in the way that a picture, sculpture, or architectural monument means? Can music assert, predicate, describe, imitate, *refer* – in the way that speech permits?

Literary discourse (as against everyday practical speech) problematizes the relation between what Roman Jakobson calls the referential, the poetic, and the metalingual (or codifying) functions of language. Our contributors have therefore inevitably focused on the extent to which musical utterance manifests the capacity to operate these functions, the ways in which it can be conceived to do so, and the similarities and differences between the meaning-effects produced in musical expression, on the one hand, and literary discourse, on the other. Understandably, then, most of the essays take, as their principal test cases for the consideration of our topic, texts that contain both music and words: song, opera, oratorios, program pieces, radiographs (Hamm), and the like. Only Newcomb and Grey chose to test the thesis that "pure" music, instrumental music unsupplemented with words, *can* narrate, can tell a story, complete with events, characters, plot-trajectories, and an identifiable thematic content. Arguably, this is the best course to pursue, because any analysis of the relation between music and words in a piece that contains a verbal text or gloss, in the form of a title, epigraph, or program notes, will tend to ignore the problematic relationship between the literal and figurative levels of the verbal matter. The tendency will be to treat the verbal text as a fairly easily discernible literalist statement which the musical matter "translates" in one way or another.

This tendency informs Solie's study of the ideology of gender in Schumann's *Frauenliebe* songs, Kramer's analysis of prefiguration in Haydn's *Creation*, Lewin's discussion of power-relations in Mozart's *Figaro*, and Rosand's characterization of the representation of madness in operas by Monteverdi and Handel. In these essays, the verbal content of the pieces analyzed can be taken for granted as the immediate referent of music insofar as it can be said to "refer" at all. By concentrating on musical pieces that contain no verbal matter, Newcomb and Grey are forced to confront the problem of identifying an *equivalent* of a verbal content in musical expression in musical (or musicological) terms alone.

NARRATION IN INSTRUMENTAL MUSIC: GREY AND NEWCOMB

Thomas Grey uses a survey of nineteenth-century musical theorists' notions of the idea-contents ("heroism," "pastoralism," "bacchic fury") of Beethoven's symphonies to pose the question of the "metaphorical" meanings that might reside in the "sound surfaces" of instrumental works such as Beethoven's Seventh Symphony. Concentrating on the metaphoric content and narrative function of the "introduction," he discovers that the music produces a particular kind of *figurative* structure, the "tonal prolepsis," which can be said to narrativize the musical structure of the whole piece on a level quite different from that on which a distinctive cognitive content or *Grundidee* might be identified by a literalist reading of the musical code of the work. For example, Grey does not accept the "tonal progression C–F–E, in which E functioned as the flatted supertonic of the dominant" in the Vivace, as a sign of the "idea" of "bacchic fury." He views it, rather, as a "prolepsis" of the "full-scale transposition of the rounded opening group of the movement to C" in the Finale. The suggestion is that the musical figure of prolepsis endows the work with a kind of cognitive content quite distinct from the thematic material identified by nineteenth-century commentators.

We might call this kind of cognitive content "narrational" knowledge, i.e. the kind of tacit knowledge necessary for the telling and following of "stories." This is a kind of extramusical or transmusical knowledge, because it is implicit in narrational discourse in general: in jokes and fables, epics, novels, pictorial sequences, and even in architecture (or at least, in the decorative surfaces of architectural monuments). Such knowledge is required in any effort to "follow" a story as much as it is required for the production of a discourse that is intended "to be followed" rather than to be grasped "synoptically" as a synchronic structure of relationships. Such knowledge, like knowledge of one's mother tongue, need not be attended by or incarnated in any given corpus of "information." It presupposes some kind of awareness of such categories as "characters," "actions," "events," "conflict," development over time, crisis, climax, denouement, and so on, *and* of the possible kinds of *relations* among these without which storytelling and storyhearing would be inconceivable. We may call such knowledge, following Louis O. Mink, "narrational" – a kind of preknowledge of how to narrativize which precedes any explicit knowledge of any given story that *might* be told about any *thing* whatsoever.

Considered as a figure of sound, prolepsis can be said to mediate between "the Form of Expression" of Beethoven's Introduction and its "Substance of Expression." This "substance" is nothing

other than what is meant by the English translation of the term
"prolepsis": i.e. anticipation. By the use of this figure, the composer signals that something will happen later on that will "fulfill"
or actualize what is now indicated as only a possibility or potentia-
lity. Grey calls the effect of this figure "prefiguration." The music
in which this figure is sounded does not – because, without the aid
of speech, it cannot – posit a "Substance of Content" of the sort
identified as "bacchic fury." In a word, the music expresses a
figure of "narrativity" itself: a "substance" of narrative without
either concrete story elements or a plot.

As thus envisaged, music utilizing the figure of prolepsis can be
said to project a *possible* story. This suggests that endings of musical
pieces which "resolve" figures of conflict posited during the course
of their articulation might involve the use of the figure of antana-
clasis (bending back) or metalepsis (transumption). The important
point is that Beethoven's Seventh can be said to have a cognitive
content of a specifically conceptual kind, but that it indicates,
refers, or represents this content only by way of musical, rather
than verbal, figures. Moreover, music can be said to figure its
content not, as in verbal speech, indirectly, but rather directly. On
this view, music can be said to indicate *literally* the figurative
nature of its conceptual content, which content is "figuration"
itself.

But figuration need not be only diachronic in its articulation. A
given figure of speech, such as synecdoche or metaphor, may
operate on the paradigmatic axis of meaning-production. In this
case, the force of meaning is not produced by projecting "the
principle of equivalency onto the axis of combination" (Jakobson's
definition of the "poetic" function), but is produced, rather, by the
thickening, deepening or condensing of connotative significance at
specific points on the syntagmatic chain. Figures like prolepsis,
metalepsis, metonymy, repetition, produce the narrative effect, but
only a part of it: because, in fact there can be no narrative effect (or
diegesis) without utilizing discursive or descriptive (*mimetic*) procedures.

Grey tells us something important about musical diegesis – and
especially about how beginnings and endings can be joined by
figurations that operate across the diachronic axis of musical
articulation to produce the "narrative effect" without really
"telling a story" at all. The next question must be: can musical
utterance represent the kinds of "characters" and "events" that we

would imagine to inhabit the genres of prose narrative, from the simple fable all the way up to the polylogical novel?

Anthony Newcomb suggests that, in musical discourse, *themes* function like *characters* in novels. If this is so, then it is necessary to show how musical themes can be endowed with the kind of depth and complexity that we associate with characters in novels. In his analysis of "narrative strategies" in Mahler's Ninth Symphony, Newcomb attempts to show how depth of character is produced by the "intersection" of three elements: "formal paradigm," "thematic recurrence," and "plot archetype." Plot archetypes provide a content more "conceptual" than verbal at the level of what we have called, following Hjelmslev, "the Substance of the Content."

But this conceptual content turns out to be, in the Mahler case, the sinusoidal plot type of the Romantic *Bildungsroman* as interpreted by M. H. Abrams in his book, *Natural Supernaturalism*. The conceptual paradigm of Mahler's Ninth, often interpreted as an expression of death-anxieties, is "laid out" in the "contrast" between "diatonic purity" and a "subverting, corrupting chromatism." The "effect is one of placid stability undermined" in a succession of "collapses," to each of which (what we must necessarily construe as) a heroic protagonist responds with a noble, life-affirming exertion. The meaning of the piece, then, "arises ... through an interaction of conceptual plot and the musical paradigm."

One "meaning" of Mahler's Ninth, therefore, is the "story" which Newcomb is able to extract from the "interaction" between what we might call the Substance of the (Musical) Expression and the Substance of a (Cognitive) Content. The former consists of a series of figures similar to Grey's "prolepsis", e.g. what Newcomb calls "slippage," "crux," "repetition"; while the latter consists of the plot type of the Romantic *Bildungsroman*.

But what are the grounds for positing this plot-type as a content of the piece? They appear to be two: first, the general diffusion of the Romance plot-type in the culture of Mahler's time – Newcomb tells us that "Mahler's Ninth works with the same conceptual paradigm" as that formulated in Schiller's "Forward to Elysium"; and second, Freud's theory of the psyche as a mechanism which, according to Newcomb, effects "the transformation of experience by memory". The latter theme serves as the content of the narrative "middle" sections of the various movements and of the symphony as a whole. The symphony's "many returns ... prepared by

mimetic collapses and laborious rebuildings that precede them"
are "attempts to work the primary experience through to a proper
end ..." Thus, "The incorporation of the past as past within the
present through the play of repetition is an essential, perhaps *the*
essential, element in Mahler's last movement."

Now, if this reading of the symphony is creditable, then it gives
us some insight into the relation between Romanticism and that
Modernism which is usually interpreted as a reaction against
(among other things) Romanticism. We can see how, in the case of
the "modernist" Mahler at least, a Romanticist world-view – in
the guise of Schiller's injunction to "look, not backward to
Arcadia, but forward to Elysium" – is the sublimated *content* of
modernist atonal *form*. "Diatonic" harmonics equals spiritual
"purity," while "chromatism" equals "corruption." The symphony as a whole *affirms* the desirability of a Romanticist purity
over against the debilitating urgencies of Modernist corruption.
But, on Newcomb's account, what Alpers calls the "mode" of the
piece remains distinctively modernist in its refusal finally, in its
ending, to "affirm" or even to "assert" the possibility of human
"triumph" over temporality. "The question as to whether the
symphony presents the *triumph* of temporality or the *suspension* of
temporality is left in a state of ambiguous uncertainty." The
difference between this uncertainty and the chest-thumping "cer-
tainty" of Romanticist heroism is the difference between Modernism and Romanticism in general.

The *story*, then, that we must construct on the basis of our
understanding of the musical form and the culturally provided
plot-content is a story of the "working through" of the ambiguities
and ambivalences of a Romantic world-view chastened by the
experiences of a modern world deprived of its enabling illusions.
This story is not so much *implicit* in the symphony (it cannot be
deduced analytically from the music as such) as rather *latent* within
it. The story is, in a word, the Unconscious of the text, a latent
content of the text's Unconscious. In psychoanalytical terms, it
corresponds to the "dream-thoughts" as against the "dream-
contents" expressed on the musical surface. Such latent matter can
be got at only through the postulation of some universal structure
of consciousness or master-narrative considered to be even more
basic, more primary than the dream-images themselves: for
example, the Freudian Oedipal drama or "family romance."

Newcomb does not go quite this far. Instead, he posits a specific

version of this psychic theatre, the Romance version, which differs
from the Freudian version by virtue of its sublimation of the son's
conflict with the father or the social system which the father
represents, into a melodramatic conflict of the "pure" youth coming
to grips with a *metaphysical* enemy: time, death, mortality. This
sublimation of the conflict between life and death, grasped in
symbols of a conflict between "purity" and "corruption," is the
mark of ideological discourse in general. Another mark of ideologization is the tendency to leave the apprehension of the *social*
dimensions of individual unhappiness unspecified – in a word, to
leave the conflict and its resolution in a condition of cognitive
ambiguity and, moreover, to celebrate this ambiguity as a kind of
higher knowledge or wisdom. Thus, we are compelled to ask
whether the "ambiguous uncertainty" that Newcomb posits as the
content of the ending of Mahler's symphony is a function of
Mahler's ideology (is it really the "meaning" of the piece?), or
Newcomb's (does he share the Romantic illusion that the meaning
of life is the conflict between purity and corruption, that the
problem is "time" rather than our social condition, and that the
height of wisdom is to leave the question of the conflict between
"the triumph of temporality and the suspension of temporality" in
a "state of ambiguous uncertainty"?), or of an ideology of music
which sees music's value in the circumstance that it can, in Newcomb's phrase, "embody" the "question [of the relation between
"triumph ... or suspension"] concretely without having to *imply*
an answer" (my emphasis)?

IDEOLOGY AND NARRATIVITY

The question of ideology is central to contemporary discussions of
narrative inasmuch as narrativization is viewed as the principal
discursive instrument of ideologization – considered as the production of self-repressing or self-disciplining social subjects. On this
view, ideology is less a specific thought-content or world-view than
a process in which individuals are compelled to introject certain
"master-narratives" of imaginary social and life-histories or archetypal plot-structures, on the one side, and taught to think narrati-
vistically, on the other. That is, they are taught to imagine themselves as actors or characters in certain ideal story-types or fables,
and to grasp the meaning of social relations in narrational, rather
than analytical, terms. Ideologies are apprehended as generic

class- or group-fantasies addressed to the imaginary dimensions of consciousness where infantile dreams of individual wholeness, presence, and autonomy operate as compensatory reactions to the actual, severed and alienating conditions of social existence. The effect of ideology is to reconcile the individual to the feelings of alienation (produced by real social "abjection") by providing compensatory illusions of personal ennoblement through "heroic" endurance of pains actually caused by social, rather than by ontological, conditions of existence. The ideology-effect deflects the awareness of the social causes of alienation onto the cosmos where abstractions such as "purity" and "corruption," "good" and "evil" do battle for the individual "soul."

HOW IDEOLOGY WORKS: KRAMER, SOLIE AND ROSAND

The ways in which ideology does its work or plays its game can be seen in Kramer's study of Haydn's *Creation*, Solie's analysis of Schumann's *Frauenliebe* songs, and Rosand's treatment of Handel and Monteverdi.

Let us begin with Kramer's treatment of music as "a bearer of meaning" in his analysis of Haydn's *Creation*. Unlike Newcomb and Grey, who deal with instrumental pieces, Kramer does not have to extract the equivalent of a verbal meaning from the music, because *The Creation* already has a verbal text. But the text is uncertain. There are at least two and possibly three verbal texts. On the one hand, there is the *manifest* biblical account of the effects of the generative word(s) of the two Testaments; on the other, there is the text of Laplace's nebular hypothesis postulated by Kramer as an element of the work's *possible* conceptual content. Kramer wishes to determine the extent to which the musical setting can be said to refer to or to represent the cognitive contents of these texts. He wishes, as he puts it, to "correlate" the musical with the verbal content of the work by showing how the score "condenses" and "reinterprets" the "discursive field" by musical *means*. It is not a text–context relationship that is involved, Kramer tells us, but rather a "dialogical" one.

The key to the understanding of this correlation is a theory of musical metaphor, construed apparently on the basis of Peirce's theory of signs and Austin's theory of performative utterances ("speech acts"). Taking the introduction of "the Representation of

Chaos" as a "preparation" for the appearance of "Logos,"
Kramer identifies an "unharmonized C" as an "*Ur*-sound" which
both signifies the primal chaos and serves as a "nucleus" of "everything to follow." In Grey's terms, this unharmonized C is a figure
of prolepsis; Kramer says that it "prefigures" the "harmonic significance" of the C minor that finally appears in measure 4.

In his analysis of the "melodic representation of [the] divine
word ... that closes the music of chaos," Kramer hears in "this
figure ... a musical representation of the Spirit of God descending
to hover over the waters." Here Kramer can be said to be moving
from the Expression plane to the Content plane of the musical
discourse. The movement enacts or performs a "figure of descent,"
of "divine catabasis."

Kramer grants that "agreement about the form [of this Representation of Chaos] seems impossible to reach," but, he avers,
"certain formal intentions ... are unmistakable": "recapitulation
and movement towards an extended dominant." Moreover, he
insists, these intentions "contradict each other." The dominant, he
says, "commands immediate expectation," but Haydn "drives the
intelligibility of the dominant into the structural background ...
[the] classical recapitulation ... is abrogated." The "paradoxes"
are what yield the figurated "fullness" of the utterance of the
divine word. And the effect: to make the "light hearable." The
"ear of reason" is elevated over and made privy to a knowledge to
which the "eye of reason" must remain blind.

Music, Kramer concludes, "becomes representational not in
direct relation to social or physical reality, but in relation to
tropes." The (or a) "musical likeness" of Chaos or of "the spirit of
God descending" or of the "divine word" does not represent these
objects mimetically but, rather, metaphorically. Thus, Kramer
says, "The musical likeness is the equivalent of a metaphor ...,"
and "music becomes representational not in direct relation to
social or physical reality but in relation to *tropes*." In a word, the
references in Haydn's *Creation* are to figures of thought, such as, for
example, "paradoxicality." Indeed, it is only by referring us to a
figure of thought such as "paradoxicality" by way of the "contradiction" between the musical figures of "recapitulation" and
"movement" that Haydn can posit the (catachretic) figure of a
"seeing ear" – the "ear" that "hears" the "divine light," and, in
hearing it, grasps "the divine truth inscribed in the order of
nature." Thus, Haydn's narrative of Creation, in contrast to that

given in the words of both Genesis and St. John's Gospel, effects a synthesis of religious and scientific versions of truth – "touch[ing] our human senses as a primary image for Enlightenment itself."

Now, the ideology of knowledge revealed in this analysis is that which seeks to convince that any "contradiction" that might *appear* between religious faith and scientific reason is *only* apparent, that in reality the two visions are resolvable in an apprehension of a higher truth than that which can be given by perception or by a thought unaided by revelation. The organ posited as the instrument of this insight is not that of any of the senses used alone or in combination, but rather that of an organ (the ear) which has taken over the function of another (the eye). The "hearing eye," like Addison's "shining voices" of the heavenly "orbs," figures forth – catachretically (like Milton's "blind mouths") – a truth unknowable to reason's demands for a merely logical coherence.

But is this ideology Haydn's or Kramer's? More Kramer's than Haydn's, I would say; but there seems to be a truth in it which points, metaphorically or figuratively, to a specifically "musicological" ideology: namely, the belief that the *meaning* borne by musical utterance has to do with rhythms, meters, and modes of *bodily* existence. Arguably, it is these that give to speech what Jakobson calls its "sound shape" in both poetic and prosaic, and therefore narrative, utterance. For whatever else narrative discourse may be, it differs from dissertative discourse in virtue of its efforts to capture in language the conflicts, dissonances, and contradictions of human existence *and* social being. *Its* resolutions or closes are always forced, arbitrary, partial in some way. By moving to a plane of pure relationships, beyond the messy ambiguities of incarnated existence, music can give expression to, represent, and mimetically reproduce the *kinds* of conflicts and contradictions that *are* structurally resolvable. But resolvable only in a figurative way: as catachresis, irony, oxymoron, and other figures are resolvable by being *transumed* in a *vision*, metaphysical or mystical, of a "coincidentia oppositorum."

The question of knowledge and power as the basis of ideologization is addressed in Ruth Solie's essay on "The Gendered Self in Schumann's *Frauenliebe* Songs." She analyzes the ideology of gender informing Chamisso's poem cycle and Schumann's setting of it. She argues that both the verbal texts and their musical settings reflect the patriarchalist–mysogynist social code of early nineteenth-century Europe. They do so, moreover, not so much by speaking to or about women as, rather, by *impersonating* women. Here are two males presuming to "masquerade" as women and speak with women's voices. The ideological content of the song-cycle, then, is not so much its *mis*representation of women (indeed, the songs convey what the patriarchalist social system demanded of women in the way of subjection and abjection all too accurately), as, rather, the trick that is played on women by providing them with (falsely feminized) male voices.

Solie thus identifies the (expression of the) Content of the song cycle as an idealized or imaginary story of the woman whose being is comprised solely of her function as a "reflecting mirror" of her "heroic" husband. It is thus he and not she who emerges as the real protagonist of the cycle and as the ideal "author" of whatever pseudo-subjectivity the woman can ever lay claim to. Solie interprets the cycle, then, as an *apparatus* for the "alienation" of women from themselves and others and their transformation into little more than dummies of their ventriloquist male rulers.

How this apparatus operates can be seen most clearly in her analysis of Song 3 of the cycle, a passage of which she characterizes as "the most strikingly alienated stanza in the song." This song ("Ich kann's nicht fassen"), she says, "is about misperception," about the heroine's "having been 'tricked' ('berückt') and unable to understand her own experience." The word "tricked," she points out, "is first set with an appropriate diminished seventh chord, and its implications more fully played out in the song's ending, which proceeds from deceptive (and altered) plagal cadential patterns [that are] further marked by a devious Picardy-esque shift to the major mode ..." Thus, Schumann subverts the heroine's "melodramatic wish for death by a major-mode setting, and her hopes for 'unendliche Lust' with a sudden turn to minor ... Whereas the poetic text moves, albeit limply, toward affirmation ... the composer, cycling yet again, returns her not once but twice to her original state of tricked bewilderment."

The grounds for this interpretation apparently lie in the semantic contrast between a "negative" expression (a wish for death) and the putative "positivity" of a major mode setting and, conversely, between a "positive" expression (of hope for endless joy) and the presumed "negativity" of a minor mode setting. A negative is cancelled out or subverted by a positive, and a positive is cancelled out or subverted by a negative. What she has done is to identify the expressive dimension of the Content of Schumann's song.

On Solie's account, Schumann's music emphasizes and as it were "doubles" the affective or conative force of the poem's implicit verbal content. Schumann excises certain elements of the poems and substitutes other, more extreme versions of their misogynistic meanings. And, finally, he fills in "gaps" in Chamisso's narrative in order to figure forth an imaginary *Frauenleben*, the sole "meaning" of which is the idealized *Herrenleben* that is the music's deep content.

All this is convincing, but it should be said that, on Solie's account of the matter, the question of the Substance of the Content of both the poem cycle and its musical setting remains unspecified. For if, as she argues, this is a song cycle in which males impersonate women and speak in an (imaginary) woman's voice, then it is the *latent* content of these *men's* voices, and not what they explicitly say or what is implicitly present in what they say, that constitutes the ultimate ideological dimension of the text. The explicit semantic content of the text is not ideological inasmuch as it is the *literal* meaning and as such is directly apprehendible by its auditor-readers. It is difficult to believe that any woman could not see through this dimension of the songs. How could any woman have been "tricked" by this representation of her life? So, there must be something more going on here than a "trick."

In order to get at this something more, we must ask: what is the "conflict" for which Schumann's song cycle might be considered an "imaginary" resolution? Solie suggests that gender relationships were undergoing radical, and to males radically threatening, transformations in the early nineteenth century. The patriarchalist response to these transformations, she argues, was to set up and disseminate the myth of "das Ewig-Weibliche." Solie says that this myth was not available to earlier cultural formations, but in fact the myth is as old as myth itself. Therefore, it is not the myth itself, which appears everywhere that patriarchy prevails, but its specific inflection in Chamisso–Schumann's use of it that provides its historically specific ideological content.

Considered as an impersonation by males of an imaginary female voice, the song cycle might be viewed as an index of the ambivalence felt about *male* identity – and especially about the identity of the male *artist* – during this particular historical period. The period witnessed a deep transformation of the patterns of male homosocial bonding in which both the ideal of manliness and that of the possible relationships that males might have with other

males, including homoerotic ones, were undergoing radical re-
definition. Moreover, the domain of work, including artistic work,
was being restructured; specifically, while middle-class women
were being relegated to the domestic sphere as the sole place of
their legitimate activity, the domain of artistic work was being
"feminized" – which is to say, marginalized by being made the
sphere of a sensibility more "feminine" than "masculine" in
nature. Considered as the domain of "feeling" rather than of
"rationality," artistic activity came to be thought of as being
inhabited by social types whose gender-ambiguity marked them as
suspect in every regard.

I have no quarrel with Solie's analysis of the musical content of
Schumann's songs, although I would like to have it documented
that major always denotes positive and minor negative or at least
was presumed to have been apprehendible as such at the time
Schumann composed this piece. The crucial point for me turns
upon the fact that the words being glossed by Schumann's music at
the point in the text focused on by Solie are "Traum" (dream) and
"berückt" (tricked). In fact, the passage is not, as Solie claims,
about "misperception," but about "miscomprehension" and "dis-
belief" ("Ich kann's *nicht fassen, nicht glauben*") and their cause
("es hat ein *Traum* mich *berückt*"). It is a "dream" that "has
tricked" her. Can the word *berückt* be read as a "subversion" of the
insight contained in the phrase "a dream has tricked me" or "I
have been taken in by a dream"? Or can it be plausibly interpreted
as a reinforcement of the insight contained in the expression? For,
on Solie's account, the heroine has indeed "been taken in."

But is this not an affirmation – on the figurative level – of the
truth contained in the expression of "tricked bewilderment" on the
literal level of the heroine's verbal utterance? Is not Schumann
suggesting, against the "moves ... towards affirmation" of Chamisso's text, that the heroine has indeed been tricked by a "dream"
and that her perception of her own "bewilderment" is a true
perception of her condition? Is not Schumann's subversion of the
heroine's melodramatic wish for death and her hopes for endless
joy more *realistic* than Chamisso's representations of these feelings
as evidence of her true passion?

Of course, we cannot decide the matter definitively. If Schumann's music is a subversion of Chamisso's verbal text, what is
being subverted: the literal or the figurative, the denoted or the
connoted content of the verbal assertion? When the heroine asserts

that, "Es hat ein Traum mich berückt," she is speaking figuratively: she asserts that she has been "tricked" by a "dream."
"Traum" here has to be read as "illusion," and it is set in a
diminished seventh chord. Why a diminished seventh? What does a
setting in diminished seventh *do*? Does this setting subvert the force
of the assertion and its possible truth or does it reinforce the sense of
the "illusory" nature of the dream that is causing the heroine's
incapacity to "comprehend" and "believe" her feelings and perceptions? Does it mean that she really has been tricked or that she
has not?

Solie's discussion of the "figure of woman" in the *Frauenliebe*
cycle reveals the relation between the expression plane and the
content plane of a musical discourse that has been added to the
verbal discourse of Chamisso's poem cycle. This musical supplement is a product of a specifically musical figuration of an
already figured verbal "content." In the process of supplemen-
tation, the techniques of condensation, displacement, and iconici-
zation are used to "revise" the verbal text in conformity to impulses both conscious and unconscious. The ideology of the piece
consists of the relationships obtaining between these two kinds of
impulses. This permits the distinction between what is *implicit* in
the text and what is or remains only *latent* within it. The former
content can be derived by logical analysis from explicitly stated
assertions about the nature of "reality" – "a woman's love and
life." The latter can only be derived by analysis of the figuratively
connoted content of what is only *denoted* on the literal and manifest
levels of the text (musical and verbal).

The distinction between the implicit content of a text and what
is latent within it poses distinct problems for the interpreter desiring to grasp the relationship of the text to its context and thus its
ideological function. The implicit is what is logically entailed, both
as necessary presuppositions and as possible conclusions, by what is
explicitly said on the literal level of the text's articulation. One can
take what has been said explicitly and derive from it a long chain of
possible beliefs, convictions and assertions, to which the speaker
can be said to be implicitly committed by *logical* necessity.

Thus, when Chamisso's text has the imaginary woman speaker
present herself as living only insofar as she can bathe in the
reflected glory of her husband, "the Lord of All," the implication is
that husbands are "Lords of All" and that women properly live
only insofar as they can bathe in the reflected glory of their

husbands. So, too, when Schumann sets the phrase in which the heroine expresses her hope for "endless joy" in a diminished seventh chord, the literal implication is that Schumann intends to "diminish" the basis of such hope.

If, however, one reads both the verbal expression "endless joy" and the musical expression "diminished seventh" as figures, which they undeniably are, then the question becomes: what literal meaning had to be repressed, avoided, or swerved away from, so that it could only be expressed indirectly or figuratively? In fact, "endless joy" is an example of the figure of hyperbole and "diminished seventh" is or at least functions here as an instance of the figure of litotes or understatement. Could we gain a more complete understanding of the work under study, and moreover of its ideologizing function, by augmenting our logical analysis of what it explicitly says with a rhetorical analysis of what it figuratively expresses and therefore latently contains?

Such an operation is, or seems to be, the purpose of Ellen Rosand's study of the representation of madness by musical means in her analysis of operas by Monteverdi and Handel. She begins by pointing out that, in dramatic conventions in the West, madness is often represented by a character's lapse from speech into song. The musical setting of the speech of a character represented in the libretto as mad often serves to intensify the madness-effect by "subordinating its own logic to the illogic of the text," thereby "reinforcing and complementing" the sense of the words. But, according to Rosand, music can figure madness in its own right and does so by the violence it enacts upon whatever stylistic regularities it has originally laid down as the manifest sign of its own "normality."

This is a nice insight, telling us something important about musical expression in general. If one test of sanity is the capacity to use grammatically correct *speech* and logically coherent discourse, then any lapse into singing in the midst of speaking and discoursing must be viewed as a kind of temporary insanity. Or, to put it another way, if a test of sanity is to be able to operate the difference between the literal and the metaphoric uses of speech, then any lapse into singing in the midst of speaking indicates a lapse into pure figuration. (A seventeenth-century definition of madness was the attempt to *live* a metaphor – in the manner of Don Quixote or, later, Madame Bovary.) On this view, one could argue that musical expression or the conjoining of music and words inevitably erases any possibility of distinguishing between the literal and the figurative levels of utterance. This does not mean that an analysis of what is being expressed in musical utterance is impossible; but it does mean that techniques of figurative, rather than of logical or grammatical, analysis are called for.

Rosand shows us the ways in which music can represent madness, not by referring us to a specific conceptual content of the idea of madness prevailing at a given time and place (such as "melancholia" or "hydrophobia" or "paranoia"), but rather by the way in which music can do violence to and undercut its own feigned "normality." It is the sheer "conventionality" of a given style of expression, whether in words or in music, that is exposed when "madness" is allowed to irrupt into the scene of expression or representation. Or is it the madness of conventionality itself, the violence that it enacts upon the self and subject of speech, that is being figuratively suggested in music charged with the task of representing madness? Rosand suggests as much when she concludes: "The portrayal of madness is an exercise in operatic consciousness raising. For just as each individual mad-scene sheds light on the stylistic conventions of its own period, so all such portrayals, in exploiting the tension between text and music, raising it to a level of primacy, call attention to the precariousness of 'normal' reciprocity, of the balance of operatic discourse in general." But, we might add, so too for music in general and beyond that, all poetic speech or stylized utterance. So even for Schumann's song cycle which, in its attempt to impersonate the woman's voice, also "calls attention to the precariousness of 'normal' reciprocity" and the impossibility of representing either a "life" or a "love" except by figurative means.

VOICE, MODE, AND LATENCY IN POETIC AND MUSICAL EXPRESSION: ALPERS

In the case of a musical setting of a poem or piece of prose, we are inclined to concentrate on the extent to which the music translates or glosses the verbal text or, as stressed by Solie and Rosand, the ways in which the music revises and edits the text, reinforcing, supplementing, or subverting its manifest meaning. The danger, I have tried to suggest, is that the manifest meaning may be stressed at the expense of the latent meaning. Among the kinds of latent meaning that might be supposed to inhabit the repressed sectors of a literary text is that which is manifested in the *mode* in which it is cast.

The relevance of the concept of mode to any interest we might have in a historical or ideological analysis of works of art is indicated by Paul Alpers's characterization of mode in literature. He defines mode as "the ... manifestation, in a given work, not of its attitudes in a loose sense, but of its assumptions about human nature and our situation" and, more specifically, assumptions about human "strength [or weakness] relative to world ..." The presumption of strength or weakness is manifested, as Northrop Frye tells us, in two kinds of relationships represented in literary texts: first, the protagonist's relationship to his or her environment, both physical and social; and, second, the artist's presumed relationship to his or her intended audience.

The only difficulty with translating these precepts into operational terms is that the specifically poetic text (with the possible exception of epic genres) typically takes for granted the problematic nature of both relationships as the condition necessitating its composition. It is the *problematic nature* of these relationships that constitutes a latent content of the poetic utterance, however confident it appears to be in the expression of "strength relative to world" on its manifest level of expression. Thus, for example, Alpers shows us how Herbert's "Vertue" plays off a "fairly direct equation of rhetorical and spiritual firmness" against the "suggestion" that "not only the poet's physical being but also his poetry is subject to mortality. The firm conclusions of [the poem's] rhetoric are made out to share the mutability of natural things ..." Moreover, the trope of the third stanza, in which "the death of natural beauty" is figured as "a sequence of musical cadences," suggests to Alpers a "manifestation of a sense of vulnerability central to the poem's [own] rhetoric."

"How does the poem negotiate the tension between spiritual vulnerability and firmness?" Alpers asks. Is Herbert's (or the poem's) voice one which, as Helen Vendler has it, "never gives"? Or is it one that "yields" to an apprehension of its own mortality in what Alpers calls "the rhetorical force" of the last line ("Then chiefly lives")? Or does it both yield and not yield? Does it both affirm and deny, at one and the same time, its own mortality? If so, the poem states a logical contradiction and expresses a feeling of ambivalence about the doctrine of the immortality of the soul. Or does it, rather, simply *posit* the aporetic nature of an *incarnated* spirit, consciousness, or conscience in the elaboration of the rhetorical figure of "paradox"? If so, the contradiction expressed on one level (the Expression of the Content) is deprived of its force at another level (that of the Substance of the Content), in much the same way that what appear to be "contradictory" character traits of a person become, when apprehended as "paradoxical," both interesting and attractive as evidence of that person's "depth."

Alpers raises the question of how one might set Herbert's "Vertue" to music. Obviously, it could be set in any number of ways. Would there be any obligation on the part of the composer to "remain true" to the poem's form or its content or to both of these? It is difficult to say. Should, for example, the composer credit his or her readings of the text, in the way Harbison apparently took responsibility for discerning the real content, not only of Learned Hand's speech, but also the contents of the poems by Lindsay, Crane, Fried, and Snyder? Should the composer consult critics' interpretations of those literary works they have chosen to set to music? What would be gained in the way of understanding the task either of translation or of revisionary setting?

Actually, Alpers's readings of the poems he has chosen to deal with show that something could be gained from such a collaboration. What he has done is to suggest that the meaning of the poetic text is not a matter of form alone nor of content alone but is rather a function of the modalities in which the relations between forms and contents are figured. Thus he alerts us to the difference between the ways in which a discourse produces meaning by way of "codification," on the one hand, and by way of "poeticization," on the other. The difference is that which Alpers specifies as obtaining between genre and mode. We can ourselves characterize genre as a codifying protocol, mode as a poeticizing one.

Roman Jakobson pointed out that the metalingual and the poetic functions of verbal utterances *both* work to project the "principle of equivalence [by which referents are endowed with "meaning"] from the paradigmatic onto the syntagmatic axis" of articulation. But, he insisted, these two functions are opposed in the *kind of equivalences* they feature: whereas the metalingual or codifying function makes unities out of equivalences ("A = A": *Horse* is a species of the class *Equus caballus*), the poetic function makes equivalences out of unities (A = Not-A: "My music shows ye have your closes"; "America, like a hounded shark"; "Women have served ... as looking glasses" and so on). The principle of equivalence utilized in "*Horse* is a species of the class *Equus caballus*" is that of direct predication; the code is implicit but derivable by grammatical analysis of and logical deduction from the explicitly stated elements of the utterance. The principle of equivalence utilized in "My music shows ye have your closes" is not met-alingual; it does not tell us what the elements of the object-language of the phrase ("My," "ye," "your," "shows," "have," "music," and "closes") *mean*. There is a code implicit in the phrase, but it is a local and arguably ideolectal code of figurative conden-sation and tropical displacement. This code is not derivable by a grammatical analysis of and logical deduction from the explicitly stated elements of the utterance. The *meaning* of the phrase, con-sequently, is latent, which is to say psycho-physiological, rather than implicit. The structure of the phrase can be analyzed rhe-torically, but such analysis will not provide a basis for a literal translation or paraphrase of its full semantic content. Recall Marshall Brown's reminder: the structure of a text is not to be confused with its meaning; a structure is a *means* of meaning-production.

The semantic content of a text consists as much of the specific figurations and tropes by which the principle of equivalence is projected from the paradigmatic onto the syntagmatic axis of articulation as it does of what the phrase seems to be literally asserting. These specific figurations and the tropes that effect their specific successivity *mean* precisely by their evasion of every litera-list, lexical, and grammatical expectation.

Thus, the referent of "music" in Herbert's phrase "My music shows ye have your closes" is utterly indeterminable. Even if it is read as a metaphor for the poem or the poetry of the poet, the idea that music could "show" anything, even in the sense of "manifes-ting," "displaying," or "demonstrating," is absurd – a catachresis; but the notion that this "music" could "show" that the "Sweet spring" apostrophized in line 1 of the stanza has *its* "closes" (like the "box where sweets compacted lie," to which the spring is likened by apposition in line 2) is even more absurd. For even if "closes" is read as "cadences" (a sixteenth-century usage), thereby saving the logic of "music" as a figure for poetry, it makes no sense to say that either music or poetry "shows" that "spring" has its "cadences." But the "logic" of the phrase consists of the figures of alliteration ("*My m*usic", "*y*e ... *y*our") and internal rhyme ("shows, ... closes") and the poetic necessity of having an end-rhyme for "roses" which ends line 1 of the stanza. Too much meaning or not enough? Or meaning of a kind different from both grammatical sense and extra-textual referentiality?

So, what might the composer's obligations to the poetic text

which he or she might decide to set to music? On Alpers's view of
the nature of the poetic text, the composer should be especially
attentive to the mode in which the work is cast, the feeling of
strength or weakness relative to world that pervades the text. In
other words, it is not so much a matter of finding musical equiv-
alents of what the text literally says or what it suggests by the use of
specific figures of speech and tropes. It is a matter of suggesting by
musical means the *mode* of relationship to the world that is the
poem's own latent content.

FORMALISM AND IDEOLOGY: CONE AND LEWIN

A consistently formalist approach to the study of musical artworks
is represented in the essays by Edward T. Cone and David Lewin.
In Cone's consideration of the nature of voice in song and of the
persona of the singer in Schumann's Lieder, there is no reference to
the social context in which specific notions of both voice and
persona function as elements of a specific ideology of poetic creativity. There are many references to the cultural and specifically
musical context of Schumann's songs, but the relationships presumed to exist between the sung text and the cultural context are
those of a perfect identity of formal contents. Indeed, Cone appears
to have embraced the ideology of poetic creativity predominant in
Schumann himself if not in Romantic aesthetics in general. This
embrace results in deep insights into the internal dynamics of the
songs referred to by Cone in his explication of the relations obtaining between words and music in specific Lieder. It yields forceful
instruction for the performance of these songs. It leads to the
identification of a specific kind of irony in a composer traditionally
thought to be lacking in irony altogether. In a word, it permits us
to view and to hear Schumann's songs from within their culturally
provided interior.

But the interpretation of vocal persona as the persona of the
composer (rather than that of the poet-singer) remains historically
unmediated by any reference to the ideology of poetic creativity
prevailing during Schumann's time. As a result, at the level of the
theoretical payoff of Cone's essay, he ends up reasserting and
affirming the very Romantic ideology of poetic creativity which he
wished to analyze.

That Cone is more an advocate than an analyst of this Romantic
ideology is indicated by the extent to which he adverts to a

hypostatized notion of a poetic–musical "consciousness" seemingly perfect in self-knowledge and control of its own thought-contents and processes. While Cone refers to the "conscious" and "subconscious" elements of the hypothesized composer's persona, he nowhere suggests that this kind of persona might have an "unconscious," which is to say, be the un-conscious bearer of values, fantasies, and illusions as well as of genuine insights – especially regarding the nature of "personae" themselves – of a given time, place and social-cultural condition. The ignoring of the possibility of an unconscious dimension of the composer's persona no doubt reflects a suspicion of a currently dominant notion of selfhood, Freudian or generally psychoanalytical, which is itself ideological in nature. But without a theory of consciousness that features some version of an unconscious and generally ideological motivation in the composition of selves and personae, the notion of a specifically poetic creativity remains subject to the "Promethean" illusions of its Romantic formulation.

David Lewin's perspicuous reading of a phrase in Mozart's *Figaro* is similarly formalist in method and similarly seeks to avoid consideration of the possibility that the work or its composer(s) operated under any kind of unconscious motivation. His essay, however, is much more pragmatically oriented than Cone's, being more concerned with the derivation of possible "stage directions" from a rigorously formalist analysis of the score than with the "persona" of either the author of the libretto or the composer. What emerges from Lewin's analysis, however, is something like an ideology of the stage director and indeed of the musical analyst that resembles the Promethean and timeless "composer's persona" projected by Cone.

In Lewin's essay, there is no suggestion that the social roles of the director or the analyst might be historically specific, that what it meant to be a "stage director" or a "musical analyst" was different in Mozart's time, place, and social–cultural condition from what it means in our own historical moment. Indeed, both stage direction and analysis are viewed as Promethean activities: the latter leaves no element of the text and score undisclosed, the former supposes a level of self-conscious knowledge of and control over the singer-actor similar to that posited by Cone for the "composer's persona."

Nonetheless (and perhaps this is a result of the *pragmatic* purpose informing Lewin's analytic exercise), ideology – and moreover ideology understood as a practice which reinforces structures of domination and subordination – insinuates itself into Lewin's handling of his materials. It appears in his characterization of the themes of the opera and especially of the passage he analyzes. Note that Lewin recommends "the idea of command" as the "point of departure for continuing and elaborating our [his] analysis-cum-direction" of the opening of the first-act trio of *Figaro*, "Cosa sento!" According to his interpretation of the passage, it is an allegory of outrage and confusion passing over into the Count's "taking command of self and situation" and then "issuing a command."

Lewin makes a persuasive case for the idea that the Count's utterance "Cosa sento!" refers to the music of measures 1–3 (a "loud agitated tutti that elaborates a dominant seventh harmony, demanding resolution") and portrays the "confused outrage" of the Count expressed in his words only in measures 2–3. This provides the basis for the generalization that, first, the Count takes his cues primarily from the music, rather than from the words preceding, and that, second, "Mozart . . . consistently displaces the actual words forwards in time" in relationship to the musical motives that always precede them. Whence, then, the interpretation of the Count's persona: "Mozart's Count does not give impetus to the music by his verbal utterances, as an effective authority figure should . . . Rather, he consistently takes his verbal cues from whatever music he has just heard." And the consequent direction to the actor playing the role of the Count: "the actor should take the loud agitated music of measures 1–3, and not Basilio's earlier disparaging gossip [about the Count] as a cue for the reaction 'Cosa sento!'" Thus, Lewin concludes, "Throughout the first half of the trio . . . the Count continues to take his cues, both thematic and tonal, from preceding music," while "Basilio and Susanna struggle to take control of those cues. They contend in initiating themes and harmonic moves to which the Count responds; each thereby tries to win the authority of the Count to use against the other."

What we have here, then, according to Lewin, is a dramatic musical representation of the loss and recovery of "control," "authority," and the power of command by the Count; a power struggle between subaltern figures, the music master Basilio and the Count's inamorata Susanna, to expropriate that authority for use against one another; and the triumph – at least in Basilio's solo following upon the passage in question – of a "fawning hypocrite"

(Basilio) over both the lecherous aristocrat (the Count) and the lying and dissimulating woman (Susanna).

The whole passage and especially Basilio's solo, as analyzed by Lewin, fairly cries out for an ideological analysis of the extent to which it participates in or resists complicity with the dominant structure of social relationships, class and gender roles especially, of the historical moment in which they were composed. In the "infinite tennis game" between Basilio and the Count, Lewin perceives a figure of "a struggle for power and control between the two males" in which the woman, Susanna, "has no place whatsoever." In Lewin's interpretation, Basilio's victory in this game derives from the "hypocritical fawning" which, in both Da Ponte's text and Mozart's musical setting, is, in contrast to Beaumarchais's original version, elevated from the status of a "flat character trait" into a supreme instantiation of "manipulative mastery" through parody. Basilio's music not only "apes his master's model right up to the final cadence, as if he were about to confirm the Count's tonic closure," it trumps (could we say "deconstructs"?) the model by substituting "C minor-to-F" for the Count's "final harmonies, F-to-B♭."

Moreover, this manipulative mastery is extended to encompass Susanna as well, and by a similarly parodistic gesture, in this case, to the love aria (*Non so più*) previously sung by Cherubino to Susanna. This gesture functions, according to Lewin, as a weapon in the "duel" between Basilio and Susanna "for the Count's authority"; it serves to "outwit and foil Susanna" by making sure that "she knows [Basilio's] suspicion" that she has been dallying with Cherubino and "suspects his certain knowledge." Lewin "imagines" (his term) that "while Basilio's solo is manipulating the Count," he (Basilio) is "casually perusing" a score of Cherubino's song (which may have been dropped in flight from the approaching Count) and "darting one sly leer at Susanna." Thus, while "manipulating the Count in all sorts of ways," Basilio can also keep "a firm grip on Susanna."

Now, Lewin's manifest admiration of the genius of Mozart and the talent of Da Ponte takes the form of a celebration of the power, indeed the *manipulative* power, of the former over the latter and of both over Beaumarchais, the original author of the story. Beyond this: it leads to the suggestion that Mozart and Da Ponte must have admired the manipulative *power* of the "fawning hypocrite," manipulator of men, and suborner of women represented by the char-

acter Basilio in Beaumarchais's story. Beyond that: it leads Lewin
to celebrate the manipulative power of music over words in
general. And, finally, beyond that: in his (admittedly "imaginary") characterization of Basilio as a manipulator whose principal
instrument is, on the one hand, his music and, on the other, his
talents as a "musical analyst" (he is imagined as "casually perusing" the score of Cherubino's song while his "solo is manipulating
the Count"), Lewin appears to be indulging himself in a fantasy of
the power of "analysis" over "performance."

Such celebrations of manipulative power are easily recognizable
as compensatory responses to the apprehension of those who make
them of their own relative social powerlessness. This is not to
demean Lewin or his interpretation of the passage in question. On
the contrary, his analysis of this passage amply demonstrates the
especial fascination which manipulative power held for Mozart, his
generation, and the social groups of his historical epoch. Moreover,
in their ascription of this power to such a petit bourgeois figure as
Basilio, who is after all only a "music master," Mozart, Da Ponte,
and Beaumarchais alike can be seen as participating in a fantasy of
"the democratization of power" that overrides any consideration
of birth or social status (though not of gender). This is a fantasy
quite other than that of "the power of democracy." Lewin shows
the extent to which this fantasy of the democratization of power, a
fantasy which would be theorized in different ways by thinkers as
diverse as Diderot, Hegel, Stendhal, Marx, and Nietzsche, pervaded the consciousness of Mozart himself. But Lewin leaves this
fantasy "unanalyzed." He simply or, rather, complexly shows how
the fantasy works in Mozart's music to endow it with a content or
meaning that can serve as a basis for the "stage director's" manipulative control of the "actor-singers" subject to his "command."

CONTEXTUALIZATION AND RECEPTION: HAMM, NEUBAUER, AND RABINOWITZ

The question of the relation of the musical work to its historical
context is raised in a variety of ways in this volume, but most
explicitly and most radically by Charles Hamm, John Neubauer,
and Peter Rabinowitz. Unlike those who relate the musical work to
the context of its original time of production and its ideological
content, these three critics take their point of departure from the
postmodernist notions of the openness of the work of art and of the

function of the performer and/or audience in the production of the work's possible meaning.

Thus, in his consideration of the reception in black South Africa of Lionel Richie's "All Night Long (All Night)," Hamm first stresses the difficulty of imputing any specific meaning to the work itself; it is, in his view, a "generic" pop hit. This means that the song is a mélange of codes and pseudo-codes which do not – on Hamm's reading – add up to any determinable meaning. Specific meanings are produced, Hamm says, "only at the moment of reception" and are "shaped by the cultural capital of the listener."

Hamm stresses the multiplicity of contexts – national, regional, ethnic, class, political, etc. – that could have determined how Richie's piece might have been received. Moreover, he suggests that these contexts are so different from that in which the song was originally written and produced that any reference either to the tradition of rock 'n' roll, on the one hand, or to anything identifiable as a clear reference in the lyrics, on the other, would be irrelevant to an interpretation of its true or dominant meaning. Indeed, Hamm notes that the non-meanings or "ambiguities deliberately built into Richie's song" were perhaps the source of its popularity. Individuals and groups in a wide variety of social contexts could read into the song a host of meanings that could endow it with a "power" it would otherwise lack.

Hamm's broader purpose appears to be to challenge the conventional notion of the "canonic" musical work as an "ideal object" possessing "an immutable and unshifting 'real' meaning that is to be unfolded by the scholar." He concludes his essay by asking whether "classical" music might not be as "generic" in its "content" as Richie's pop hit and as open, therefore, to as many interpretations as there are contexts in which it might be heard.

The implications of Hamm's position could be unsettling to critics, I should think. According to Hamm, the critic's role would not consist of determining the real or true meaning of a given musical work, but rather – insofar as one were interested in meaning at all – in identifying the contexts in which it may have been heard and surveying the various meanings imputed to it by listeners in those contexts. What is the status of this suggestion? Is it descriptive of the difference between a musicologist's interest and that of the ethnomusicologist or historian of music? Or is it prescriptive of what musicologists ought to be doing when they study any piece of music, old or new, native or exotic, traditional or experimental? If the latter were the case, in what would the musicologist's expertise consist? If there is nothing specifically musical about the *meaning* of a given piece of music, this could imply either that musicologists should not concern themselves with meaning or that they should concentrate on ethno-historical studies of musical works. In the former case, one could justify the most austere formalism; in the latter, the most fulsome historicism.

Similar issues and choices are raised by the essays of John Neubauer and Peter Rabinowitz. Both address the issue of whether, not only modernist and postmodernist, but also classical works of art can be said to contain "intrinsic meaning." Neither suggests that there is no meaning in musical compositions, but both appear to believe that whatever meaning may have been built into a work by the composer is either irretrievable or, if retrievable, enjoys no special status in the determination of a work's potential meaning. Neubauer bases his conclusions on a conception of the ineluctable "openness" of the artistic work, while Rabinowitz founds his on the power of the listener legitimately to "attribute" meanings to works of art which their composers could not even have imagined.

Thus, Neubauer begins his essay with a consideration of the constraints which institutions (both formal and informal) bring to bear upon composers, performers, and listeners alike. He then proceeds to reflect on the crucial role of the "performer" of the musical piece, the relation between performing and listening, and the similarities between performing and reading. He concludes by questioning the possibility of distinguishing – on ontological grounds – among "closed," "open," and "in progress" works. Thus, he points out, even performance "authenticists" such as Koopman and Harnoncourt, who pretend to perform earlier works "as they really were," run up against the limitations of systems of musical notation that will "encode only a fraction of what composers have in their mind . . . " He goes on to remark on the irony of Harnoncourt's preference of eighteenth-century "Classical" over nineteenth-century "Romantic" music; it turns out that the former granted an interpretive freedom to performers that the latter denied. Thus, while "advocates of authentic performance practices seek to recreate a lost pristine tradition," they "actually . . . offer exhilarating new interpretations that manifest a contemporary preoccupation with performance. Authentic performance practices destabilize the text by privileging the performer and blurring the line that separates him from the author."

This circumstance allows us to recognize how important is the performer's (and by extension, the listener's) share in the realization of any given work's potential meaning. Not that the performer or listener is *perfectly* free. (Who is?) The institutional constraints on listening and performing are quite as effective as they are on composition. The challenge, Neubauer concludes, is to work out an analytical model that will focus on the relationships of composition, performance, reception, and institutional structures all at once.

This is a tall order, and it appears to be the project on which Peter Rabinowitz has embarked. Like Neubauer and Hamm, Rabinowitz begins by questioning the notion of the musical (or artistic) "thing in itself" and quickly moves on to consider the ways in which conventions "shape and control the experiences of the listener." He envisages a "model of listening" based on a "model of reading" that would feature the identification of "levels" of comprehension (technical and attributive), on the one hand, and certain "rules of listening" (rules of notice, signification, configuration, and coherence), on the other. This combination of levels and rules would, on Rabinowitz's account, permit conceptualization of the active aspect of listening and determination of the ways in which the listener "attributes" meaning to the work even when it is so "open" as to defy interpretation. He speaks of "attributive screens" which function like a grammar and syntax of listening and correspond to the codes (linguistic and cultural) that must be operated in the acts of reading, writing, and speaking alike.

A similar notion of speech and writing led in poststructuralism, and especially in the work of Jacques Derrida and Paul de Man, to the doctrine of the "undecidability" of the literary work of art. Rabinowitz does not go this far. He remains within the structuralist ambit, envisaging the possibility of communication between cultures and across different epochs within the same cultural tradition in virtue of the possibility of the critic's translating between different "attributive screens." But this is to place the critic's activities in a position denied to composers, performers, and other listeners. Rabinowitz appears to suggest that critics, unlike other listeners, would not so much "attribute" meaning to other people's "attributive screens" as rather actually *know* what these "attributive screens" consist in.

However, as the history of poststructuralism demonstrates, when one begins to theorize the idea of the "open work," it is difficult to resist extending it to include the theorist's own ideas. And so too with the notion of the audience's share in the production of meaning. If the work of art is conceived less as an object possessing a determinable form and identifiable content than as a kind of Rorschach blot onto which the audience can freely project whatever its "attributive screen" suggests, why should not the critic's work be conceived in exactly the same way? Yet, surely Charles Hamm would not wish us to believe that the meaning of his essay is solely or even primarily a function of the various contexts in which it is received and read. Nor would Neubauer wish us to consider his essay as an "open work."

But how should we mediate the differences between our intention to communicate clearly and effectively and our audiences' power and right to interpret what our discourse *means* as well as what it explicitly *asserts*? Hamm, Rabinowitz, and Neubauer force us to consider this question anew, particularly with respect to our responses as critics and theorists to musical discourse.

It is of course difficult to find a single thread running through such diverse and diversely conceived essays and impossible to derive a moral from consideration of them. Nonetheless, it seems possible to say the following: what the contributors to the present volume appear to envision is a kind of "historical–formalist" approach to musical criticism. On the evidence of these essays, we can see the extent to which this new approach is indebted to recent work in structural linguistics, semiotics, textology, narratology, literary hermeneutics (including reception theory, speech-act theory, New Historicism, poststructuralism, and deconstruction), cultural materialism, and feminist theory. We can see how much practitioners of the new approach have learned from recent literary theory about the ways in which the artistic text can be related to its historical context. We also see how literary theorists might learn from musicological theorists about the formal aspects of literary texts, the ways in which they might fail to mean and escape explanation. But in addition we can see the difficulties confronting efforts to construe musical works on the analogy to literary texts and how attempts to relate both of these to their historical context(s) require a full theorization of what is meant by "history" itself.

Beyond that, it should be remembered that the very effort to import literary theory into musicology implies fundamental *differences* between literature and music. It is unlikely that any set of critical or theoretical principles devised to deal primarily with verbal discourse can effectively address the principal problems of musical criticism and theory. What literary theory and criticism can contribute to musicology and music criticism is insight into the nature of discourse in general. It would follow that musicology could profit from this exchange only insofar as music could be considered as a form or mode of discourse. And in that case, the exchange would run both ways, for if music were a form or mode of discourse, then literary theory would have as much to learn from musicology as music criticism has to learn from literary studies.

Index

dissonance, rhythmic *cont.*
  emancipation of, 85, 289
Donizetti, Gaetano; work: *Lucia di Lammermoor*, 243
Donne, John, 43, 65
Doyle, Arthur Conan, 81
Dryden, John, 143, 153 n. 28, 155
Duchamp, Marcel, 4
Dussek, Johann Ladislaus, 53

Ebers, C. F., 101, 104, 105 n. 27
Eco, Umberto, 7, 9–10, 14
Elevation music, 149
Elgar, Sir Edward, 47 n. 18; work: *Enigma Variations*, 47 n. 18
Eliot, T. S., 13, 78, 200
Ellmann, Richard, 89 n. 29

farcical mode, 172 n. 4
Feder, Lillian, 265 n. 19
Felman, Shoshana, 86 n. 22
feminism, *see* criticism
Fétis, François-Joseph, 99
Fetterley, Judith, 220
Fiori, Umberto, 22 n. 4
Fish, Stanley, 16–18, 39
Flaubert, Gustave, 78, 82
Fletcher, Angus, 61, 63
formalism, 93, 239–40, 288–90, 310–11, 316, 318; musical, 91, 139–40, 162
Foster, Stephen, 22
Foucault, Michel, 7–8 n. 12, 91, 265 n. 19
fragmentation, 85–86
Frankfurt School, 5
Freud, Sigmund, 133, 135–36, 225, 233, 295–96, 311
Fried, Michael, 193–215, 291, 308
Frisch, Walter, 176 n. 7
Fry, Paul H., 61
Frye, Northrop, 62–63, 92, 161 n. 37, 307

Gadamer, Hans-Georg, 7
gaps, *see* narrative
Gay, Peter, 222, 226 n. 29
gaze, 227
gender, 219–40, 303, 313–14; ideology of, 292, 300; and social hierarchy in Haydn's *Creation*, 159–60

Genette, Gerard, 85 n. 19, 106
genre, xv, 3, 8, 24, 59–61, 64–65, 70, 97–98, 110, 176, 223, 294, 308, 315
gesture, rhythmic, 41; musical, 165, 167, 263, 286
Goethe, Johann Wolfgang von, 59, 95, 97, 102, 141
Goodman, Nelson, 7–8, 19, 140 n. 5
Gounod, Charles, 115 n. 45
Graff, Gerald, 38
Granville-Barker, Harley, 175
Greene, Thomas, 159
Greimas, A. J., 92, 194–95, 212–13, 215
Grey, Thomas, 41, 119 n. 7, 176, 288, 290, 292–95, 298
Guillén, Claudio, 60 n. 1

Haley, Bill, 22, 35
Hallmark, Rufus, 189–90
Hamm, Charles, 39, 288–90, 292, 314–15, 318
Hand, Learned, 193, 195–99, 201, 208–10, 213, 291, 308
Handel, George Frederic, 253 n. 11, 265, 269, 285–87, 292, 305; works: "Largo," 253 n. 11; *Orlando*, 265–87
Hanslick, Eduard, 93, 96, 113 n. 41, 116, 139
Harbison, John, 193–215, 291, 308; work: *The Flower-Fed Buffaloes*, 193–215, 291
Hardy, Thomas, 78, 80–81, 85–86, 89, 91
Harker, Dave, 22
Harnoncourt, Nikolaus, 11–13, 16, 316
Hartman, Geoffrey, 71, 73
Haydn, Joseph, 48, 53, 55, 89, 139–62, 291–92, 298–300; works: *The Creation*, 55, 139–62, 291–92, 298–300; London symphonies, 151
Hegel, Georg Wilhelm Friedrich, 314
Heine, Heinrich, 177–92
Herbert, George, 64–70, 307; work: "Vertue" ["Virtue"], 64–70, 307–309
hermeneutics, xiii, 7, 21; aesthetic, 290; historical, 290; literary, 318; musical, 100, 140, 161, 290, 318; political, 290; *see also* representation